"Acceptance and mindfulness [met ___ ___ ___ ___ ___ tures around the world. That is a part of what makes this work so relevant to cultural issues on the one hand, and in need of culturally competent application on the other. This ground-breaking volume walks through both sides of this issue in a way that will uplift, energize, and empower practitioners. Highly recommended."

—**Steven C. Hayes, PhD**, codeveloper of acceptance and commitment therapy (ACT)

"*Mindfulness and Acceptance in Multicultural Competency* addresses challenges in the application of mindfulness- and acceptance-based interventions to diverse groups. The emphasis throughout the book is on the principles of these approaches rather than on their topographical or surface characteristics. There is a breadth of topics, including cultural issues, such as cultural competence and cultural adaptation of interventions, as well as sociocultural issues, such as discrimination, prejudice, stigma, and minority status....This book provides a useful conceptual framework to guide research and clinical practice."

—**Gordon C. Nagayama Hall**, professor of psychology and director of clinical training at the University of Oregon

"Most therapists aspire to be culturally competent, but what does this mean for those using mindfulness and acceptance-based treatments? Are these interventions effective with diverse groups? Should they be adapted to reduce cultural bias? If so, how? Can clinicians use mindfulness- and acceptance-based methods to improve their own cultural competence? Fascinating and practical, this book provides compelling answers to these and other important questions."

—**Ruth Baer, PhD**, professor of psychology at the University of Kentucky and editor of *Mindfulness-Based Treatment Approaches*

THE
MINDFULNESS & ACCEPTANCE
PRACTICA SERIES

As mindfulness and acceptance-based therapies gain momentum in the field of mental health, it is increasingly important for professionals to understand the full range of their applications. To keep up with the growing demand for authoritative resources on these treatments, *The Mindfulness and Acceptance Practica Series* was created. These edited books cover a range of evidence-based treatments, such as acceptance and commitment therapy (ACT), cognitive behavioral therapy (CBT), compassion-focused therapy (CFT), dialectical behavioral therapy (DBT), and mindfulness-based stress reduction (MBSR) therapy. Incorporating new research in the field of psychology, these books are powerful tools for mental health clinicians, researchers, advanced students, and anyone interested in the growth of mindfulness and acceptance strategies.

Visit www.newharbinger.com for
more books in this series.

MINDFULNESS &
ACCEPTANCE IN
MULTICULTURAL
COMPETENCY

A Contextual Approach to Sociocultural
Diversity in Theory & Practice

Edited by
AKIHIKO MASUDA, PhD

CONTEXT PRESS
An Imprint of New Harbinger Publications, Inc.

Publisher's Note

This publication is designed to provide accurate and authoritative information in regard to the subject matter covered. It is sold with the understanding that the publisher is not engaged in rendering psychological, financial, legal, or other professional services. If expert assistance or counseling is needed, the services of a competent professional should be sought.

Distributed in Canada by Raincoast Books

Copyright © 2014 by Akihiko Masuda
New Harbinger Publications, Inc.
5674 Shattuck Avenue
Oakland, CA 94609
www.newharbinger.com

Cover design by Amy Shoup
Acquired by Catharine Meyers
Edited by Marisa Solis

Library of Congress Cataloging-in-Publication Data on file

Printed in the United States of America

16   15   14

10   9   8   7   6   5   4   3   2   1

First printing

Contents

Part II
Cultural Adaptation of Acceptance- and Mindfulness-Based Methods

PART III
Application of Acceptance- and Mindfulness-Based Approaches to Diversity Issues

Introduction

Akihiko Masuda, Ph.D.
Georgia State University

... it becomes critically important that those persons coming to the field with professional interest and enthusiasm recognize the unique qualities and characteristics of mindfulness as an alternative practice, with all that implies, so that mindfulness is not simply seized upon as the next promising cognitive behavioral technique or exercise, decontextualized, and "plugged" into a behaviorist paradigm with the aim of driving desirable change, or of fixing what is broken.

> —Jon Kabat-Zinn, "Mindfulness-Based Interventions
> in Context: Past, Present, and Future,"
> *Clinical Psychology: Science and Practice* (2003)

Despite consensus over the importance and significance of cultural values and behaviors in treatment, investigators have actually varied in their specific assumptions or focus for cultural competency.

> —Stanley Sue, Nolan Zane, Gordon Hall, &
> Lauren Berger, "The Case for Cultural
> Competency in Psychotherapeutic Interventions,"
> *Annual Review of Psychology* (2009)

Mindfulness and Acceptance Overview

A growing interest in mindfulness and psychological acceptance has swept across the fields of Western medicine and mental health in recent years. Their rapid popularity, despite originating in ancient spiritual traditions (e.g., Buddhism and Christianity; Hayes & Wilson, 2003; Kabat-Zinn, 2003), can be attributed to several key factors. First, a growing body of evidence has pointed to the potential applicability of mindfulness- and acceptance-based principles and practices to a wide range of physical health and psychosocial issues (Brown, Ryan, & Creswell, 2007; Kashdan & Rottenberg, 2010). Second, there has been a shift in our understanding of psychological health and psychopathology (Hayes, Follette, & Linehan, 2004). Despite the dominance of symptom-focused treatments, we have begun to acknowledge the benefits of a holistic approach, which serves a client as a whole individual. The teachings of mindfulness and acceptance theories, such as "living fully and purposefully here and now," parallel this holistic stance. Finally, clinicians and researchers have begun to recognize and even embrace the ubiquitous nature of human suffering (Segal, Williams, & Teasdale, 2002). The wisdom drawn from this awareness is that some struggles that we experience are not to be fought against. Rather, they are essential parts of our lives, from which we can learn to enrich ourselves and others (Hayes, Strosahl, & Wilson, 2012).

As part of this mindfulness- and acceptance-based movement, a number of new cognitive and behavioral therapies (CBTs) have emerged, integrating mindfulness, acceptance, and values into their conceptual models and practices (Hayes, Villatte, Levin, & Hildebrandt, 2011). Examples of these treatments include acceptance and commitment therapy (ACT; Hayes, Strosahl, & Wilson, 1999), dialectical behavior therapy (DBT; Linehan, 1993), mindfulness-based cognitive therapy (MBCT; Segal et al., 2002), and similar others (Hayes et al., 2004). To date, DBT, MBCT, and ACT have been applied to diverse treatment settings, such as independent practice (Bach & Moran, 2008; Marra, 2005), Veterans Affairs (VA) clinics

(Kearney, McDermott, Malte, Martinez, & Simpson, 2012), university counseling services centers (Kurash & Schaul, 2006), substance use treatment clinics (Hayes & Levin, 2012), medical settings (Grossman, Niemann, Schmidt, & Walach, 2004; McCracken, 2011), and e-health settings (Ljótsson et al., 2010), to name a few. Similarly, these treatments have been used to promote quality of life for individuals who are struggling with a wide range of issues, such as depression (Segal et al., 2002), anxiety (Arch et al., 2012), disordered eating (Safer, Telch, & Agras, 2001; Telch, Agras, & Linehan, 2001), substance use and addiction problems (Hayes & Levin, 2012), physical health issues (Grossman et al., 2004), and many others.

Mindfulness and Acceptance in Mindfulness- and Acceptance-Based Approaches

It is important to note that in the literature the terms "mindfulness" and "acceptance" are viewed differently among investigators. Some view mindfulness as enhanced attention to and awareness of present-moment experience (Brown & Ryan, 2003). Others define mindfulness as a multifaceted phenomenon, including observing, describing, accepting whatever one is experiencing without judgment, and acting with awareness (Baer, Smith, & Allen, 2004). Also, in the psychotherapy literature, these terms are often used to refer to different aspects of therapy. For example, in some contexts mindfulness and acceptance are viewed as a set of therapeutic techniques (e.g., breathing exercises), and in other contexts as a particular process targeted in therapy (e.g., open awareness to the present-moment experience with compassion). Or, these terms are used as an overarching conceptual model of well-being and behavior change (Baer, 2010; Hayes & Wilson, 2003). Being cognizant of these related, yet distinct, aspects of acceptance and mindfulness in therapy is crucial in understanding and critically evaluating a given psychotherapy.

Considering the varying definitions and conceptualizations of mindfulness and acceptance becomes even more important when we critically evaluate the cultural competency and cultural adaptation of acceptance- and mindfulness-based approaches (chapter 2). More specific, when employing this framework, one may conclude that cultural adaptation of a given therapy (e.g., ACT) may be necessary for particular aspects of therapy (e.g., techniques) but not for others (e.g., conceptualization). In other words, this framework allows us to see which aspects of psychotherapy require cultural modification, rather than hastily rejecting an entire therapy when we find a tiny incompetency within the treatment. Finally, it is crucial to be cognizant that our preanalytically determined worldview (philosophical perspective) influences how we understand these aspects of mindfulness and acceptance (Hayes, Hayes, & Reese, 1988; Hayes, Levin, Plumb-Vilardaga, Villatte, & Pistorello, 2013), as we outline extensively later in this volume.

Mindfulness- and Acceptance-Based Approaches within Diverse Sociocultural Contexts

The effects and mechanisms of mindfulness- and acceptance-based interventions are not yet fully investigated across diverse settings, populations, and clinical issues (Woidneck, Pratt, Gundy, Nelson, & Twohig, 2012). Accumulating evidence in these areas is crucial, as our society has become increasingly diverse (Sue, 1999; Sue, Zane, Hall, & Berger, 2009). Although evidence is growing in the area of diversity (Fuchs, Lee, Roemer, & Orsillo, 2013; Woidneck et al., 2012), it remains unclear (1) whether mindfulness- and acceptance-based interventions are appropriate for culturally diverse populations; (2) whether cultural adaptation is necessary to enhance their effectiveness when applied to individuals from a given sociocultural background; (3) whether their essential concepts, processes, and principles, such as the construct of mindfulness, are culturally biased; and (4) if these approaches contribute to overcoming sociocultural challenges, such as stigma and prejudice.

Reflecting these unanswered questions, the present volume addresses three major themes raised in recent debates on cultural competency and mindfulness- and acceptance-based interventions. Part I addresses fundamental culturally related issues that clinicians and researchers have faced for years and their relevance to the current mindfulness- and acceptance-based movement. Part II focuses on the cultural competency of three major acceptance- and mindfulness-based approaches (i.e., DBT, MBCT, and ACT). Finally, part III presents and evaluates the application of mindfulness- and acceptance-based approaches to diversity-related issues, such as multicultural competency training, stigma and prejudice, and spirituality. Efforts to investigate the integration of cultural competency and mindfulness- and acceptance-based approaches are in their infancy, and many of the claims presented in this volume are still speculative. However, data thus far suggest the potential utility of mindfulness- and acceptance-based principles and interventions for serving a diverse group of clients.

Cultural Competency and Mindfulness- and Acceptance-Based Approaches

Part I of this volume starts by addressing long-standing culturally related issues that investigators have faced in Western medicine and mental health, presented by Drs. Janice Cheng and Stanley Sue (chapter 1). Although chapter 1 primarily focuses on ethnic minority populations, issues and future directions addressed by Cheng and Sue are pertinent to other sociocultural contexts. Focusing on meta-level issues, Cheng and Sue argue that the *ways* our field operates contribute to the inadequacy in addressing cultural competency and health disparity. Cheng and Sue then warn that clinicians and researchers in the acceptance and mindfulness movement must be cognizant of these meta-level issues in moving the field forward.

Fully grasping cultural competency is an extremely challenging task (Sue et al., 2009; Whaley & Davis, 2007). While many of us intuitively acknowledge its importance, we often do not know what cultural competency is and how best to approach it. While the challenge is often attributed to its multifaceted and multi-level nature (Whaley & Davis, 2007), as Cheng and Sue address, it can also be attributed to the inadequate strategies used for building our knowledge (Sue, 1999; also see chapter 1). We believe that part of these inadequate strategies can be attributed to the lack of conceptual and philosophical clarity when we approach this subject (Hayes et al., 2013; Hayes, Muto, & Masuda, 2011; Sue et al., 2009).

So what can be the most parsimonious *way* of understanding cultural competency that also brings effective strategies to promote it? The focal issue is not ontological (what cultural competency is), but pragmatic (Hayes, Barnes-Holmes, & Wilson, 2012); how can we effectively promote cultural competence? In the field of psychology, the cultural competency of therapists is often understood *topographically* and *descriptively* in terms of its form or appearance. For example, cultural competency is defined as a set of awareness, knowledge, and skills with particular *content*. A major problem of a content-focused approach is that it does not necessarily tell us how to teach and learn cultural competency. As Cheng and Sue state in the present volume, we need to more fully develop and refine *causal-based knowledge* (e.g., behavior change principle) in order to understand and promote cultural competency. Furthermore, a content-focused account does not adequately address the fact that the *forms* of culturally competent awareness, knowledge, and skills vary across and within clients, therapists, and therapeutic interactions of the two, depending on the context (Hall, Hong, Zane, & Meyer, 2011; Whaley & Davis, 2007). Partially responding to this concern, experts in diversity psychology have recently suggested that *process*-based accounts, which view cultural competency as the *process* or *quality* of problem-solving skills in the context of working with a given client, may be more adequate to the complex task of cultural competence (Whaley & Davis, 2007). Nevertheless, the shift from a content-based to a process-based account does not necessarily address the pragmatic issue of how to promote cultural competence, either. We believe that principles of behavior change, which are based on a functional-contextual perspective, may be a useful alternative.

Functional Contextualism as Essential Worldview

Masuda (chapter 2) argues that a functional conceptual framework, which is based on the philosophical perspective of functional contextualism, helps us to develop and organize knowledge of cultural competency and to promote it in a pragmatic and contextually sensitive manner. Specifically, he postulates that reconceptualizing cultural competency in terms of "the act of a given person in his or her historical and situational context" will allow researchers and clinicians to identify cultural competency tailored to a given context, to identify strategies to promote it, and to measure and evaluate these strategies. Cultural competency from a functional-contextual perspective may be summarized as follows: (1) The cultural competency of a given therapist is not within the therapist, nor in the therapist's behavior, but is held within the context of the intricate interaction between a therapist and a client in a given moment. (2) A therapist's behavior is said to be culturally competent when it effectively serves a predetermined purpose (e.g., the promotion of wellness of the very person the therapist serves). (3) Culturally competent therapist behavior for a given client is not necessarily culturally competent in the context of working with another client. Culturally competent actions, when working with a given client today, may not be competent at all when working with the same client next week. (4) Culturally competent behavior necessitates an ongoing awareness and acknowledgment of present-moment experience with this client, as it is, fully and purposefully, while keeping the purpose of therapeutic work with this client in mind. (5) If we do not see the moment-by-moment as well as the contextual nature of cultural competency, we are likely to remain hopelessly stuck, full of bias and judgmental righteousness.

Partially in response to Masuda's claim, Dr. Anderson and her colleagues (chapter 3) argue that learning a mindfulness- and acceptance-based approach, such as ACT, does not necessarily build a therapist's cultural competency by itself. Given how cultural competency is defined in diversity psychology and multiculturalism (Whaley & Davis, 2007), embodying cultural competency is to acknowledge ourselves and our clients *fully* as contextual beings. For a clinician, this requires continuous efforts to see and relate to herself or himself as well as the clients. For a functional and contextual therapist, one must develop skills to identify ideographically specific contextual factors that contribute to issues that that client presents. Anderson and colleagues argue that learning ACT itself in principles and techniques may not promote such sensitivity. They introduce essential theories from the diversity literature and urge mindfulness- and acceptance-based therapists to participate in multicultural competency training and build awareness, knowledge, and skills in order to develop and refine individually crafted therapeutic work with a given client.

DBT, MBCT, and ACT: How Culturally Competent Are These New Therapies?

Part II of this volume examines the cultural competency and cultural adaptation of three major mindfulness- and acceptance-based CBTs: DBT, MBCT, and ACT. This is no easy task. As the concept of cultural competency is multidimensional and multi-leveled, a given therapy can be viewed at multiple levels with different foci. In the literature, a given form of psychotherapy is often viewed as a set of techniques as well as an overarching model of psychological health and behavior change. Once again, what is not fully articulated in the literature is that understanding and embodying these methodological and conceptual aspects of therapy is heavily influenced by one's philosophical standpoint (i.e., worldview, fundamental way of making sense of the world). According to Hayes (Hayes et al., 1988), the philosophical stance that a person follows determines how he or she approaches and understands a phenomenon of interest, in this case mindfulness-based interventions and cultural competence. As such, we must recognize the essential standpoint through which we understand and evaluate the cultural competency of mindfulness- and acceptance-based approaches (Hayes, 2005; Hayes et al., 1999).

DBT, MBCT, and ACT as a Whole

Philosophically, DBT, MBCT, and ACT are more or less functional, contextual, and process focused (Hayes, Villatte et al., 2011; Segal et al., 2002). That is, when evaluating their cultural competency from their lenses, the focus is placed on the *function* (e.g., "Does ACT promote the quality of life in this given client?") of a given behavior of a clinician or client in a given situational and historical *context*, not merely on the topographical form (e.g., what was said or done to the client). Effective forms and styles of therapy vary contextually, depending on the client and therapist and their therapeutic interactions in a given moment. As such, evaluating mindfulness- and acceptance-based therapies merely in form is not valid or clinically useful. Furthermore, DBT, MBCT, and ACT also adopt a process-based account in order to capture the ongoing nature of their therapeutic work.

Dialectical behavior therapy (Linehan, 1993) is the most rigorously studied mindfulness- and acceptance-based intervention to date. Although DBT is most often practiced in the promotion of the quality of life among women diagnosed with borderline personality disorder, its broader clinical applicability is significant (Dimeff & Koerner, 2007; Marra, 2005). Dr. McFarr and her colleagues (chapter 4) present cultural competence considerations in DBT, while focusing on their work in Spanish-speaking adult populations in the United States.

Mindfulness-based cognitive therapy (Segal et al., 2002) is a group intervention typically conducted over eight weeks. MBCT was originally developed as an integration of CBT and mindfulness-based stress reduction (Kabat-Zinn, 1990) to aid in preventing the relapse of depression among those with chronic depression. Dr. Hazlett-Stevens and her colleague (chapter 5) explore the cultural competency and adaptation of this fairly structured treatment intervention with a diverse sample of clients.

Finally, Drs. Pasillas and Masuda (chapter 6) explore the cultural competency of acceptance and commitment therapy (Hayes, Strosahl et al., 2012) and address concerns and recommendations when adapting ACT to a given client with a unique sociocultural background. These three chapters provide careful examination of cultural competency from conceptual and technical standpoints and offer a number of clinical examples.

Application of Mindfulness and Acceptance to Culturally Relevant Issues

Finally, part III of this volume presents the application of mindfulness- and acceptance-based principles and interventions to a range of culturally relevant topics that researchers and clinicians face. These include cultural adaptation or translation of a treatment protocol to another verbal community, multicultural competency training, spirituality, stigma, prejudice, and internalized shame.

Cultural Adaptation of Treatment to a Different Verbal Community

DBT, MBCT, and ACT, originally developed within English-speaking contexts, have been translated into other languages and adapted across the world. One of the major dissemination and adaptation efforts is the translation of English-written protocols into the native tongue of a target verbal community (e.g., Japanese). What is crucial in protocol translation is the adherence to functional and contextual adaptation, rather than to a content-based literal translation. In other words, therapists must be cognizant of the purpose of a given treatment strategy (i.e., its function), not the word-to-word correspondence. To explore these issues further, Dr. Drossel and her colleagues (chapter 7) address the pitfalls of content-focused literal translation and present how function- and context-focused treatment adaptation promotes sensitivity and effectiveness within other verbal contexts, while maintaining the unique quality and characteristics of mindfulness- and acceptance-based interventions.

Multicultural Competency Training

Multicultural competency training is typically designed to promote adequate awareness, knowledge, and skills of clinicians around culturally relevant topics. While clinicians and therapist trainees are enthusiastic about advocating the importance of multicultural competency, actually participating in such trainings, especially experiential ones, may be more difficult. For some, multicultural competency training, or even just thinking about it, evokes intense fear of making mistakes, offending others, looking stupid, and/or appearing "racist." For others, multicultural competency training is yet another disappointing moment of witnessing the insensitivity of others. Literature suggests that not adequately addressing these issues within the context of multicultural competency training undermines its very purpose. In chapter 8, Dr. Twohig and his colleagues present how an acceptance- and mindfulness-based approach is applied in the context of multicultural competency training. Specifically, they argue that an acceptance- and mindfulness-based approach is particularly useful in undermining the impact of these negative effects within the training, while illuminating participants' intrinsic motivation for building cultural competency.

Religion and Spirituality

Psychotherapy and religion have had a long, complex, and, at times, acrimonious history. The cultural image of religious dogma oppressing the enlightened psychotherapy scientists and clinicians has been with us for centuries (Cummings, O'Donohue, & Cummings, 2009). In the 20th century, a movement led Western society away from organized religion to a more secular, or at least less institutionalized, religious viewpoint. However, it is unfair to describe the West, and particularly the United States, as atheistic or secular; indeed, polls show that the majority of Americans believe in God. This image has also been unfair to the science of psychology, as many scholars have pointed to ways in which science and religion are compatible. From the perspective of acceptance- and mindfulness-based treatments, Dr. Murrell and her colleagues (chapter 9) address issues of religion and spirituality in the context of the therapeutic relationship. Using clinical examples, they postulate that validating and encouraging discussion about concerns regarding mismatch—or perceived mismatch—between a client's and therapist's religious and spiritual values are central to an effective course of therapy. From that center point, they conclude that acceptance- and mindfulness-based therapies share a number of similarities with various religious and spiritual traditions.

Prejudice, Stigma, and Internalized Shame

Stigma and prejudice toward individuals based on their group membership is a major source of human despair across nearly all domains of society. The verbal and sociocultural processes in these realms result in negative emotional and health consequences for the victims of discrimination based on social categorizations, such as race and ethnicity, mental illness, and sexual minority status, to name a few. Given their significant impact, stigma and prejudice are important targets for reducing human suffering and improving the quality of life of people who have been historically marginalized.

In recent years, there have been growing efforts to understand and modulate stigma and prejudice from mindfulness- and acceptance-based models of complex human behavior. The psychological flexibility model (Hayes, Luoma, Bond, Masuda, & Lillis, 2006) is an example of such a model. This model, although originally developed as a conceptual and intervention framework for psychopathology and psychological health, has been applied to various forms of stigma and prejudice (chapters 10–12).

As discussed extensively in this volume, the psychological flexibility model views stigma and prejudice as a generalized verbal process that involves normal and useful language/verbal abilities gone awry (Hayes, Niccolls, Masuda, & Rye, 2002). More specific, stigma and prejudice are roughly defined as the process of objectification and dehumanization of the self or others as a result of their participation in normal verbal processes of categorization, association, and evaluation. According to this model, various forms of stigma and prejudice, though varying in content, may not be qualitatively distinct from one another. This conceptual position is supported in part by the finding that prejudiced attitudes toward various groups tend to co-occur and comprise a single latent variable (Bäckström & Björklund, 2007). As such, interventions may be more efficacious if they target the verbal processes that underlie stigma and prejudice, instead of focusing on the content of beliefs and biases toward specific groups.

The salient features of a psychological flexibility–based intervention for stigma and prejudice are its focus on (a) the underlying verbal processes of categorization, association, and evaluation rather than the specific topographical content of stigmatizing thoughts; and (b) the promotion of intrinsic and prosocial actions alternative to or incompatible with stigmatization and discrimination, rather than directly challenging and making efforts to refute stigma and prejudice. In chapter 10, Drs. Lillis and Levin explicate the application of the psychological flexibility model to issues related to social categorizations and present an ACT-based invention targeting racial prejudice. In chapter 11, Dr. Luoma addresses two major sets of stigma—stigma directed toward others and stigma directed toward the self—and then details treatment components of an ACT-based stigma-reduction intervention. Finally, Dr. Skinta (chapter 12) discusses the link between perceived stigma from others, internalized stigma, and psychological distress in the stigmatized and presents the integration of a compassion-based intervention and ACT designed to promote quality of life among sexual minorities.

Summary

This volume represents the first attempt in a book-length form to address and review the current status of mindfulness- and acceptance-based approaches on culturally related issues. The following chapters elucidate three major themes that have emerged in recent debates on cultural competency and acceptance- and mindfulness-based interventions. The first major theme involves the importance of cultural competency and the identification of useful ways to understand and promote it. The second major theme reflects cultural competency and cultural adaptation of mindfulness- and acceptance-based treatment approaches, namely DBT, MBCT, and ACT. Experts in each treatment modality discuss its cultural competency and practical tips in adapting the intervention method to a given client. Finally, the third major theme is the application of mindfulness- and acceptance-based approaches to culturally relevant issues, such as the cultural adaptation of a treatment protocol to another language community, multicultural competency training, spirituality, and a variety of forms of stigma and prejudice.

Efforts to understand and integrate cultural competency and acceptance- and mindfulness-based approaches are still in their infancy. Nevertheless, preliminary evidence suggests that mindfulness- and acceptance-based approaches may contribute to the field of cultural competency and sensitivity. We hope that this book will serve as a stepping-stone for advancing our understanding of cultural competency and the promotion of cultural competency in mindfulness- and acceptance-based approaches.

References

Arch, J. J., Eifert, G. H., Davies, C., Vilardaga, J. C. P., Rose, R. D., & Craske, M. G. (2012). Randomized clinical trial of cognitive behavioral therapy (CBT) versus acceptance and commitment therapy (ACT) for mixed anxiety disorders. *Journal of Consulting and Clinical Psychology, 80*(5), 750–765.

Bach, P. A., & Moran, D. J. (2008). *ACT in practice: Case conceptualization in acceptance and commitment therapy.* Oakland, CA: New Harbinger Publications.

Bäckström, M., & Björklund, F. (2007). Structural modeling of generalized prejudice: The role of social dominance, authoritarianism, and empathy. *Journal of Individual Differences, 28*(1), 10–17.

Baer, R. A. (2010). *Assessing mindfulness and acceptance processes in clients: Illuminating the theory and practice of change.* Oakland, CA: Context Press/New Harbinger Publications.

Baer, R. A., Smith, G. T., & Allen, K. B. (2004). Assessment of mindfulness by self-report: The Kentucky inventory of mindfulness skills. *Assessment, 11*(3), 191–206. doi: 10.1177/1073191104268029.

Brown, K. W., & Ryan, R. M. (2003). The benefits of being present: Mindfulness and its role in psychological well-being. *Journal of Personality and Social Psychology, 84*(4), 822–848.

Brown, K. W., Ryan, R. M., & Creswell, J. D. (2007). Mindfulness: Theoretical foundations and evidence for its salutary effects. *Psychological Inquiry, 18*(4), 211–237.

Cummings, N., O'Donohue, W., & Cummings, J. (2009). *Psychology's war on religion.* Phoenix, AZ.: Zeig, Tucker & Theisen.

Dimeff, L. A., & Koerner, K. (2007). *Dialectical behavior therapy in clinical practice: Applications across disorders and settings.* New York: Guilford Press.

Fuchs, C., Lee, J. K., Roemer, L., & Orsillo, S. M. (2013). Using mindfulness- and acceptance-based treatments with clients from nondominant cultural and/or marginalized backgrounds: Clinical consideration, meta-analysis findings, and introduction to the special series. *Cognitive and Behavioral Practice, 20*(1), 1–12.

Grossman, P., Niemann, L., Schmidt, S., & Walach, H. (2004). Mindfulness-based stress reduction and health benefits: A meta-analysis. *Journal of Psychosomatic Research, 57*(1), 35-43. doi: 10.1016/s0022-3999(03)00573-7.

Hall, G. C. N., Hong, J. J., Zane, N. W. S., & Meyer, O. L. (2011). Culturally competent treatments for Asian Americans: The relevance of mindfulness and acceptance-based psychotherapies. *Clinical Psychology: Science and Practice, 18*(3), 215–231.

Hayes, S. C. (2005). Eleven rules for a more successful clinical psychology. *Journal of Clinical Psychology, 61*(9), 1055–1060.

Hayes, S. C., Barnes-Holmes, D., & Wilson, K. G. (2012). Contextual behavioral science: Creating a science more adequate to the challenge of the human condition. *Journal of Contextual Behavioral Science, 1*(1–2), 1–16.

Hayes, S. C., Follette, V. M., & Linehan, M. M. (2004). *Mindfulness and acceptance: Expanding the cognitive-behavioral tradition*. New York: Guilford Press.

Hayes, S. C., Hayes, L. J., & Reese, H. W. (1988). Finding the philosophical core: A review of Stephen C. Pepper's world hypotheses: A study in evidence. *Journal of the Experimental Analysis of Behavior, 50*, 97–111.

Hayes, S. C., & Levin, M. E. (2012). *Mindfulness and acceptance for addictive behaviors: Applying contextual CBT to substance abuse and behavioral addictions*. Oakland, CA: Context Press/New Harbinger Publications.

Hayes, S. C., Levin, M. E., Plumb-Vilardaga, J., Villatte, J. L., & Pistorello, J. (2013). Acceptance and commitment therapy and contextual behavioral science: Examining the progress of a distinctive model of behavioral and cognitive therapy. *Behavior Therapy, 44*(2), 180–198.

Hayes, S. C., Luoma, J. B., Bond, F. W., Masuda, A., & Lillis, J. (2006). Acceptance and commitment therapy: Model, processes and outcomes. *Behaviour Research and Therapy, 44*(1), 1–25.

Hayes, S. C., Muto, T., & Masuda, A. (2011). Seeking cultural competence from the ground up. *Clinical Psychology: Science & Practice, 18*(3), 232–237.

Hayes, S. C., Niccolls, R., Masuda, A., & Rye, A. K. (2002). Prejudice, terrorism and behavior therapy. *Cognitive and Behavioral Practice, 9*(4), 296–301.

Hayes, S. C., Strosahl, K. D., & Wilson, K. G. (1999). *Acceptance and commitment therapy: An experiential approach to behavior change*. New York: Guilford Press.

Hayes, S. C., Strosahl, K. D., & Wilson, K. G. (2012). *Acceptance and commitment therapy: The process and practice of mindful change* (2nd ed.). New York: Guilford Press.

Hayes, S. C., Villatte, M., Levin, M., & Hildebrandt, M. (2011). Open, aware, and active: Contextual approaches as an emerging trend in the behavioral and cognitive therapies. *Annual Review of Clinical Psychology, 7*, 141–168.

Hayes, S. C., & Wilson, K. G. (2003). Mindfulness: Method and process. *Clinical Psychology: Science and Practice, 10*(2), 161–165.

Kabat-Zinn, J. (1990). *Full catastrophe living: Using the wisdom of your body and mind to face stress, pain, and illness*. New York: Delacorte Press, 1990.

Kabat-Zinn, J. (2003). Mindfulness-based interventions in context: Past, present, and future. *Clinical Psychology: Science and Practice, 10*(2), 144–156.

Kashdan, T. B., & Rottenberg, J. (2010). Psychological flexibility as a fundamental aspect of health. *Clinical Psychology Review, 30*(4), 467–480.

Kearney, D. J., McDermott, K., Malte, C., Martinez, M., & Simpson, T. L. (2012). Association of participation in a mindfulness program with measures of PTSD, depression and quality of life in a veteran sample. *Journal of Clinical Psychology, 68*(1), 101–116.

Kurash, C., & Schaul, J. (2006). Integrating mindfulness meditation within a university counseling center setting. *Journal of College Student Psychotherapy, 20*(3), 53–67.

Linehan, M. M. (1993). *Cognitive-behavioral treatment of borderline personality disorder*. New York: Guilford Press.

Ljótsson, B., Falk, L., Vesterlund, A. W., Hedman, E., Lindfors, P., Rück, C., et al. (2010). Internet-delivered exposure and mindfulness-based therapy for irritable bowel syndrome: A randomized controlled trial. *Behaviour Research and Therapy, 48*(6), 531–539.

Marra, T. (2005). *Dialectical behavior therapy in private practice: A practical and comprehensive guide.* Oakland, CA: New Harbinger Publications.

McCracken, L. M. (2011). *Mindfulness and acceptance in behavioral medicine: Current theory and practice.* Oakland, CA: Context Press/New Harbinger Publications.

Safer, D. L., Telch, C. F., & Agras, W. S. (2001). Dialectical behavior therapy for bulimia nervosa. *The American Journal of Psychiatry, 158*(4), 632–634.

Segal, Z. V., Williams, J. M. G., & Teasdale, J. D. (2002). *Mindfulness-based cognitive therapy for depression: A new approach to preventing relapse.* New York: Guilford Press.

Sue, S. (1999). Science, ethnicity, and bias: Where have we gone wrong? *American Psychologist, 54*(12), 1070–1077.

Sue, S., Zane, N., Hall, G. C. N., & Berger, L. K. (2009). The case for cultural competency in psychotherapeutic interventions. *Annual Review of Psychology, 60*, 525–548.

Telch, C. F., Agras, W. S., & Linehan, M. M. (2001). Dialectical behavior therapy for binge eating disorder. *Journal of Consulting and Clinical Psychology, 69*(6), 1061–1065.

Whaley, A. L., & Davis, K. E. (2007). Cultural competence and evidence-based practice in mental health services: A complementary perspective. *American Psychologist, 62*(6), 563–574.

Woidneck, M. R., Pratt, K. M., Gundy, J. M., Nelson, C. R., & Twohig, M. P. (2012). Exploring cultural competence in acceptance and commitment therapy outcomes. *Professional Psychology: Research and Practice, 43*(3), 227–233.

PART I

Mindfulness- and Acceptance-Based Accounts of Culture and Diversity

CHAPTER 1

Addressing Cultural and Ethnic Minority Issues in the Acceptance and Mindfulness Movement

Janice Ka Yan Cheng, Ph.D.
University of California, Davis

Stanley Sue, Ph.D.
Palo Alto University and University of California, Davis

Acceptance- and mindfulness-based treatments for psychological disorders have received growing attention in recent years. Acceptance- and mindfulness-based treatments are considered the "third wave" of behavioral and cognitive therapy (Hayes, Luoma, Bond, Masuda, & Lillis, 2006). Examples of such therapies include dialectical behavior therapy (DBT; Linehan, 1993), acceptance and commitment therapy (ACT; Hayes, Strosahl, & Wilson, 1999), mindfulness-based cognitive therapy (MBCT; Segal, Williams, & Teasdale, 2001), and mindfulness-based stress reduction (MBSR; Kabat-Zinn, 1990). While cognitive behavioral therapy (CBT) focuses on changing the dysfunctional thought processes and negative emotions directly, acceptance- and mindfulness-based therapies emphasize the importance of acknowledging and recognizing one's contextual demands and emotions, without attempting to avoid or change them. The goals of acceptance- and mindfulness-based therapies are to increase individuals' moment-to-moment awareness and to clarify what is most important to them.

As the mental health systems increasingly advocate evidence-based practice, a number of empirical questions related to the application of acceptance- and mindfulness-based therapies with culturally diverse populations arise (S. Sue, 1999). For example, are acceptance- and mindfulness-based approaches appropriate for culturally diverse populations? Are cultural adaptations or modifications necessary to enhance the effectiveness of treatment? Are the basic assumptions and therapeutic process of acceptance- and mindfulness-based approaches culturally biased? Can acceptance and mindfulness models provide a means for promoting cultural competency and resolving social problems? Although other books on acceptance- and mindfulness-based treatments are available in the market, this book is the first to directly address these important issues. The intent of this chapter is to discuss fundamental culturally related issues that researchers and clinicians must face.

Importance of Cultural Competency

Finding culturally competent interventions and modifying existing forms of treatment to meet the needs of ethnic minority populations have bedeviled psychology for decades. There is evidence that our current forms of mental health treatment have been especially inadequate for ethnic minority populations. For example, in the mental health system, the underutilization of mental health services by ethnic minorities is a persistent disparity, especially among immigrants. Almost four decades ago, S. Sue and McKinney (1975) found that ethnic minorities tended to underutilize mental health services, compared to White individuals. Although different efforts have been made to improve mental health services for ethnic minority clients, recent reports continue to document that mental health services were often inaccessible, inappropriate, or poorly delivered (U.S. Department of Health and Human Services [DHHS], 2001, 2012). Alegría et al. (2008) examined the utilization of mental health services among those with depression and found that 40.2% of non-Latino Whites did not access any mental health treatment in the past year, compared to 63.7% of Latinos, 68.7% of Asians, and 58.8% of African Americans. Furthermore, among those with depression who accessed depression treatment, African Americans were more likely to receive inadequate care. The disparities in utilization appear to be related to the incongruence between the cultural values and expectations of ethnic minority clients and the practices of mental health services based on a Western-based paradigm. The underutilization of services persists even after controlling for prevalence rates of mental disorders (DHHS, 2012).

Some recent studies reveal that utilization and treatment outcomes for ethnic minority groups are enhanced by the provision of culturally competent services (Griner & Smith, 2006; Smith, Domenech Rodríguez, & Bernal, 2011). Thus, the development of cultural competency in services at the provider, agency, and systems

23

levels has been a top priority among ethnic minority groups. D. W. Sue and his colleagues have categorized cultural competency into three basic characteristics of mental health providers, namely (1) cultural awareness and beliefs, (2) cultural knowledge, and (3) cultural skills (D. W. Sue, Arredondo, & McDavis, 1992; D. W. Sue et al., 1982). A culturally competent counselor or provider is sensitive to her/his personal values and biases and how these may affect perceptions of the client, the client's problem, and the counseling relationship. The counselor has knowledge of the client's culture and expectations for the counseling relationship. In addition, the counselor is able to intervene in a manner that is culturally appropriate and relevant. We believe that the acceptance and mindfulness models may provide a promising method for promoting cultural competency and addressing social issues. However, to enhance the potential fruits that emerge from acceptance and mindfulness models, several pitfalls that have been associated with research and practice in psychology in general and mental health in particular must be addressed.

Critical Tasks in Developing Culturally Competent Acceptance and Mindfulness Interventions

We have previously indicated basic problems that confront the science and practice of psychology (S. Sue, 1999; S. Sue, 2009)—problems that are pertinent to acceptance and mindfulness interventions: (1) inadequacy of knowledge concerning ethnic (or nonmainstream) cultural populations, (2) culturally biased perspectives, and (3) sacrificing considerations of external validity in the promotion of internal validity in research. After presenting these issues and concerns, we offer some recommendations on how to improve the application of acceptance- and mindfulness-based therapies with culturally diverse populations.

Lack of Knowledge about Ethnic Minority Groups

Research on acceptance- and mindfulness-based treatments is still in a relatively early stage of development, and the available knowledge on their effectiveness in ethnic minority clients is especially sparse. For example, if we are interested in identifying what mental health treatment works *for whom* and under *what conditions*, very little empirical research is available to address this issue (DHHS, 2001). Woidneck, Pratt, Gundy, Nelson, and Twohig (2012) conducted a review of the literature to explore the utility of ACT with racially/ ethnically diverse populations due to the increased popularity of ACT. Findings indicated that a total of 42 studies were conducted in 10 different countries. All studies reported gender information, but only 21 of the studies provided race/ethnicity information. Interestingly, all the studies providing race/ethnicity information were conducted in the United States. Among these 21 trials, seven of them included 20% or more participants from a single non-White racial or ethnic group. Most studies did not report whether treatment effects differed by ethnic groups (probably due to small sizes). Woidneck et al. (2012) concluded "although the process-oriented nature of the ACT model suggests that it may be particularly amenable to adaptation for use with a variety of diversity related issues, this cannot occur without more research explicitly examining process differences in diverse populations" (p. 231).

Fuchs, Lee, Roemer, and Orsillo (2013) conducted a meta-analysis of acceptance- and mindfulness-based treatments with clients who are not traditionally the focus of psychological treatment outcome studies (e.g., non-White individuals, older adults, and individuals whose first languages were not that of the majority group). The review yielded 32 studies that met the inclusion criteria. Results showed that the effects of treatment outcomes varied by study, ranging from small to large. Fuchs et al. (2013) noted that the median number of participants in each study was only 28. Overall, findings from these reviews suggest that although some progress has been made in the inclusion of ethnic minorities, ethnic minorities are still underrepresented in most clinical trials. The specific acceptability and effectiveness of acceptance- and mindfulness-based treatments among ethnic minorities remains inconclusive due to the lack of empirical evidence. Given the dearth of research on acceptance- and mindfulness-based treatments among ethnic minorities, we must remain cautious when applying clinical findings to populations that are not well represented in the majority of clinical studies.

Cultural Bias in Intervention Models

Cultural bias in models of human beings involves an error in mistaking *emic* phenomena for *etic* phenomena. Emics are accounts of behaviors as seen from a particular culture—a culture-specific description. On the other hand, etics are accounts that are applicable to all cultures—a universally valid account. Problems occur when theories are assumed to be universally true when their validity is confined to one culture or population. Darley (2001) notes that:

> …psychology…has adopted the perspective that our task is to discover the basic mechanisms of human memory, emotion thought and action and to demonstrate by experiments that we have gotten it right. We demand that the generalizations that find their way into our Journals be empirically supported, preferably based on experimentation that allows for clear causal inference…. We believe that…we are discovering truths of human functioning that transcend culture and context. We are universalistic in our scientific aspirations….
>
> Unfortunately, a nasty thing happened on our way to our universal generalizations: culture and context turned out to have a much more fundamental effect on our generalizations than we expected. This has come home to social and cognitive psychologists in the discoveries of cultural psychologists (p. 3).

Perhaps one can argue that (1) non-Hispanic White Americans are not so different from ethnic minority groups that it would negate generalizing findings from one group to another or (2) in the absence of empirical research on all groups, it may be best to employ the treatment that has been found to be effective, albeit on one group. Can't we simply assume that research findings are universal and generalizable to all individuals, regardless of their backgrounds? Although some psychological theories or research findings can be generalized from one group to another, problems occur when assumptions of universality are made. These assumptions of universality are often inaccurate or even biased. Our position is that empirical studies must be conducted on diverse groups in order to draw valid conclusions, a practice that is consistent with sound scientific principles.

Is it possible that acceptance and mindfulness interventions are based on emic assumptions in which the benefits from recognizing one's contextual demands and emotions and increasing moment-to-moment awareness are culturally limited? For example, is it possible that in some cultural groups, psychological denial and avoidance are healthy (see Lazarus, 1993, for a discussion of healthy denial)? Conversely, might some cultural groups find acceptance and mindfulness principles especially congruent with their cultural beliefs and practices? Hall, Hong, Zane, and Meyer (2011) have argued that acceptance- and mindfulness-based psychotherapies are consistent with Buddhist meditation practices and, therefore, are more easily modified for use with Asian Americans. Research has increasingly demonstrated the effectiveness of acceptance and commitment therapy with Asians (see Hayes, Muto, & Masuda, 2011, and discussions by Hwang, 2011, and Leong & Kalibatseva, 2011). Obviously, much more research is needed to identify the effectiveness, underlying processes, and generality of findings associated with acceptance- and mindfulness-based therapies.

External and Internal Validity

Why is the current knowledge on acceptance- and mindfulness-based treatments in ethnic minority groups so limited? Although the area of acceptance- and mindfulness-based treatments is relatively new, we do not believe that the notion of underdevelopment can fully explain the lack of knowledge on acceptance- and mindfulness-based treatments in ethnic minority groups. Rather, it is our position that the current practice of scientific psychology in favor of internal validity over external validity hinders the quality, quantity, and funding of ethnic minority research. This bias is one of the major challenges faced by researchers and clinicians who are interested in studying the utility of acceptance- and mindfulness-based treatments with ethnic minority groups.

As noted by S. Sue (1999), the primary goal of psychological science is to describe, explain, predict, and modify phenomena through scientific research. One of the most important tasks in psychological science is the ability to make causal inferences through empirical research. We want to understand if a treatment leads to better clinical outcomes, that is, the cause-and-effect relationship. In order to draw causal relationships, research must involve internal and external validity. Internal validity refers to the extent to which conclusions can be drawn about the causal effects of one variable on another. On the other hand, external validity refers to the extent to which one can generalize the findings to populations and settings of interest. Both internal and external validity affect our ability to draw causal inferences, and both should be considered as equally important. If internal validity is low, it undermines the level of confidence upon which we can draw conclusions and make causal inferences. If external validity is low, the generalizability of a phenomenon to other populations and settings is questionable.

Although it is apparent that the scientific principles of internal and external validity are equally important, internal and external validity are not equal partners in practice. Because of the strong demand to make cause-and-effect relationships, experimental designs are generally considered as more rigorous than observational and correlational designs. Randomized controlled trials (RCTs) are the most widely accepted methodology for examining treatment effects, including acceptance- and mindfulness-based therapies. Unfortunately, it is unlikely that experiments are both high in internal and external validity. On the one hand, experimental designs (e.g., RCTs) allow researchers to draw causal inferences about a phenomenon under a highly controlled environment through the use of different techniques, such as setting strict inclusion and exclusion criteria (e.g., including patients with only one type of disorder) and random assignments. A controlled setting (e.g., academic research center) is typically an ideal setting for researchers to minimize noise and maximize internal validity. On the other hand, for researchers to achieve external validity, it is most ideal to conduct the experiment in a natural environment where noise and extraneous variables normally exist. Thus, tension always exists between internal and external validity. In practice, researchers pay much more attention to internal validity over external validity. Far more papers submitted for publications are rejected because of issues related to internal validity, such as design flaws, than for external validity problems. Research papers often pay little attention to the generalizability of the findings, or even simply assume the findings can be applied to other populations (S. Sue, 1999). However, Rothwell (2005) noted that the external validity of RCTs is often poor. Multiple factors, such as trial setting, selection of participants, and characteristics of participants, affect the external validity of RCTs. Nevertheless, the external validity of RCTs is often neglected by researchers, journals, and funding agencies. Far more research articles focus on reporting the internal validity of RCTs than on how findings should be applied in practice. Readers who are interested in the effectiveness of different types of psychotherapy are often given inadequate information to judge whether research findings can be applied to a certain population. In addition, the scoring criteria for judging the quality of RCTs focus far more on assessing internal validity. What this means is that intervention research, including that relevant to acceptance and mindfulness therapy, is far more focused on internal validity than on generality across different cultural groups and populations.

Representativeness of Research Samples

Perhaps because psychology has largely been developed in Western countries, especially in the United States, research has been conducted predominantly on participants from the United States. For example, Arnett (2008) conducted an analysis of articles published in six premier APA journals. From 2003 and 2007, 73% and 74% of the first authors and other authors were affiliated with an American university, respectively; 68% of the samples were in the United States. This pattern of American dominance has not changed during the past 20 years. Nevertheless, Americans compose less than 5% of the world's population, and yet, formal psychological theories have been most developed in the United States. This indicates that the vast majority of theories of psychopathology and well-being are derived from one country that represents only a small proportion of the world's population. Henrich, Heine, and Norenzayan (2010) argued that knowledge in psychology is based on Western, Educated, Industrialized, Rich, and Democratic (WEIRD) samples. Henrich et al. (2010) has comprehensively reviewed empirical findings in multiple domains and demonstrated that the behaviors of WEIRD samples are atypical of human beings throughout the world. Furthermore, researchers often implicitly assume that the findings based on the WEIRD samples are universally generalizable to all human beings. The reliance on the WEIRD database along with the implicit assumption of its generalizability has led to a biased representation of humanity (Arnett, 2008; Henrich et al., 2010). Thus, it is important for researchers and clinicians to evaluate whether the therapeutic process of acceptance- and mindfulness-based therapies is culturally sensitive, and if cultural adaptations or modifications can enhance treatment outcomes for ethnic minority clients. Initial evidence shows that the applicability of acceptance- and mindfulness-based treatments to ethnic minority groups is encouraging (Fuchs et al., 2013; Woidneck et al., 2012).

Culturally adapted acceptance- and mindfulness-based treatments especially have promise for application with ethnic minority clients (e.g., Hall et al., 2011).

Underrepresentation of Ethnic Minority Psychologists

Researchers and clinicians who are interested in ethnic minority research in general and acceptance- and mindfulness-based treatments in particular must face the fact that ethnic minority psychologists are persistently underrepresented, despite different efforts having been made to promote the recruitment and retention of ethnic minority professionals in psychology. For example, the APA Minority Fellowship Program (MFP) was founded in 1974 to provide professional development activities, career guidance, and financial support to promising doctoral students and postdoctoral psychologists (Jones & Austin-Dailey, 2009). The APA established the guidelines in an effort to enhance psychologists' knowledge and skills in multicultural education, training, research, practice, and organizational change (American Psychological Association, 2003). Nevertheless, ethnic minorities are still underrepresented in the field of psychology, especially at the doctoral and faculty representation levels. Maton, Kohout, Wicherski, Leary, and Vinokurov (2006) conducted a thorough analysis of the trends, between 1989 and 2003, in the representation of ethnic minorities in higher education in psychology. The encouraging trend was that there was a steady increase in the percentage of ethnic minority students obtaining bachelor's degrees from 1989 (13.6%) to 2002 (24.3%). Similarly, there was a steady increase in the percentage of master's degrees received by ethnic minority students from 1989 (10.6%) to 2003 (21.5%). Nevertheless, the troubling trends indicated that although there was a modest increase in the percentage of ethnic minorities receiving PhD degrees from 1989 (8.0%) to 1999 (15.1%), there has been no growth since then. The percentage of ethnic minority PhD recipients represented less than half of population representation. The representation for ethnic minority students entering PsyD departments was less than two-thirds of population representation. The even more disquieting trend was that ethnic minority full-time faculty represented less than two-fifths of population representation.

The lack of diversity among psychologists, especially at doctoral and faculty levels, has hindered the development of acceptance- and mindfulness-based treatments for different cultural groups. While it is stereotypic to suggest that members of certain cultural groups all have the same perspective or cultural beliefs, it is true that heterogeneity does increase different perspectives and viewpoints. The lack of ethnic minority psychologists means there is an inadequate representation of ethnic perspectives as well as visibility in administrative positions and leadership roles to advocate for important issues related to research and practice of acceptance- and mindfulness-based treatments, such as research funding and cultural competency in psychotherapy. In research, the apparent problems include the inadequate numbers of ethnic minority researchers, journal reviewers, and grant reviewers. In practice, there are not enough ethnic minority practitioners to deliver mental health services to culturally diverse clients. It is discouraging because the client-therapist match has been found to enhance treatment outcomes (Griner & Smith, 2006). The underrepresentation of ethnic minority psychologists has also made it difficult for ethnic minority students to find role models, mentors, and student peers for support. In a national survey of psychology graduate students, ethnic minority students were more likely to report a link between the academic barriers they experienced and their racial/ethnic status, compared to European American students (Maton et al., 2011). Ethnic minority students, compared to European American students, perceived that their racial/ethnic group was represented stereotypically or was not represented at all. Importantly, more ethnic minority students, relative to European American students, believed that psychology would offer something special to their ethnic group. This suggests that despite the fact that ethnic minority students encounter challenges associated with their ethnic backgrounds, ethnic minority students believe that they can address diversity issues and make an impact in our nation through psychological research.

Recommendations

What does the acceptance and mindfulness movement need to address in order to enhance practice, research, and theory? Despite the encouraging initial research of the applicability of acceptance- and mindfulness-based treatments to ethnic minority clients, much more innovative studies of ethnic minority clients are needed. We believe that the acceptance and mindfulness movement will be served well by engaging in several tasks.

First, the effectiveness of acceptance- and mindfulness-based treatments should be evaluated with individuals from diverse, under-served backgrounds. Much more attention should be paid to the importance of external validity, while maintaining the standards for internal validity. There should be true desire to include diverse populations in clinical research in order to improve mental health care for minority clients. Researchers should explicitly describe the samples in a way that readers can determine to whom the findings can be applied. In cases where treatments are only tested with limited populations, researchers and clinicians should not assume findings can be generalized to all populations unless they are empirically tested. By studying whether acceptance- and mindfulness-based treatments can be applicable to people from diverse backgrounds, researchers essentially contribute to the understanding of the universality of mental health treatments for all individuals.

Second, the processes underlying effective treatment using acceptance and mindfulness approaches should be identified. With this identification, aspects of the treatment that are more etic or emic can be ascertained. That is, are principles associated with acceptance and mindfulness more consistent with certain cultures or cultural patterns?

Third, evidence suggests that psychotherapeutic interventions are enhanced when they are culturally modified to meet the needs of diverse client populations (Griner & Smith, 2006; Smith et al., 2011). For example, such modifications in treatment can involve a method of delivery (e.g., responding to the ethnic language of clients, varying the style of interaction, or providing a cultural context for interventions) or the introduction of certain content in treatment (e.g., integrating ethnic cultural issues in the therapeutic interaction, discussing ethnic community supports, etc.). Discovering the kinds of cultural modifications that may be beneficial in acceptance and mindfulness therapy is a critical task.

Fourth, in addition to RCTs, a range of alternative research strategies should be considered when studying the feasibility and effectiveness of a treatment. As discussed, researchers who are interested in treatments for ethnic minority clients often encounter the fact that there is limited research available. Ethnic minority clients are often underrepresented in clinical trials. Community-based participatory research (CBPR) involves collaboration between community members and researchers to identify problems, inform research design, implement the study, and disseminate research findings. CBPR often utilizes qualitative methods—including focus groups, in-depth interviews, and ethnographies—to generate valuable baseline knowledge for the development of an intervention. CBPR is particularly useful in providing a deeper understanding of structural and cultural factors affecting mental health care and empowering community members to engage in all aspects of the study. Furthermore, single treatment open trials (STOTs) and single case design experiments (SCDEs) can provide preliminary evidence of the feasibility and effectiveness of a treatment prior to investing in a costly RCT (see Lau, Chang, & Okazaki, 2010, for a discussion of alternative strategies).

Finally, recruitment and retention of ethnic minority students, faculty, and staff are important. Undergraduate and graduate programs should offer courses in ethnic minority research and diversity issues. Training programs should expose trainees to clients from diverse backgrounds. Increasing the heterogeneity and participation in psychology will serve to increase perspectives and commitment to different cultural groups.

Summary

In this chapter, we have discussed some fundamental issues in the current practice of psychological science that may hinder the development of acceptance- and mindfulness-based treatments. Despite increased attention to diversity issues, ethnic minorities are still underrepresented in the field of psychology. Baseline knowledge on the effectiveness of treatments for ethnic minority groups is limited. While psychological science strives to maximize internal validity in order to draw causal inferences, external validity is often jeopardized. The current practice of psychological science has led to the failures in programs and practices, such as the underutilization of mental health services by ethnic minority clients.

We have made recommendations for the application of acceptance- and mindfulness-based therapies with culturally diverse populations. They include evaluating the effectiveness of treatments with individuals from diverse backgrounds, investigating the processes underlying effective treatment, examining the kinds of cultural modifications that may enhance treatment outcomes, utilizing a wide range of research strategies, and promoting the recruitment and retention of ethnic minority students and faculty. By engaging in these tasks, we believe that we are in a better position to address the fundamental issues related to the practice of psychological science in general and the application of acceptance- and mindfulness-based therapies in particular.

References

Alegría, M., Chatterji, P., Wells, K., Cao, Z., Chen, C. N., Takeuchi, D. et al. (2008). Disparity in depression treatment among racial and ethnic minority populations in the United States. *Psychiatric Services, 59,* 1264–1272.

American Psychological Association. (2003). Guidelines on multicultural education, training, research, practice, and organizational changes for psychologists. *American Psychologist, 58,* 377–402.

Arnett, J. J. (2008). The neglected 95%: Why American psychology needs to become less American. *American Psychologist, 63,* 602–614. doi: 10.1037/0003-066X.63.7.602.

Darley, J. (2001). We fail to contribute to policy debates. *APS Observer, 14,* 3.

Fuchs, C., Lee, J. K., Roemer, L., & Orsillo, S. M. (2013). Using mindfulness- and acceptance-based treatments with clients from nondominant cultural and/or marginalized backgrounds: Clinical considerations, meta-analysis findings, and introduction to the special series: Clinical considerations in using acceptance- and mindfulness-based treatments with diverse populations. *Cognitive and Behavioral Practice, 20*(1), 1–12. doi: 10.1016/j.cbpra.2011.12.004.

Griner, D., & Smith, T. B. (2006). Culturally adapted mental health interventions: A meta-analytic review. *Psychotherapy: Theory, Research, Practice, Training, 43,* 531–548. doi: 10.1037/0033-3204.43.4.531.

Hall, G. C. N., Hong, J. J., Zane, N. W. S., & Meyer, O. (2011). Culturally competent treatments for Asian Americans: The relevance of mindfulness and acceptance-based psychotherapies. *Clinical Psychology: Science and Practice, 18,* 215–231.

Hayes, S. C., Luoma, J., Bond, F., Masuda, A., & Lillis, J. (2006). Acceptance and commitment therapy: Model, processes, and outcomes. *Behaviour Research and Therapy, 44,* 1–25. doi: 10.1016/j.brat.2005.06.006.

Hayes, S. C., Muto, T., & Masuda, A. (2011). Seeking cultural competence from the ground up. *Clinical Psychology: Science and Practice, 18,* 232–237. doi: 10.1111/j.1468-2850.2011.01254.x.

Hayes, S. C., Strosahl, K., & Wilson, K. G. (1999). *Acceptance and commitment therapy: An experiential approach to behavior change.* New York: Guilford Press.

Henrich, J., Heine, S. J., & Norenzayan, A. (2010). The weirdest people in the world? *Behavioral and Brain Sciences, 33,* 61–135. doi: 10.1017/S0140525X0999152X.

Hwang, W. (2011). Cultural adaptations: A complex interplay between clinical and cultural issues. *Clinical Psychology: Science and Practice, 18,* 238–241. doi: 10.1111/j.1468-2850.2011.01255.x.

Jones, J. M., & Austin-Dailey, A. T. (2009). The Minority Fellowship Program: A 30-year legacy of training psychologists of color. *Cultural Diversity and Ethnic Minority Psychology, 15,* 388–399. doi: 10.1037/a0017558.

Kabat-Zinn, J. (1990). *Full catastrophe living: Using the wisdom of your body and mind to face stress, pain, and illness.* New York: Dell Publishing.

Lau, A. S., Chang, D. F., & Okazaki, S. (2010). Methodological challenges in treatment outcome research with ethnic minorities. *Cultural Diversity and Ethnic Minority Psychology, 16,* 573–580. doi: 10.1037/a0021371.

Lazarus, R.S. (1993). Coping theory and research: Past, present, and future. *Psychosomatic Medicine, 55,* 234–247.

Leong, F. T. L., & Kalibatseva, Z. (2011). Effective psychotherapy for Asian Americans: From cultural accommodation to cultural congruence. *Clinical Psychology: Science and Practice, 18,* 242–245. doi: 10.1111/j.1468-2850.2011.01256.x.

Linehan, M. M. (1993). *Cognitive-behavioral treatment of borderline personality disorder.* New York: Guilford Press.

Maton, K. I., Kohout, J. L., Wicherski, M., Leary, G. E., & Vinokurov, A. (2006). Minority students of color and the psychology graduate pipeline: Disquieting and encouraging trends, 1989–2003. *American Psychologist, 61,* 117–131. doi: 10.1037/0003-066X.61.2.117.

Maton, K. I., Wimms, H. E., Grant, S. K., Wittig, M. A., Rogers, M. R., & Vasquez, M. J. T. (2011). Experiences and perspectives of African American, Latina/o, Asian American, and European American psychology graduate students: A national study. *Cultural Diversity and Ethnic Minority Psychology, 17,* 68–78. doi: 10.1037/a0021668.

Rothwell, P. M. (2005). External validity of randomised controlled trials: "To whom do the results of this trial apply?" *Lancet, 365,* 82–93.

Segal, Z. V., Williams, J. M. G., & Teasdale, J. T. (2001). *Mindfulness-based cognitive therapy for depression: A new approach to preventing relapse.* New York: Guilford Press.

Smith, T., Domenech Rodríguez, M. M., & Bernal, G. (2011). Culture. *Journal of Clinical Psychology, 67,* 166–175. doi: 10.1002/jclp.20757.

Sue, D. W., Arredondo, P., & McDavis, R. (1992). Multicultural counseling competencies and standards: A call to the profession. *Journal of Counseling and Development, 70,* 477–486.

Sue, D. W., Bernier, J. B., Duran, M., Feinberg, L., Pedersen, P., Smith, E. et al. (1982). Position paper: Cross-cultural counseling competencies. *The Counseling Psychologist, 10,* 45–52.

Sue, S. (1999). Science, ethnicity, and bias: Where have we gone wrong? *American Psychologist, 54,* 1070–1077.

Sue, S. (2009). Ethnic minority psychology: Struggles and triumphs. *Cultural Diversity and Ethnic Minority Psychology, 15,* 409–415. doi: 10.1037/a0017559.

Sue, S., & McKinney, H. (1975). Asian Americans in the community mental health care system. *Journal of Orthopsychiatry, 45,* 111–118. doi: 10.1111/j.1939-0025.1975.tb01172.x.

U.S. Department of Health and Human Services (DHHS). (2001). *Mental health: Culture, race, and ethnicity. A Supplement to Mental Health: A Report of the Surgeon General.* Retrieved from http://www.surgeongeneral.gov/library/mental health/cre.

U.S. Department of Health and Human Services (DHHS), Agency for Healthcare Research and Quality. (2012). *National healthcare disparities report: 2011* (AHRQ Publication No. 11-0006). Retrieved from http://www.ahrq.gov /research/findings/nhqrdr/nhdr11/nhdr11.pdf.

Woidneck, M. R., Pratt, K. M., Gundy, J. M., Nelson, C. R., & Twohig, M. P. (2012). Exploring cultural competence in acceptance and commitment therapy outcomes. *Professional Psychology: Research and Practice, 43,* 227–233. doi: 10.1037 /a0026235.

CHAPTER 2

Psychotherapy in Cultural Context: An Overview

Akihiko Masuda, Ph.D.

Georgia State University

Acceptance, mindfulness, and values are recent "hot topics" in the field of psychotherapy and applied psychology (Baer, 2006; Hayes, Follette, & Linehan, 2004). A number of new cognitive and behavioral therapies have emerged that integrate mindfulness, acceptance, and values into their models and practice (Hayes, Villatte, Levin, & Hildebrandt, 2011). Examples of such interventions include acceptance and commitment therapy (ACT; Hayes, Strosahl, & Wilson, 1999), dialectical behavior therapy (DBT; Linehan, 1993), mindfulness-based cognitive therapy (MBCT; Segal, Williams, & Teasdale, 2002), and many others. These interventions have been applied in a wide range of health service settings for diverse individuals with a broad array of psychological and physical health issues (Hayes, Villatte et al., 2011).

Given their rapid expansion in recent years, it is quite natural for many to wonder about the cultural competency of acceptance- and mindfulness-based psychotherapies. For example, experts in diversity psychology (Hall, Hong, Zane, & Meyer, 2011) have raised concerns, such as whether cultural adaptation is necessary for these interventions when applied to ethnic minority individuals and whether their essential concepts and processes, such as acceptance, are culturally biased. As discussed elsewhere (Sue & Zane, 1987), we cannot fully grasp the heart of psychotherapy without considering the cultural context in which it occurs. Nevertheless, understanding the intricate interplay between psychotherapy and cultural context is extremely challenging. Despite extensive triumphs and progress in this area (Sue, 2009), we still have a long way to go.

To overcome this challenge, Sue and his colleagues (Sue, Zane, Hall, & Berger, 2009) suggest the adaptation of a bottom-up, pragmatic theoretical framework to systematically organize our knowledge and strategies. As such, the present chapter provides an empirically based conceptual framework, upon which some of the recent acceptance- and mindfulness-oriented psychotherapies are based. Because every conceptual model is developed from a particular worldview, we first present our essential philosophical assumptions and analytic goals. Subsequently, I will explicate a conceptual account of complex human behavior and discuss *culture* and *psychotherapy* within this conceptual framework. Finally, we will discuss whether acceptance, mindfulness, and values are culturally biased and delineate the potential contributions of the acceptance- and mindfulness-based approach to the issues of cultural diversity and competence.

Our Essential Perspective

There are almost infinite ways of viewing culture, psychotherapy and culture, and relevant topics (e.g., cultural competence; Sue et al., 2009). Although having diverse ideas can be viewed as a strength, it may also hinder advancement in the welfare and betterment of individuals (Sue et al., 2009). According to Hayes and his colleagues, this somewhat chaotic phenomenon in the topic of culture and psychotherapy is partially attributable to (a) different levels of analysis (e.g., biological, psychological, and social levels of analysis) used to understand culture and psychotherapy and the tension between these different levels of analysis (Hayes & Toarmino, 1995), (b) different worldviews (Hayes, Hayes, & Reese, 1988), and (c) the lack of a coherent theoretical framework for systematizing and refining our knowledge and skills (Hayes et al., 1999). As such, one way to clearly elucidate our position is to present our worldview, conceptual model, and the level of analysis at the outset.

Levels of Analysis

As the "biopsychosocial model" has flourished in the field of behavioral science, the link between culture and psychotherapy has been discussed at multiple levels (Chiao et al., 2010; Sue et al., 2009; Wang & Sue, 2005; Whaley & Davis, 2007). Different levels of analysis have distinct units of understanding (biological, psychological, and social), each with particular analytic goals. We consider no particular level of understanding (e.g., biological) to be superior to others (e.g., psychological; Hayes & Toarmino, 1995).

41

Psychological accounts of human behavior are conducted at the level of the individual. This level of analysis focuses on the *act of a whole individual*. The psychological level of analysis is relevant to, but different from, a biological or intraorganism level of understanding; biological levels focus on a part of an individual (e.g., brain or particular trait) as the fundamental unit of understanding. For example, at a psychological level of analysis, it is the entire person who thinks, not the brain or a particular cognitive schema, and it is the whole person who speaks, not the mouth or the language centers of the brain. Similarly, the psychological level of understanding is pertinent to, but distinct from, a group, social, or cultural level of analysis, because these levels focus on the practices of a *group* of individuals or a system, rather than the act of each individual member that composes that group.

These distinctions may be confusing because all cultural practices are also psychological events, but not vice versa, just as all psychological events are also biological events, but not vice versa (Hayes & Toarmino, 1995). This allows cultural phenomena to be discussed at a group/cultural level, at a psychological level, and at a biological level. Because such a reductionist approach is possible, however, knowledge applicable to a group may be incorporated into a psychological level of understanding without sensitivity to the idiographic nature of a given person. As Hall and his colleagues (2011) point out, a piece of information at the group level (e.g., "Asians are hardworking people") is not necessarily applicable to a given individual member of that group.

Functional Contextualism

Whether it is explicitly recognized or not, all people are bound to their worldview (i.e., philosophical perspective; Hayes et al., 1988). A worldview provides ways of making sense of the world, including personal experience. The author of the present chapter takes the perspective of functional contextualism (Biglan & Hayes, 1996). This fundamental worldview underlies a number of acceptance- and mindfulness-based psychotherapies that have been developed in recent years (Hayes, Villatte et al., 2011), as well as in many spiritual traditions, such as Buddhism (Hayes, 2002).

An essential aspect of functional contextualism is the view of an "act-in-context" as an ongoing process (Hayes et al., 1988). In this chapter, the terms "act" and "behavior" are used interchangeably, and at a psychological level of analysis, these terms refer to everything a person does and says as a whole organism, including feeling, thinking, and overtly behaving. As such, the terms "behavior" and "action" capture a wide range of activities and psychological processes (e.g., friendship, love, anxiety, compassion, culture, mindfulness, acceptance, values, and cultural competence), which are viewed in terms of "the behavior of a whole person in a historical and situational context."

The behavior of a given person cannot be separated from the context in which it occurs. This is because its very nature (e.g., function, purpose, and meaning) is found only within its intricate interaction with the context. Take the example of the present author speaking Japanese. He is bilingual and speaks Japanese and English. When he talks to his sister, he speaks Japanese. When he talks to his wife, he speaks English. From a functional and contextual perspective, simply viewing his behavior as speaking a particular language is incomplete because the behavior is essentially situational and historical. In any given moment, a behavior is the manifestation of his learning history intricately interacting with a current situational context, and it serves a particular purpose (e.g., communicating with his sister). A functional and contextual way of viewing a behavior is said to be *holistic* and *idiographic* since a given person has his or her own unique experience.

The goal of functional contextualism is the prediction-and-influence of the behavioral phenomenon of interest (Biglan & Hayes, 1996). An analysis is said to be "true" or "valid" to the extent that it leads to the achievement of this goal. Prediction-and-influence is one goal, not two separate ones. Prediction is used in a restricted sense that is bound to influence (Biglan & Hayes, 1996). For example, if the focus of analysis is the therapist's behavior of cultural competency, a functional contextualist asks not only "What is cultural competency?" but also "How can we influence the behavior of cultural competence?"

From a functional-contextual perspective, the first question cannot fully be answered without answers to the latter question. Additionally, we can identify an infinite number of cultural factors in analysis of cultural competence. And yet, functional contextualism takes only particular kinds of cultural factors into consideration. Once identifying the target behavior, we look for cultural factors that contribute to the occurrence of that behavior, and, at the same time, that can be influenced by the client or therapist or both. Finally, functional contextualism focuses on the "act-in-context" for this pragmatic purpose. From this perspective, it is the context that maintains the behavior of a whole person, and we can only influence the behavior through acting on the context where it occurs.

Functional and Contextual Theory of Complex Human Behavior

Relational frame theory (RFT) is a theory of complex human behavior that is based on functional contextualism (Hayes, Barnes-Holmes, & Roche, 2001). RFT postulates that almost all of our behaviors are learned, shaped, and maintained verbally. This conceptual position overlaps with conventional *behavioral principles* (Ramnerö & Törneke, 2008). RFT expands conventional accounts by highlighting the predominantly verbal nature of our behavior while also taking into consideration the context in which the behavior occurs for the purpose of behavior change (Hayes et al., 2001).

Verbal behavior (e.g., cognitive process, mental activity) is roughly defined as a process of describing, relating, and evaluating an event in terms of other events (Hayes et al., 2001). For example, the word "tree" is a symbolic representation of the actual experience of seeing, touching, and smelling a tree. We can think about a tree, describe a tree, and relate a tree to other objects because we can relate a symbolic, verbal representation (i.e., the word "tree") to actual experience. We can see the complexity of this symbolic relating when we think, ruminate, wonder, rationalize, believe, try to make sense of something, and so on. As humans are social beings, verbal processing becomes a central part of living. It occurs in almost every facet of our lives (Hayes et al., 2001).

Additionally, verbal processing has become a dominant source of regulating behaviors at both psychological and group levels (Hayes et al., 2001). This regulatory function of language occurs indiscriminately, whether a behavior is adaptive or not. For example, many clinically relevant behaviors, such as staying in bed when depressed, are regulated and maintained by verbal processes such as self-talk (e.g., "I'm too exhausted," "What's the point of getting up, anyway?"). At a group level, many cultural practices are often verbally transmitted from generation to generation.

There are several reasons we should emphasize verbal processes in psychotherapy and culture. First, in many clinical and applied contexts, behavior change involves verbal processes. In psychotherapy, client behavior change is navigated by the verbal exchange between the client and the therapist (Hayes et al., 1999). In cultural competency trainings, a therapist's behavior is shaped through his or her insight as well as through feedback from others (e.g., client, colleagues). Even in a high-context *less-verbal* communication culture, behavior change involves verbal processes.

Second, the products of verbal processing, such as particular beliefs or stereotypes (e.g., "I can't move on unless I keep all of my painful memories under control"), are difficult to eliminate once formed. We may develop new attitudes (e.g., "I can move on with pain"), but we cannot replace old ones with new ones (Wilson, Lindsey, & Schooler, 2000). Furthermore, attempts to eliminate and suppress unwanted thoughts and attitudes are futile and often counterproductive (Wegner, Schneider, Carter, & White, 1987). As mentioned in the following paragraphs, the rigidity of verbal ideas is particularly relevant to psychotherapy and cultural competency training.

Third, verbal processing can change the functions of other behavioral processes (Hayes et al., 2001). For example, suppose a person occasionally takes medicine for a physical or emotional ailment. Once hearing "medicine is toxic," she begins to avoid taking all medications without actually experiencing negative effects. As noted elsewhere (Hayes, Niccolls, Masuda, & Rye, 2002), this indirect learning is quite efficient and economical in many contexts, but it could be quite debilitating in other contexts.

One of the most debilitating features of verbal processing is that it can obscure here-and-now experience (Hayes et al., 1999). This is in part because, through verbal processing, we respond to a particular event (or person) in terms of its relation to other events. A salient example is stereotyping behavior. Because verbal processing is stereotype-generating by nature (Hayes et al., 2002), attempts to eliminate stereotypes and preconceptions are perhaps futile. Given the rigidity of verbal ideas, acceptance- and mindfulness-based psychotherapies, such as ACT, teach the client to coexist wisely with verbal processing, rather than trying to get rid of it.

A Functional and Contextual Account of Culture

What is culture from a functional and contextual point of view, and how is a functional and contextual account of culture different from extant views? In a recent article, Whaley and Davis (2007) define culture as "a dynamic process involving worldviews and ways of living in a physical and social environment shared by the groups, which are passed from generation to generation and may be modified by contacts between cultures in a particular social, historical, and political context" (p. 564). Whaley and Davis's account of culture, like those of many others, is based on a group level of analysis, whereby the focus is placed on the process of a group.

A functional and contextual account of culture varies, depending on the level of analysis and its analytic goal. At a group level, the definition of culture is translated into "the practice of a group in context." For example, cultural practices are thought to be behavioral events considered in terms of their prevalence in a population and analyzed in terms of contextual features that affect the social propagation and maintenance of these behaviors. As such, a culture is viewed as a set of functionally interrelated cultural practices (Hayes & Toarmino, 1995).

Contextual features that maintain a strong cultural practice may be entirely different from those that promote psychological adjustment of a given individual (Hayes, Muto, & Masuda, 2011). For example, staying married can be a cultural practice supported in diverse social communities. In these contexts, many people are often prohibited from getting a divorce even if staying in a marriage is extremely detrimental. Many cultural practices are maintained by contextual features that only emerge at the level of the group.

Psychotherapy is often viewed at the psychological level, where the focus is placed on a *given individual* interacting with another individual (Hall et al., 2011; Hwang, 2011). At this level of analysis, "culture" and "cultural factors" are translated into the framework of "behaviors of a *given person* in a historical and situational context." In this analysis, cultural factors are translated into the target behavior or contextual factors. As stated earlier, not all cultural factors are included in the analysis. Only the cultural factors that are relevant to the target behavior and that are systematically arranged by the client or the therapist are included in the analysis. For example, imagine that you are about to work with a 21-year-old Asian American male who wants to improve his communication skills with his family members, particularly with his parents. From a functional and contextual perspective, understanding the verbal and social contexts in which his communication with family members occurs is relevant. However, from a pragmatic point of view, if the verbal context cannot be arranged systematically, the analysis remains incomplete.

Acceptance, Mindfulness, and Values

The conceptualizations of acceptance, mindfulness, and values vary across researchers and practitioners (Hayes & Wilson, 2003). A functional and contextual perspective views acceptance, mindfulness, and values as ongoing *processes* of "behavior in a given context" (Biglan &

Hayes, 1996); these processes are particular *ways of relating* to our verbal processes.

Acceptance, Mindfulness, and Values as Behavioral Processes

In acceptance- and mindfulness-based psychotherapies, such as ACT, the focus is on the promotion of vital living. Vital living is marked by consciously being in contact with the present moment without needless defenses while persisting with and changing behavior in the service of chosen values (Hayes, Luoma, Bond, Masuda, & Lillis, 2006; Hayes, Villatte et al., 2011). As discussed elsewhere, verbal processes often keep us from contacting here-and-now experiences and amplify excessive defenses. Vital living is the presence of openness to one's experience, not necessarily the replacement of defenses with openness, in addition to the behavioral commitment to a life that is worth living.

Acceptance, mindfulness, and values reflect flexible and vital living through allowing us to coexist with our verbal behavior. Acceptance is a behavioral process of a whole person in a given context consciously allowing difficult psychological events (e.g., a negatively evaluated verbal event, such as anxiety) to be present and felt so as to be able to move in a valued direction. Mindfulness is characterized by purposeful awareness of the present moment in a way that is nonjudgmental and accepting of one's internal and external experience. Being nonjudgmental does not mean the absence of verbal judgment. Rather, it is the awareness of such verbal processes and the ability to choose a course of action freely, whether judgment is present or not. Finally, values are verbal processes that increase the likelihood of intrinsically reinforcing activity (see Hayes et al., 1999).

Acceptance, mindfulness, values, and vital living are behavioral processes with particular qualities (i.e., flexibility, openness, sensitivity, and vitality), and they are not bound to specific forms of attitudes or actions. For example, socializing with someone is a sign of acceptance to some individuals in particular contexts, and it can be an escape from reality for others. Similarly, experiencing anxiety as it is and acting inconsistently with it by continuing to talk may be a sign of vitality and flexibility. Experiencing anxiety as it is and not acting on it when almost being hit by a moving bus may not be so vital. We cannot see if a given behavior is flexible, open, sensitive, and vital merely in its form. To do so, we have to view it functionally and contextually.

Acceptance, Mindfulness, and Values as Therapeutic Techniques

The terms "acceptance," "mindfulness," and "values" are also used to describe a set of particular techniques and therapeutic styles (Hayes & Wilson, 2003). When viewed as techniques and styles, they are often viewed exclusively in their form (i.e., as topographical features). While topographical features can be the proxy of effective treatment and cultural competency, an exclusive emphasis on form obscures their principle-based nature. Acceptance, mindfulness, and value-based techniques are called such because they target the *processes* of acceptance, mindfulness, and values. From a functional and contextual perspective, topographical adherence to a treatment protocol does not necessarily affect the target processes (Ramnerö & Törneke, 2008). What is crucial in acceptance- and mindfulness-based psychotherapies is the functional and contextual adherence (Hayes, Muto et al., 2011).

Are Acceptance, Mindfulness, and Values Culturally Biased?

Experts in diversity psychology have recently argued that acceptance- and mindfulness-based therapies are culturally biased (Hall et al., 2011). We agree and disagree with this position, depending on how we conceptualize acceptance- and mindfulness-based psychotherapies, either topographically (i.e., as a set of techniques) or functionally and contextually (i.e., as a conceptual model). Specifically, a topographically defined psychotherapy is likely to be culturally biased because not all techniques will serve the same functions in different sociocultural contexts.

At the conceptual level, however, we believe that acceptance- and mindfulness-based psychotherapies are less culturally biased. This is in part because their conceptual models, especially the one presented in this chapter, are contextual and process based. As Whaley and Davis (2007) stated, a process-oriented account is less prone to cultural stereotypes than a topography- and content-oriented model. Furthermore, a growing body of evidence points to a broad applicability of acceptance- and mindfulness-based conceptual accounts (Hayes et al., 2006; Hayes, Muto et al., 2011; Hayes, Villatte et al., 2011). For example, diminished openness to one's difficult experience seems to be more or less applicable to emotional struggles experienced by a 21-year-old African American male as well as to those experienced by a 61-year-old Caucasian American female. Diminished value-directed living is likely to be related to a lower quality of life in a 41-year-old Asian American male who is physically disabled as well as in a 31-year-old Mexican American female who self-identifies as a "queer." In all cases, strategies that promote acceptance, mindfulness, and values seem to improve quality of life. That said, evidence is still limited, and we need to continue to investigate this assertion further.

Although the conceptual account does not change, topographical adaptation is inevitable for acceptance- and mindfulness-based psychotherapies when applied to a given individual. As mentioned earlier, what defines acceptance- and mindfulness-based psychotherapies are their functions in a given context, not necessarily their topographical presentations. For example, ACT is called ACT because it is designed to promote vital living through improving acceptance, mindfulness, values, and relevant processes (Hayes et al., 2006). As such, "cultural adaptation" or "individually tailored treatment" in form is assumed and expected when applied to a given individual (or group of individuals).

Cultural Competence: From an Acceptance and Mindfulness Perspective

Cultural competence is multifaceted, and the problems giving rise to cultural competency can be argued at multiple levels (e.g., treatment level, agency level, and systems level; Sue et al., 2009). That being said, this section focuses on the behaviors of a therapist in the context of psychotherapy as well as in the context of competency training.

At the level of therapist behavior (e.g., psychological level of analysis), Whaley and Davis (2007) view cultural competence as "a set of problem-solving skills that includes (a) the ability to recognize and understand the dynamic interplay between the heritage and adaptation dimensions of culture in shaping human behavior; (b) the ability to use the knowledge acquired about an individual heritage and adaptation challenges to maximize the effectiveness of assessment, diagnosis, and treatment; and (c) internalization (i.e., incorporation into one's clinical problem-solving repertoire) of this process of recognition, acquisition, and use of cultural dynamics so that it can be routinely applied to diverse groups" (p. 565). Similarly, Sue and colleagues (Sue et al., 2009) view cultural competence as a multidimensional process of "scientific mindedness (i.e., forming and testing hypotheses), dynamic sizing (i.e., flexibility in generalizing and individualizing), and culture-specific resources (i.e., having knowledge and skills to work with other cultures) in response to different kinds of clients" (p. 529). Concurring with Whaley and Davis (2007) as well as Sue et al. (2009), we believe that these behavioral processes are crucial for embodying an effective psychotherapy with a client in a given treatment as well as for working effectively with a diverse group of individuals. In this final section, we introduce several suggestions regarding cultural competence and cultural competency training. We especially focus on the impact of verbal processes and how they could promote and hinder our competency.

51

First, we cannot stress enough that no degree of knowledge about group memberships and the characteristics of those groups, no matter how detailed, can substitute for the individual level of knowledge when working with a given person (Hayes & Toarmino, 1995; Hwang, 2011). When the goal of analysis and intervention is behavior change of a given client (e.g., improvement in quality of life of *this* person), the case conceptualization and intervention should focus on the idiographic nature of that person. Only the individual level of understanding allows a therapeutic strategy specific to *this* person.

Second, choosing the cultural factors that should be taken into consideration depends on the goal of analysis/intervention as well as whether these factors can be systematically arranged in order to influence the behavioral phenomena of interest. For example, the goal of case conceptualization is not to gather an exhaustive number of cultural factors relevant to a given client, but to achieve its identified treatment goal.

Third, once becoming aware of one's own biases and stereotypes toward the client, the therapist does not have to make efforts to dispute the occurrence of these events. Verbal processing by nature is stereotype generating, and efforts to control the occurrence of stereotypes can disable us with fear. The problem is not having these events, but the impact that verbal processing may have on our actions. We can experience stereotyping views toward a particular individual and still connect with him or her genuinely and effectively. Acceptance- and mindfulness-based psychotherapies focus on learning to notice biases and stereotypes as they occur without acting on them. This stance can allow the therapist to choose and focus on his or her value-directed action in therapy without needlessly struggling with verbal content.

Fourth, acceptance- and mindfulness-based psychotherapies may provide balance in cultural competency training. They direct our focus to the promotion of what to do to be culturally competent (e.g., perspective taking, art of psychotherapy) in addition to what not to do. In cultural competency trainings, the focus is often placed on problem solving of culturally incompetent behaviors (e.g., biased thoughts, automatic behaviors). Nevertheless, the absence of culturally incompetent behaviors does not necessarily mean the prosperity of culturally competent behaviors.

Fifth, it is important to be mindful of one's own sense of self-righteousness. An attachment to the perceived sense of being right can be more harmful than useful even when we are doing the "right" thing. This is also the case for cultural competency trainings. Pointing out or correcting others' cultural incompetency from the sense of righteousness can even represent an act of stigmatization. Embracing the conflicts between the pursuit of cultural competency and the inevitability of posing stereotypes on self and others will provide a human level of cultural competency training.

Finally, it is important that those of us who highly value cultural competency consider whether specific training in group-level cultural competence is necessarily relevant or important for psychologists. We must first consider the function of cultural competency training in therapy and research settings. If our job is to promote cultural diversity and competency and to find common goals to promote the betterment of human beings and the world, then idiographic approaches, which consider the context of the individual, may be enough for adequate cultural competence.

Conclusion

Given the recent expansion of acceptance- and mindfulness-based psychotherapies in a wide range of clinical and applied areas, many wonder about the cultural competence of these psychotherapies and the extent to which cultural adaptation is necessary. Nevertheless, "culture and psychotherapy" is an extremely challenging topic. The present chapter provides a conceptual framework for organizing our knowledge to promote cultural competency and treatment effectiveness particularly at an individual level. I hope that this chapter initiates dialogue and efforts for further advancing diversity and cultural competency in the field of psychotherapy and applied psychology.

References

Baer, R. A. (2006). *Mindfulness-based treatment approaches: Clinician's guide to evidence base and applications.* San Diego, CA: Elsevier Academic Press.

Biglan, A., & Hayes, S. C. (1996). Should the behavioral sciences become more pragmatic? The case for functional contextualism in research on human behavior. *Applied & Preventive Psychology, 5*(1), 47–57. doi: 10.1016/s0962-1849(96)80026-6.

Chiao, J. Y., Hariri, A. R., Harada, T., Mano, Y., Sadato, N., Parrish, T. B. et al. (2010). Theory and methods in cultural neuroscience. *Social Cognitive and Affective Neuroscience, 5*(2–3), 356–361. doi: 10.1093/scan/nsq063.

Hall, G. C. N., Hong, J. J., Zane, N. W. S., & Meyer, O. L. (2011). Culturally competent treatments for Asian Americans: The relevance of mindfulness- and acceptance-based psychotherapies. *Clinical Psychology: Science and Practice, 18*(3), 215–231. doi: 10.1111/j.1468-2850.2011.01253.x.

Hayes, S. C. (2002). Buddhism and acceptance and commitment therapy. *Cognitive and Behavioral Practice, 9*(1), 58–66. doi: 10.1016/s1077-7229(02)80041-4.

Hayes, S. C., Barnes-Holmes, D., & Roche, B. (2001). *Relational frame theory: A post-Skinnerian account of human language and cognition.* New York: Kluwer Academic/Plenum Publishers.

Hayes, S. C., Follette, V. M., & Linehan, M. M. (2004). *Mindfulness and acceptance: Expanding the cognitive-behavioral tradition.* New York: Guilford Press.

Hayes, S. C., Hayes, L. J., & Reese, H. W. (1988). Finding the philosophical core: A review of Stephen C. Pepper's world hypotheses: A study in evidence. *Journal of the Experimental Analysis of Behavior, 50,* 97–111.

Hayes, S. C., Luoma, J. B., Bond, F. W., Masuda, A., & Lillis, J. (2006). Acceptance and commitment therapy: Model, processes and outcomes. *Behaviour Research and Therapy, 44*(1), 1–25. doi: 10.1016/j.brat.2005.06.006.

Hayes, S. C., Muto, T., & Masuda, A. (2011). Seeking cultural competence from the ground up. [Article]. *Clinical Psychology: Science & Practice, 18*(3), 232–237. doi: 10.1111/j.1468-2850.2011.01254.x.

Hayes, S. C., Niccolls, R., Masuda, A., & Rye, A. K. (2002). Prejudice, terrorism and behavior therapy. *Cognitive and Behavioral Practice, 9*(4), 296–301. doi: 10.1016/s1077-7229(02)80023-2.

Hayes, S. C., Strosahl, K. D., & Wilson, K. G. (1999). *Acceptance and commitment therapy: An experiential approach to behavior change.* New York: Guilford Press.

Hayes, S. C., & Toarmino, D. (1995). If behavioral principles are generally applicable, why is it necessary to understand cultural diversity? *The Behavior Therapist, 18,* 21–23.

Hayes, S. C., Villatte, M., Levin, M., & Hildebrandt, M. (2011). Open, aware, and active: Contextual approaches as an emerging trend in the behavioral and cognitive therapies. *Annual Review of Clinical Psychology, 7,* 141–168. doi: 10.1146/annurev-clinpsy-032210-104449.

Hayes, S. C., & Wilson, K. G. (2003). Mindfulness: Method and process. *Clinical Psychology: Science and Practice, 10*(2), 161–165. doi: 10.1093/clipsy/bpg018.

Hwang, W.-C. (2011). Cultural adaptations: A complex interplay between clinical and cultural issues. *Clinical Psychology: Science and Practice, 18*(3), 238–241. doi: 10.1111/j.1468-2850.2011.01255.x.

Linehan, M. M. (1993). *Cognitive-behavioral treatment of borderline personality disorder.* New York: Guilford Press.

Ramnerö, J., & Törneke, N. (2008). *The ABCs of human behavior: Behavioral principles for the practicing clinician.* Oakland, CA: New Harbinger Publications.

Segal, Z. V., Williams, J. M. G., & Teasdale, J. D. (2002). *Mindfulness-based cognitive therapy for depression: A new approach to preventing relapse.* New York: Guilford Press.

Sue, S. (2009). Ethnic minority psychology: Struggles and triumphs. *Cultural Diversity and Ethnic Minority Psychology, 15*(4), 409–415. doi: 10.1037/a0017559.

Sue, S., & Zane, N. (1987). The role of culture and cultural techniques in psychotherapy: A critique and reformulation. *American Psychologist, 42*(1), 37–45. doi: 10.1037/0003-066x.42.1.37.

Sue, S., Zane, N., Hall, G. C. N., & Berger, L. K. (2009). The case for cultural competency in psychotherapeutic interventions. *Annual Review of Psychology, 60*, 525–548. doi: 10.1146/annurev.psych.60.110707.163651.

Wang, V. O., & Sue, S. (2005). In the eye of the storm: Race and genomics in research and practice. *American Psychologist, 60*(1), 37–45. doi: 10.1037/0003-066x.60.1.37.

Wegner, D. M., Schneider, D. J., Carter, S. R., & White, T. L. (1987). Paradoxical effects of thought suppression. *Journal of Personality and Social Psychology, 53*(1), 5–13. doi: 10.1037/0022-3514.53.1.5.

Whaley, A. L., & Davis, K. E. (2007). Cultural competence and evidence-based practice in mental health services: A complementary perspective. *American Psychologist, 62*(6), 563–574. doi: 10.1037/0003-066x.62.6.563.

Wilson, T. D., Lindsey, S., & Schooler, T. Y. (2000). A model of dual attitudes. *Psychological Review, 107*(1), 101–126. doi: 10.1037/0033-295x.107.1.101.

CHAPTER 3

Supporting Multicultural Competence within Acceptance-Based Treatments: Chess Pieces in Context

Page L. Anderson, Ph.D., Kelly M. Lewis, Ph.D., Suzanne Johnson, Jessica R. Morgan, Jalika Street

Georgia State University

Notice that the (chess) board also holds an unlimited number of white pieces that hang out together—so thoughts that you really are competent and worthwhile and that things really will work out for you in the end may team up with feelings of self-confidence and memories you have of past successes in your life. But there are black pieces on the board that are just the opposite of the white ones. So, over here you may have a white piece that says, "I'm OK and things are going to work out for me." But over there is a black one that says, "Who are you kidding? You're not OK—all you've done is make a big mess of your life." It may seem like both sets of pieces can't coexist and so the black ones have to be gotten rid of. But if the pieces are merely your thoughts and feelings, can't they both be present? Can you have the thought that you're OK and the thought that you're not OK at the same time?

—Steven C. Hayes & Kirk D. Strosahl, *A Practical Guide to Acceptance and Commitment Therapy* (2005)

The chessboard metaphor is well known within acceptance and commitment therapy (ACT; Hayes, Strosahl, & Wilson, 2012), and may be used in a variety of mindfulness- and acceptance-based treatments. Recently, it was used in an exercise during a doctoral course on cognitive and behavioral therapies taught by one of the authors. Students were asked to choose a principle about which they wanted to learn more and to demonstrate how it might be used in the therapy room. One student chose to talk about defusion and then role-played with an African American classmate using the chessboard metaphor described above to demonstrate this principle. Classmates grew visibly uncomfortable as the student therapist discussed "bad black thoughts" with the African American "client."

Contextual behavioral science (CBS) researchers have repeatedly cautioned that third-wave behavior therapies are not defined by the topography of a behavioral exchange within the therapy room (Hayes, Muto, & Masuda, 2011; Hayes, Strosahl et al., 2012). That is, third-wave behavioral approaches arising from CBS emphasize the *functions* of behavior over the *form* of behavior. What is important is that therapist behaviors, such as the use of metaphor, help clients move toward values-driven action (Vilardaga, Hayes, Levin, & Muto, 2009). Thus, one must examine the function and purpose of the behavior in the therapy room. So, it is legitimate to ask, "Was this exchange appropriate from an ACT perspective?" Suppose the therapist's hypothesis is that the client's suffering is maintained by cognitive fusion, and the metaphor is used to try to loosen up those verbal processes in which the client is entangled and to support a sense of self that transcends any particular thought. Is it appropriate to use this particular metaphor with this particular client for that purpose? How does the therapist know? Can the therapist evaluate the potential utility of the metaphor a priori, or is it only possible to determine its usefulness by examining its impact on the client's behavior? Suppose that the metaphor did serve to introduce the notion of a transcendent sense of self and decrease cognitive defusion, would the use of the metaphor be ACT consistent? Is the use of the metaphor consistent with culturally competent practices?

In this role-play, we had the luxury of immediately processing the exchange with the help of many observers. The "therapist," who also was a student of color, was primarily focused on using the metaphor to try to convey defusion—the purpose of the exercise. The therapist reported that while preparing for the exercise, she was aware of racial implications in the metaphor but also knew the chessboard to be commonly used as a way to convey cognitive defusion. The student "client" said that although the metaphor did convey the concept of cognitive defusion, he was highly aware of race in the metaphor. He did not bring it up while engaged in the role-play—only when specifically asked about it in the processing of the role-play afterward did he discuss his discomfort with it. The class wondered whether the client would return if this were a real therapy session. For the students in the class, the experience highlighted the importance of tailoring treatment to the individual needs of each client. This conclusion is consistent with ACT's idiographic approach to therapy in general and with culturally competent practice (Hayes et al., 2011). It is an idea to which we will return later in the chapter.

Another consistency between acceptance-based treatments and diversity psychology's perspective on cultural competence is viewing behavior holistically and in context (Vilardaga et al., 2009). Cultural competence is essential not only at a micro level, as in the therapeutic exchange described earlier, but also from a macro-level perspective. Cultural factors exist at higher-level ecologies that, in turn, impact what goes on in the personal space of the therapy room. For example, the therapist's behavior will not only be influenced by his or her own cultural background (e.g., age, nationality) but also by the sociocultural context of his or her training. The therapist is taught within a training program, and the training program is guided by research. This research is conducted by individuals who have the privilege of framing research questions, is conducted with particular groups of people, and is peer reviewed by individuals with the privilege to do so. Does this matter for third-wave behavioral approaches?

The very existence of this book suggests that scholars and practitioners of acceptance- and mindfulness-based approaches believe that it does matter. In this chapter, we introduce some constructs from diversity psychology that inform multicultural competence and consider how such constructs fit within acceptance-based therapies.

Multicultural Competence: Awareness, Knowledge, and Skills

It is critical that psychologists develop cultural competence so that service providers can work effectively with individuals from different backgrounds, and so that the science that informs service providers is conducted in a culturally competent manner. Multicultural competence is increasingly a part of the discussion within various professional organizations, accrediting bodies, and training programs (Dadlani & Scherer, 2009).

Cultural competence involves increasing one's awareness, knowledge, and skills (D. W. Sue & D. Sue, 2008). This model is the foundation of APA's multicultural guidelines across cultural differences (American Psychological Association, 2002). *Awareness* is consciousness of our personal reactions, assumptions, values, and beliefs about people from whom we are different. It is important that therapists develop an awareness of their cultural identities and beliefs in order to better understand how their perspectives impact their perceptions of their patients (Ponterotto, Gretchen, Utsey, Rieger, & Austin, 2002; D. W. Sue & Torino, 2005). Awareness of these social identities is positively connected with how therapists conceptualize and relate to their patients (Gelso & Hayes, 2007), as well the strength of the psychotherapy relationship (Dadlani & Scherer, 2009). Awareness of bias is typically a difficult aspect of cultural competence to cultivate because it is challenging to acknowledge our own biases. However, just as psychologists are subject to errors in decision making and judgment (Kahneman & Tversky, 1973), we also are subject to biases and stereotypes. For example, Abreu (1999) found that therapists primed with words stereotyped as African American subsequently rated a fictional client as significantly more hostile than therapists primed with neutral words. We note that biases and prejudices are part of the human condition. No one is exempt from them—e.g., by holding a particular political orientation or by being a part of a minority group about which there are stereotypes. Each person must do this work of awareness building.

A second dimension in the cultural competence model is *knowledge* of culturally diverse groups. Fortunately, there is empirical literature on differences across cultural groups with regard to concepts relevant to acceptance-based therapies, including worldview (Utsey, Fisher, & Belvet, 2010), communication styles (Smith, 2011), value orientation (Kluckhohn & Strodbeck, 1961), help-seeking behavior (Arnault, 2009), and utilization of mental health services, among others. Psychologists are socialized to value such research literature as informing psychotherapy, and so the process of seeking knowledge is familiar and comfortable. Cultural competence, however, also requires willingness to acquire knowledge about a group's history, as well as the impact of oppression and stereotypes (D. W. Sue & Sue, 2008). This type of knowledge may fall outside a therapist's comfort zone or be less likely to be seen as relevant. For example, those in the helping fields are typically motivated by a desire to help. Such intentions could, in turn, make it difficult for therapists to be aware of how cultural mistrust may be operating within the therapy room. Consider a same-sex couple presenting for therapy with the goal of increasing the adaptive functioning of a child with developmental delays. It is very likely that the therapist will present and utilize principles of operant and classical conditioning to support this goal. However, the meaning of these behavioral principles may be different for a couple whose cultural history includes knowledge that these same behavioral principles were used to conduct "reparation therapy" to change sexual orientation. If the therapist is knowledgeable of such history, she or he may be better prepared to engage effectively with the couple if, for example, there are problems coming to agreement on a treatment plan.

Another reason it is important to develop knowledge about particular groups is that psychology as a field tends to be dominated by an *etic* perspective on behavior; that is, we attempt to identify universal principals of behavior that apply to all cultures. Although this goal is valuable and has led to many advances, a criticism of psychology is that principles of human behavior that are viewed as etic (or universal) in fact reflect an emic perspective of the dominant cultural group (D. W. Sue & Sue, 2008). Much of the basic psychological research with humans is conducted with White, upper-middle-class college students in the United States (Maulik, Mendelson, & Tandon, 2011). Research with clinical populations also is overrepresented by people with particular demographic characteristics (American Psychological Association, 2005). It can, in fact, be difficult to ascertain the demographic characteristics within clinical research, as they are not often fully reported (Iwamasa, Sorocco, & Koonce, 2002)—for example, studies that report only the proportion of "Caucasian" participants or the proportion of those who are "married." Thus, it requires effort to increase our knowledge about the inclusion of nondominant cultural groups.

In contrast to an etic perspective, knowledge related to cultural competence is often considered *emic*—that is, applicable within a particular group (e.g., Chinese immigrants). An emic perspective may be valuable as a starting place to consider the impact of a client's sociocultural identity and context on his or her functioning. It is important to note, however, that each client holds multiple identities. The *intersectionality* framework, rooted in the feminist and critical race theory traditions, is useful to highlight within social group variance (Cole, 2009). This framework emphasizes that each person's multiple identities interact to form a unique sociocultural context for individuals that can itself vary across contexts. For example, a therapist working on sexual issues with a client who uses a wheelchair may immediately focus on the physical disability (which is visible) and fail to recognize the salience of the client's religion or sexual orientation (which may be less visible). Although the intersectionality framework may appear conceptually similar in some ways to an idiographic approach to behavior, it is important that *knowledge* of each form of identity inform hypotheses about how cultural identities may intersect and influence behavior.

Cultural competence requires more than awareness and knowledge; it also requires *skill* in applying such knowledge to a particular person. Knowledge about universal principles (etic), about differences between cultural groups, or about a specific cultural group (emic) may be misapplied in working with a particular client. For example, knowledge about a particular group (e.g., Asians express depressive symptoms somatically) does not mean that it is true for every given member of that group. In addition, a particular social identity may or may not be relevant for the presenting issue. Given that much of the history and experience of cultural minority groups is relatively invisible to cultural majority groups, and most researchers and providers represent dominant cultural groups, much emphasis within multicultural psychology has been geared to increasing awareness of the relevance of cultural factors. Therapists can, however, overemphasize the salience of a particular cultural factor. Consider a couple who is bringing their child for parent training; the fact that the parents are a same-sex couple may or may not be relevant. Therapists must be especially cautious when emphasis on a cultural identity could reinforce a stereotype or a deficit model of the cultural group (e.g., that children raised in a family with same-sex parents will be maladjusted). A therapist's anxiety about working across differences can lead to either under- or overemphasis of cultural factors. For example, if a therapist has never worked with a person of a particular race, the therapist may work too hard to demonstrate his or her knowledge about the group when it has no applicability to presenting issues. Cultural identity and its relevance should be evaluated for each case by a therapist with the skill to identify which sociocultural issues are relevant for a client's concerns.

Power and Privilege

We have highlighted the importance of increasing awareness, knowledge, and skills in the service of cultural competence. Power and privilege are two constructs from diversity psychology that can help cultivate these aspects of cultural competence. *Power* is a dynamic of "relational influence and control" present within all social interactions, and *privilege* is the phenomenon in which a person who has power receives unearned benefits at the expense of those who do not have privilege (Piper & Treyger, 2010). Different groups hold different levels of power and privilege, based on their context and social identities.

Therapists recognize that their role confers power, and ethical codes of conduct exist, in part, to make sure that the power differential does not harm clients. Privilege, however, can be more difficult to see and is a difficult concept to apply to our own lives. Part of what makes it so challenging to accept is that when we benefit from privilege, we generally are unaware of the advantages it confers. It is far easier to see how some cultural groups are disadvantaged than to see how people in the dominant cultural group benefit. A classic paper used to introduce the idea of privilege in multicultural courses approaches this challenge by enumerating the ways in which White privilege operates in the author's life: "I can do well in a challenging situation without being called a credit to my race" and "I can count on my skin color not to work against the appearance of financial reliability" (McIntosh, 1988). Therapists seeking to increase their multicultural competence, particularly awareness, should also work to see how privilege operates in their own life and how it can affect our beliefs about and behaviors within the therapy room. Privilege is connected to many cultural identities, not only race. Privilege is also fluid; what is privileged in one context may not be in another (e.g., being Christian may yield privilege in some areas of the world, but not in others). Virtually everyone will have the experience of privilege in some identity area and should be aware of its benefits and its impact on his or her work. For example, if a clinician professes to "color blindness," he or she may not acknowledge the importance of race and cultural differences. A focus on universal behavioral principles may echo the sentiment "we are all human" and undermine the experience of minorities. Fear of magnifying differences at the expense of the therapeutic alliance may unintentionally lead to this dynamic (Qureshi & Collazos, 2011). For example, a common message of practitioners of acceptance-based therapies is that the therapist is "in the same soup" as the client. The therapist must have the awareness that this message could function to minimize the client's experience.

What does this have to do with cultural competence within mindfulness- and acceptance-based treatments? As contextual behavior scientists remind us, behavior is best viewed holistically and in context (Vilardaga et al., 2009). As a relative newcomer to the field, third-wave behavioral therapies have the potential to address some of the long-standing problems within clinical research, including the inadequacy of knowledge across different populations, biased perspectives, and lack of external validity in much of the research (S. Sue, 1999). Indeed, a goal of third-wave behavioral approaches is to create a science "more adequate to the challenge of the human condition," which naturally involves issues of diversity (Hayes, Barnes-Holmes, & Wilson, 2012). And, a recently stated goal of CBS researchers is to better adapt mindfulness- and acceptance-based treatments in a culturally competent manner (Hayes, Barnes-Holmes et al., 2012). Researchers studying constructs related to third-wave approaches can be mindful of how privilege may impact who gets to do the research, frame the questions, and design treatments based on that research.

Integrating Multicultural Theory and Acceptance-Based Treatments

Many of the philosophical and theoretical assumptions underlying CBS are consistent with basic concepts of multicultural competence. A major component of diversity training, for example, involves identifying and recognizing one's own worldview in order to better understand worldview differences that may lead to cross-cultural misunderstanding and prejudice (Qureshi & Collazos, 2011). Without recognizing the underlying assumptions of work in the psychological sciences, it may be difficult or impossible to recognize built-in prejudices in our understanding of human behavior. Consistent with this concept, CBS theorists have consciously sought to define the philosophy and worldview underlying their approach to understanding human behavior at multiple levels of analysis (Hayes & Brownstein, 1986; Hayes, Strosahl et al., 2012) from the purpose of science globally

(Hayes & Brownstein, 1986) to the micro level of understanding the individual in his or her context (Hayes, Strosahl et al., 2012).

Major components of the psychological flexibility model itself also may lend themselves well to models of cultural competence and may inform ways to increase cultural competence. In particular, this model emphasizes that psychological suffering and problematic behaviors are often a result of the regulatory function of verbal behavior (Hayes, Strosahl et al., 2012). Stigma and prejudice toward diverse groups, from this perspective, are the unfortunate result of normal, automatic human verbal processes, such as categorization and association (Hayes, Niccolls, Masuda, & Rye, 2002). Without recognizing these biases and choosing to relate to them differently, contextual behavioral accounts posit that they will continue to serve a behavior regulatory function and thus lead to discriminatory behavior. From a multicultural competence perspective, it is also assumed that all human beings, regardless of background, will have biases and prejudices of which they are unaware; awareness of these biases is the first step to increasing cultural competence and decreasing their impact on behavior (D. W. Sue & Sue, 2008). Similarly, psychological flexibility emphasizes increased awareness of thoughts we try to suppress, in order to reduce the behavior regulatory function that thoughts have on overt behavior (Hayes, Barnes-Holmes et al. 2012).

Although there are places of harmony between acceptance-based approaches and concepts of multicultural competence, there are also places of tension. Analyzing a client's behaviors within his or her sociocultural context is considered inherent in good practice of acceptance-based treatment (Hayes & Toarmino, 1995); however, treatment models may not be sufficient on their own when clinicians or researchers confront diversity-related issues in their professional work. For example, a client who has experienced sexual discrimination may struggle with verbal content related to this experience, such as, "It seems like my ideas don't matter to others because of my gender." Acceptance-based treatment recommends that clients defuse from painful or uncomfortable verbal content in order to show that language does not in itself hold meaning (Hayes, Barnes-Holmes et al. 2012). When applied to experiences of sexual discrimination, this intervention may not only invalidate the individual's experience but, when delivered by a clinician unaware of biases and prejudices, may function to silence the client's expression in order to reduce the clinician's discomfort. CBS theory argues that individualized, tailored treatment will naturally lead to cultural adaptation (Hayes et al., 2011), but a clinician who is less aware of his or her own prejudicial thinking, as well as the client's historical and cultural context and its impact, may neglect to consider such issues during the assessment.

Contextual behavioral approaches also emphasize that verbal content is difficult to eliminate or modify once formed, and thus, should not be directly targeted. ACT theorists, in particular, would argue that relating differently to internal verbal content is likely to be more fruitful than changing the verbal content itself. However, it is unlikely that targeting the individual's relationship with internal stimuli and promoting values-driven behavior change without a specific emphasis on diversity is sufficient for true cultural competence. Diversity theory argues that seeking out behavioral contexts that actually alter these biases is necessary, and that in "getting out of your cultural comfort zone" new verbal content is introduced and competes with previous biases, directly impacting behavior.

The Chessboard Revisited

How might have the behaviors of multicultural competence informed the role-play described at the beginning? A psychotherapist who had developed *awareness* of his or her own biases may be more sensitive as to whether or not this metaphor is appropriate for use with a person of color. With *knowledge* about the ways in which language supports stereotypes and biases, the therapist may have been more attuned to the racial implications of this metaphor. And, with *skills* in applying this knowledge to therapeutic endeavors, the therapist may have chosen a different metaphor to communicate the principle of defusion, without defining the black pieces as "bad." Alternatively, this metaphor could be used as an opportunity to discuss the deeply ingrained cultural message within the metaphor—that is, the association between white and "good or right" and black and "bad or wrong" and how the individual's (and culture's) entanglement in such verbal processes leads to suffering.

Recommendations for Supporting Multicultural Competence

We hope that we have highlighted that seeking cultural competence is necessary to conducting competent treatment, even when treatment is approached in an idiographic manner and is individually tailored to each client. A reader convinced of this aim may be wondering which behaviors may support cultural competence in one's own research and practice:

- Recognize that the status quo of current practice is not to assess or consider cultural identity. Develop a practice to facilitate this process. One framework that can cue therapists to assess some of the potential intersecting identities is ADDRESSING (Age, Developmental and acquired Disabilities, Religion, Ethnicity, Socioeconomic status, Sexual orientation, Indigenous heritage, National origin, and Gender; Hays, 2001).

- Consider the impact of power and privilege in your own work. This awareness can be used to better understand your client's context as well as the psychotherapy relationship. Keep in mind that individuals in positions of power are often unable to see the unearned privileges that they are afforded.

- Admit personal biases, stereotypes, and prejudices.

- Become aware of cultural norms, attitudes, and beliefs.

- Be willing to extend yourself psychologically and physically to the patient population.

- Attend diversity-related workshops and courses.

- Travel to another country or community and immerse yourself in the local culture.

- Consider the client's language preferences and ensure that treatment is conducted in the appropriate language.

- Recognize that holding a particular identity does not mean that you will be culturally competent in working with that group.

- Know how your culture is viewed by others.

- Watch movies/documentaries and read about other cultures.

- Attend cultural events and festivals.

Multicultural Skills in the Context of Therapy

- Make sure conceptualizations, assessments, and treatment plans include explicit discussion of cultural context.

- Consider that an idiographic approach to assessment and treatment may not equate to cultural competence.

- Initiate conversations about cultural difference, prejudice, and bias if potentially therapeutic. Engaging in open conversations about how these differences can strengthen the therapeutic relationship lead to more appropriate assessment/ conceptualization/treatment. Because issues of difference can be uncomfortable to speak about, clinicians can practice these skills with supervisors and colleagues. Remember that what's *not* being talked about also sends a message. Because the therapist holds a position of power, clients may be hesitant to initiate these conversations and it is not exclusively their responsibility to do so.

- Consider the extent to which your physical space and materials (e.g., website, recruitment flyers) welcome or inhibit aspects of diversity. For example, is your space (including the furniture, artwork, etc.) suited both for the population you serve (e.g., children) and for diversity within this group (e.g., accessible to children with physical disabilities)?

- Establish professional/working relationships with people of different cultures.

- Learn verbal and nonverbal cues of other cultures.

- Learn to negotiate between the person's beliefs and practices and the culture of your profession.

- Learn to develop and evaluate culturally relevant and appropriate programs, materials, and interventions.

Finally, we wish to highlight that seeking cultural competence is a lifelong process. It is a process for all of us—not only for those of us in the dominant cultural group. This chapter has emphasized multicultural competence within therapy, but multicultural competence is critically important for teaching and research, as well. Just as clinicians should keep up with the scientific literature, researchers should educate themselves in issues related to diversity and culture. Indeed, as relative newcomers to psychology, contextual behavior scientists have the potential to better integrate the two.

References

Abreu, J. M. (1999). Conscious and nonconscious African American stereotypes: Impact on first impression and diagnostic ratings by therapists. *Journal of Consulting and Clinical Psychology, 67*(3), 387. doi: 10.1037/0022-006X.67.3.387.

American Psychological Association (2002). *Guidelines on multicultural education, training, research, practice, and organizational change for psychologists—American Psychological Association.* Retrieved December 4, 2013 from http://www.apa .org/pi/oema/resources/policy/multi cultural-guidelines.aspx.

American Psychological Association (2005). APA 2000: A perfect vision of psychology. *American Psychologist, 60,* 512–522.

Arnault, D. S. (2009). Cultural determinants of help seeking: A model for research and practice. *Research and Theory for Nursing Practice: An International Journal, 23*(4), 259–278.

Cole, E. R. (2009). Intersectionality and research in psychology. *American Psychologist, 64*(3), 170–180. doi: 10.1037/a0014564.

Dadlani, M., & Scherer, D. (2009). Culture in psychotherapy practice and research: Awareness, knowledge, and skills. American Psychological Association, Division of Psychotherapy, Division 29.

Gelso, C. J., & Hayes, J. A. (2007). *Countertransference and the therapist's inner experience: Perils and possibilities.* Mahwah, NJ: Erlbaum.

Hayes, S. C., Barnes-Holmes, D. & Wilson, K. G. (2012). Contextual behavioral science: Creating a science more adequate to the challenge of the human condition. *Journal of Contextual Behavioral Science, 1*(1), 1–16.

Hayes, S. C., & Brownstein, A. J. (1986). Mentalism, behavior-behavior relations, and a behavior-analytic view of the purposes of science. *The Behavior Analyst, 9*(2), 175–190.

Hayes, S. C., Muto, T., & Masuda, A. (2011). Seeking cultural competence from the ground up. *Clinical Psychology: Science and Practice, 18*(3), 232–237. doi: 10.1111/j.1468-2850.2011.01254.x.

Hayes, S. C., Niccolls, R., Masuda, A., & Rye, A. K. (2002). Prejudice, terrorism, and behavior therapy. *Cognitive and Behavioral Practice, 9*(4), 296–301.

Hayes, S. C., & Strosahl, K. D. (2005). *A practical guide to acceptance and commitment therapy.* New York, NY: Springer Science + Business Media.

Hayes, S. C., Strosahl, K. D., & Wilson, K. G. (2012). *Acceptance and commitment therapy: The process and practice of mindful change* (2nd ed.). New York: Guilford Press.

Hayes, S. C., & Toarmino, D. (1995). If behavioral principles are generally applicable, why is it necessary to understand cultural diversity? *The Behavior Therapist, 18,* 21–23.

Hays, P. A. (2001). *Addressing cultural complexities in practice: A framework for clinicians and counselors.* Washington, DC: Greenwood.

Iwamasa, G. Y., Sorocco, K. H., & Koonce, D. A. (2002). Ethnicity and clinical psychology: A content analysis of the literature. *Clinical Psychology Review, 22*(6), 931–944. doi: 10.1016/S0272-7358(02)00147-2.

Kahneman, D., & Tversky, A. (1973). On the psychology of prediction. *Psychological Review, 80,* 237–251.

Kluckhohn, F. R., & Strodbeck, F. L. (1961). *Variations in value orientations.* Evanston, IL: Row, Patterson, & Co.

Maulik, P. K., Mendelson, T., & Tandon, S. D. (2011). Factors associated with mental health services use among disconnected African-American young adult population. *The Journal of Behavioral Health Services and Research, 38*(2), 205–220.

McIntosh, P. (1988). *White privilege and male privilege: A personal account of coming to see correspondences through work in women's studies* (Working Paper No. 189). Wellesley, MA: Wellesley College.

Piper, J., & Treyger, S. (2010). Power, privilege, and ethics. In L. Hecker (Ed.), *Ethics and professional issues in couple and family therapy*. New York: Routledge.

Ponterotto, J. G., Gretchen, D., Utsey, S. O., Rieger, B. P., & Austin, R. (2002). A revision of the Multicultural Counseling Awareness Scale. *Journal of Multicultural Counseling and Development, 30*, 153–180.

Qureshi, A., & Collazos, F. (2011). The intercultural and interracial therapeutic relationship: Challenges and recommendations. *International Review of Psychiatry, 23*(1), 10–19, doi: 10.3109/09540261.2010.544643.

Smith, P. B. (2011). Communication styles as dimensions of national culture. *Journal of Cross-Cultural Psychology, 42*(2), 216–233. doi: 10.1177/0022022110396866.

Sue, S. (1999). Science, ethnicity, and bias: Where have we gone wrong? *American Psychologist, 54*, 1070–1077.

Sue, D. W., & Sue, D. (2008). *Counseling the culturally diverse: Theory and practice* (5th ed.). New York: Wiley.

Sue, D. W., & Torino, G. C. (2005). Racial-cultural competence: Awareness, knowledge, and skills. In R. T. Carter (Ed.), *Handbook of racial-cultural psychology and counseling: Training and practice*. Hoboken, NJ: John Wiley & Sons.

Utsey, S. O., Fisher, N. L., & Belvet, B. (2010). Culture and worldview in counseling and psychotherapy: Recommended approaches for working with persons from diverse sociocultural backgrounds. In M. M. Leach, & J. D. Aten (Eds.), *Culture and the therapeutic process: A guide for mental health professionals*. New York: Routledge/Taylor & Francis Group.

Vilardaga, R., Hayes, S. C., Levin, M. E., & Muto, T. (2009). Creating a strategy for progress: A contextual behavioral science approach. *The Behavior Analyst, 32*(1), 105. Retrieved from http://www.ncbi.nlm.nih.gov/pmc/articles/PMC26 86981/

PART II

Cultural Adaptation of Acceptance- and Mindfulness-Based Methods

CHAPTER 4

Cultural Considerations in Dialectical Behavior Therapy

Lynn McFarr, Ph.D., Lizbeth Gaona, L.C.S.W.,
Nick Barr, M.S.W., Ulises Ramirez, L.C.S.W.,
Suhadee Henriquez, L.C.S.W., Aurora Farias,
L.C.S.W., and Deborah Flores, M.D.

Harbor-UCLA Medical Center

Dialectical behavior therapy (DBT; Linehan, 1993a) was developed by Marsha Linehan at the University of Washington for the treatment of borderline personality disorder (BPD). In sixteen randomized controlled clinical trials, DBT has been shown to be effective in reducing suicidal and parasuicidal behavior, expressed anger, frequency and duration of hospitalizations, and frequency of medical visits in individuals diagnosed with BPD (Koons et al., 2001; Linehan, Armstrong, Suarez, Allmon, & Heard, 1991; Linehan et al., 2006). DBT has also been adapted to treat a host of other psychiatric conditions, including eating disorders, substance-use disorders, stalking behaviors, and treatment-resistant depression, and it has been demonstrated to be effective in treating adolescents, children, and the elderly (Fuchs, Lee, Roemer, & Orsillo, 2013; Harley, Sprich, Safren, Jacobo, & Fava, 2008; Robins & Chapman, 2004; Rosenfeld et al., 2007). However, scant attention has been paid in the literature to cultural considerations in the application of DBT. Although DBT has been studied across the globe (United States of America, Canada, Germany, Netherlands, Turkey, New Zealand, Australia, Argentina, and Puerto Rico, among others), research addressing cultural considerations in the treatment of non-English-speaking populations is limited. This chapter will explore cultural considerations in the application of DBT with Latinos generally, and with Mexican American women from lower socioeconomic strata more specifically, but it is hoped that the principles of cultural attunement discussed may inform applications with other nondominant cultures as well. To that end, we will describe the biopsychosocial theory of BPD from a DBT perspective, discuss core components of the treatment, describe culturally conditioned enhancements to DBT applied with monolingual Spanish speakers, and conclude with a case example.

DBT Account of Psychopathology

BPD is characterized by a constellation of symptoms that include, but are not limited to, fears of real or imagined abandonment; intense unstable interpersonal relationships; an unstable sense of self; a history of impulsive behaviors; threats of suicide or suicidal behaviors, including self-injury; affective instability; chronic feelings of emptiness; problems with anger; and transient stress-related paranoid ideation or severe dissociation (*DSM-IV*, American Psychiatric Association, 1994).

According to DBT theory, the etiological roots of BPD reside in a dysfunctional emotion regulation system. BPD is thus primarily an emotion-regulation disorder, and criterion behaviors evinced by individuals diagnosed with BPD can be viewed as attempts to regulate emotions (e.g., cutting), or the result of emotional dysregulation (e.g., angry outbursts; Harned, Banawan, & Lynch, 2006). Evidence suggests that BPD symptoms develop in the context of an innate biological sensitivity to emotion dysregulation, coupled with an invalidating environment wherein the private, internal experiences of those diagnosed with BPD are dismissed or criticized, and/or models of adaptive coping behavior are absent.

Biological propensity to emotion dysregulation, or emotional vulnerability, is characterized by high emotional sensitivity, extreme reactivity, and a slow return to an emotional baseline. For example, an individual diagnosed with BPD may be triggered easily by an argument, have a larger than average reaction (extreme rage), and take hours or days to return to baseline. Extreme emotional reactions disrupt cognitive processing and problem solving, which can lead to maladaptive, impulsive strategies to extinguish distressing emotions in the short term (e.g., drinking, shoplifting, etc.). This can lead to problems in the environment (particularly invalidation) and impede the development of long-term problem-solving skills.

This biological predisposition is coupled with an invalidating environment, which pervasively rejects the individual's internal experiences as invalid (you shouldn't feel that way), punishes the individual for emotional displays, meets escalation of emotional behaviors with intermittent reinforcement, and oversimplifies problem solving by assuming that the BPD individual possesses skills that he or she does not. The biopsychosocial model of BPD symptom development and maintenance is transactional. Rather than a diathesis stress model positing a discrete stressor that triggers the disorder, a transactional model suggests that the individual and the environment influence and react to each other over the course of a succession of microevents, which contribute to the development and maintenance of disordered behavior. A transactional model thus places an emphasis on context and demands consideration of the influence of cultural mores, values, expectations, and norms on the development of the disorder.

DBT Treatment Methods

DBT employs four primary modes of treatment conducted concurrently (Linehan, 1993a). These include individual psychotherapy, group skills training, telephone consultation between patients and individual therapists, and a case consultation team for therapists. Many DBT patients also participate in ancillary treatments such as pharmacotherapy and substance abuse recovery maintenance processes such as Alcoholics Anonymous.

Individual Therapy

Individual psychotherapy is the central mode of DBT treatment; it helps the patient learn to inhibit and eventually extinguish maladaptive, unskillful behaviors and replace them with adaptive, skillful actions. In individual therapy sessions, the therapist collaborates with the patient to address intrapersonal or environmental factors that impede acquisition and application of behavioral skills. The therapist models the central dialectical stance of DBT, which is the harmonious blending of acceptance of in-the-moment events with strategies that support changes in patient behavior. Individual therapy is structured by a daily diary card, which the patient must bring to each therapy session. This tool tracks emotions, suicidal and parasuicidal urges and actions, and other behaviors that the therapist and patient have agreed to target for change.

Skills Group

All DBT patients are required to participate in a skills training group while in treatment. Whereas individual treatment targets a reduction in the use of maladaptive coping behaviors, suicidal and parasuicidal behavior, and the integration and generalization of skills in daily life, the skills training group is focused on teaching the four core skills of DBT: mindfulness, emotion regulation, distress tolerance, and interpersonal effectiveness. Skills training groups generally meet weekly and follow a psychoeducational format described in detail in the DBT skills training manual (Linehan, 1993b). Assigned homework targets applied learning and the use of skills in the context of the patient's daily life.

Between-Session Skills Coaching

Skills coaching is an integral part of DBT and refers to outside-of-session contact by telephone or other means between the patient and his or her individual DBT therapist. Coaching serves three primary functions. First, it helps to change maladaptive help-seeking behavior and communications of distress, and it assists with developing effective help-seeking skills. Second, coaching provides opportunities to apply generalized skills that the patient learns in sessions to his or her daily life. In particular, patients' suicidal or parasuicidal urges or behaviors may require between-session contact in order to utilize adaptive coping strategies during times of acute distress. Third, phone consultations provide opportunities to repair therapeutic ruptures and remediation of conflicts and misunderstandings that may not have been addressed in individual face-to-face sessions.

Treatment Team

Treating patients diagnosed with BPD can be extremely difficult. It is essential that DBT therapists ask for and receive support from colleagues to maintain treatment effectiveness and reduce burnout. The consultation team is DBT for the therapist and constitutes the fourth mode of DBT. The consultation team helps therapists (both individual and skills group leaders) address the personal and clinical challenges inherent in treating BPD patients. In team meetings, therapists request validation, receive assistance with case conceptualization and assessment, discuss interventions, and use DBT skills and strategies to reduce therapist burnout. Therapists' participation in a weekly treatment team is a mandatory part of DBT.

DBT Treatment Hierarchy

In pretreatment, the therapist orients the patient to treatment requirements and expectations and deploys commitment strategies to elicit agreement from the patient to work on specific goals and behavioral targets. After orienting the patient, eliciting commitment, and completing additional pretreatment requirements, the DBT therapist organizes individual sessions according to a hierarchy of primary targets (Linehan, 1993a).

In the first stage of treatment, the DBT therapist targets suicidal and parasuicidal, or level one, behaviors for change. These behaviors are tracked using diary cards, and, if present, are the primary focus of in-session clinical attention. Next, therapy-interfering, or level two, behaviors are addressed. These behaviors include any activity that interferes with the efficacy of the therapeutic process, such as arriving to session without a complete diary card, or arriving late to individual therapy or skills group. Level three targets are quality-of-life-interfering behaviors. These may include such behaviors as substance abuse (though this may also qualify as level-one or level-two behavior depending on the behavior's functions and consequences), shoplifting, disordered eating, obsessive and/or compulsive behaviors, and any other behavior that leads to interpersonal conflict.

Once patients acquire proficiency in core DBT skills, they are able to adaptively manage emotion dysregulation and distress and are ready to move to the second stage of treatment. The second stage of DBT targets symptoms of post-traumatic stress, while the third stage targets increasing self-respect and working toward personal goals.

Empirical Findings of DBT with Diverse Populations

Research shows that evidence-based psychotherapy modalities, like cognitive behavior therapy (CBT), are effective with minority populations (Miranda et al., 2005). A recent meta-analysis exploring mindfulness- and acceptance-based approaches with nondominant and/or marginalized groups yielded a total of thirty-two peer-reviewed articles, of which thirteen supported the efficacy of DBT with underserved populations (Fuchs et al., 2013). Lynch et al. (2007) and O'Hearn and Pollard (2008) have also examined the efficacy of DBT with enhancements designed to address unique patient needs, such as deafness, with promising results. However, research examining the effectiveness of standard DBT with ethnically diverse, non-English-speaking populations in community mental health settings is lacking.

The Latino population, already the nation's largest minority group, will triple in size and account for most of the nation's population growth from 2005 through 2050 (Passel & Cohn, 2008). Research examining the effectiveness of standard DBT with monolingual Latinos is urgently needed, as is data exploring the efficacy of enhancements to standard DBT to address culturally specific needs.

This chapter will discuss culturally specific enhancements of DBT for use with monolingual Spanish-speaking Latinos in community mental health settings. These enhancements are drawn from the clinical work and experience of intensively trained bilingual DBT therapists. The authors discourage unnecessary adaptations to standard DBT supported by empirical evidence, given the lack of research examining its use with monolingual Spanish speakers and the anecdotal success of the culturally specific enhancements discussed in the following paragraphs. The authors also suggest that culturally attuned enhancements that preserve and complement core principles and functions of DBT may improve treatment outcomes and patient retention.

Cultural Competency of DBT

To be culturally competent the DBT therapist needs to be mindful of his or her own worldview, biases, and expectations, while at the same time making an effort to be mindful of those of the DBT patient, negotiating the tension between adherence to evidence-based treatment standards and enhancements for the sake of effectiveness within a given cultural context. This requires a dialectical posture. The therapist needs to recognize and understand culturally influenced behaviors and provide the patient with a culturally congruent rationale for engaging in an adherent treatment process that takes this understanding into account.

Fortunately, the ideographic, deeply contextual philosophical stance of DBT is well suited for application in culturally diverse contexts. DBT treatment philosophy emphasizes ongoing assessment; an evolving, contextual understanding of individual behaviors; and a nuanced view of the transactional nature of biopsychosocial systems. This approach is inherently culturally competent and flexible, and provides a framework for translating dialectical principles into applied therapeutic interventions with ethnically diverse populations.

This dialectical stance is of particular utility for minority and culturally diverse groups, as it accounts for the transactional relationship between intrapersonal and environmental processes. Sobczak and West (2013) also point to the importance of employing a dialectical stance in the treatment of minority and underrepresented populations, because it allows the therapist to validate unique experiences (discrimination, oppression), while at the same time stressing the importance of change and self-efficacy.

Cultural Sensitivity of DBT

While DBT is by its design culturally competent, the dialectic is that it can also be enhanced to increase cultural sensitivity in its delivery to certain ethnic groups, such as low-acculturated monolingual Spanish-speaking Latinas. As with any circumscribed ethnic group, there is, of course, enormous cultural heterogeneity among Latino patients. Thus, any effort to try to identify broad cultural tendencies across such diversity is fraught with risk. It is imperative to stress that the cultural values discussed in this chapter represent broad generalizations that may or may not apply to an individual patient in a given situation. Each person is unique and influenced by a variety of cultures and subcultures, personal choices, and socioeconomic circumstances. Still, being aware of these larger value systems may help to understand a particular patient's behaviors and actions in the context of larger cultural processes.

Apart from language barriers and socioeconomic disparities, variations in the way health care is envisioned, sought out, and delivered, as well as differences in the way values are ordered and articulated, can strain the clinical health care encounter for Latino patients. In working with a population with various ethnic groups and, in particular monolingual Latinos, it is important that the DBT therapist have a general understanding of basic mores, values, expectations, cultural norms, nuances, and traditional views of wellness and healing as they relate to psychopathology.

Enhancements to Promote the Cultural Sensitivity of DBT

A culturally sensitive Spanish DBT program is adherent to DBT protocols, employs the four modes of DBT treatment, and maintains the treatment hierarchy in individual sessions and with the consultation team. Spanish team therapists advocate for the practice of standard

DBT at its purest form and simply suggest these enhancements in an effort to enhance cultural sensitivity in delivery of services. Some of the suggested enhancements originate from Latino values, while other enhancements are suggested based on therapist experience and observed behavioral changes and treatment outcomes as a result of culturally enhanced interventions and contingencies.

Providing culturally sensitive DBT entails interweaving DBT principles and assumptions (e.g., biopsychosocial theory and treatment hierarchy) with culturally specific, values-oriented interventions. This process facilitates case conceptualization and complements standard DBT treatment interventions. Examples of this will be illustrated in the following case study.

First, we will introduce the values and communication styles at work in the provision of culturally enhanced services in a Spanish DBT program. This will be followed by additional enhancements, adopting culturally familiar contingencies, utilizing *dichos* (proverbs) and *cuentos* (short stories) to reinforce the understanding of mindfulness practice, and running treatment teams in Spanish.

Values

Personalismo (personalism) refers to the value of treating people with respect and dignity, and often includes therapeutically appropriate self-disclosure about hobbies, number of children, or other aspects of the therapist's life, which have particular cultural meaning. Employing *personalismo* allows the Latino patient to feel like he or she is in a nonconfrontational, welcoming environment. A similar value, *amabilidad* (amiability) refers to a pleasant disposition, friendliness, gentility, and civility. Many Latinos are raised with the understanding that much can be achieved interpersonally if people talk nicely and give compliments.

Familismo (familism) describes inclusiveness and participation in large family networks. It also refers to the importance of collectivism or interdependence, and emphasizes collective rather than individual ownership or obligation. Generally speaking, Latino cultures include a more family-centered decision-making model than a more individualistic model. Rather than idealizing decision making based solely for personal good and self-interest, many Latino cultures view the individual's obligation to the family and broader communities' interest as paramount. Thus, the family itself can play an enormously important role in supporting and empowering the patient within the medical setting.

Formalismo (formality) and *respeto* (respect) suggest the importance of communicating respect and courtesy through the use of Spanish words such as the formal *usted* (which can be compared to using Mr. or Mrs.) in place of the familiar *tu* (which can be compared to simply using the person's first name). The use of principles of *formalismo* is particularly important when a relationship has not yet been established between the DBT therapist and the patient.

Communication Style

The therapist's communication style is of special importance when working with Spanish-speaking clients or less-acculturated Latinos. Comas-Diaz (2011) explains that high-context communication relies heavily on nonverbal processes, metaphors, and contextual factors, and allows cultural cues to shoulder the primary explanatory burden. The use of *dichos* and *cuentos* can help therapists communicate in a highly contextual manner in order to provide culturally sensitive DBT with Latinos.

Dichos and *cuentos* have been demonstrated to assist with building rapport with patients, as well as effectively explaining concepts or ideas (Santiago-Rivera, Altarriba, Poll, Gonzalez-Miller, & Cragun, 2009). Celia Falicov (1998) states that "a therapist's knowledge and timely use of *dichos* is an invaluable and aesthetic communicational resource" (p. 181). In DBT, for example, the therapist can use the *dicho* "*Quien pide con timidez, invita a negar*" ("He that asks timidly, asks for a rejection") in order to facilitate learning the "FAST" skill of the interpersonal effectiveness module or the "Appear Confident" component in the "DEAR MAN" skill (Linehan, 1993b).

Platica (small talk) is another effective communication tool that assists with rapport building in Latino cultural contexts (Organista, 2006). In practice, *platica* can be compared to initial "ice breaking" small talk with patients and is considered polite and customary before attending to formal matters. *Platica* also helps to address potential conflicts and build a foundation of trust from which to delve into deeper issues in therapy (Comas-Diaz, 2011).

Culturally Familiar Contingencies

Culturally familiar contingencies can also be adopted to improve behavioral outcomes in a culturally sensitive manner. *La Loteria Mexicana Tarjeta de Recompensa* (Mexican Bingo Rewards Card) can be used as a culturally relevant token system designed to increase attendance, diary card completion, and homework compliance in skills group. This culturally familiar contingency-management strategy functions as a token economy, employing principles of "gamification" to reward patients for following through with DBT agreements (homework completion, completing their diary card). At the end of each module, the patient with the best compliance rate receives a small reward (e.g., ten dollar gift card to local shopping center, bakery, or coffee shop).

Mindfulness

Mindfulness can be a fraught topic for some Latinos, who may have concerns that such practices may be sacrilegious or inconsistent with their personal or cultural values and beliefs. It is important to clarify with these patients that in contrast, mindfulness practice as described in DBT can be conducted in concert with religious observance and has been used with individuals from diverse cultural and religious backgrounds (Sobczak & West, 2013). In an effort to aid Latino patients in understanding mindfulness concepts, such as taking a nonjudgmental stance, and operating in one moment at a time, incorporating *cuentos* or *dichos* that specifically mention the use of not judging and living in the moment may be helpful.

Treatment Team

To further enhance cultural sensitivity, DBT consultation teams can be conducted exclusively in Spanish. One reason for this enhancement is that, as Pavlenko (2006) indicates, "languages may create different, and sometimes incommensurable, worlds for their speakers, who feel that their selves change with the shift in their language" (p. 27). When seeking consultation from treatment team members in Spanish, the presenting therapist often quotes patient statements, as well as their responses, directly. Maintaining language consistency helps consultation team members, as well as the presenting therapist, to understand the therapists' direct experience in session and to respond to subtleties that might be lost in translation. In addition, maintaining language consistency allows for a more accurate elicitation of the emotions and behavioral responses therapists may experience in sessions with patients.

Diary Card Enhancements

Enhancing patient diary cards to target specific behaviors and unique patient needs is an integral part of standard DBT. Enhancing diary cards is recommended when working with Latino patients if there is concern regarding patients' literacy levels. For example, replacing the word "sad" with a sad face can illustrate the emotion, and similar pictographs can be used to replace written target behaviors.

Case Study

Reina was a 41-year-old single mother of three who only spoke Spanish. She was unemployed and lived in a small, low-income government-subsidized apartment with her daughters, ages 16, 13, and 11. In her early thirties, she moved to the United States from Mexico in hopes of "starting a new life" and leaving behind memories of years of domestic violence from a broken marriage to a violent and alcohol-abusive husband. Since childhood, Reina remembered her mother's invalidating demands "to not be selfish" when Reina asked to play with children her age. Instead, as the oldest of six, Reina was expected to clean, care for her younger siblings, and eventually drop out of grade school to ensure her household chores were upheld. Upon intake, Reina was diagnosed with major depressive and generalized anxiety disorders. Reina reported that "my life is a disaster," and endorsed emotional instability, unrelenting chaos, constant interpersonal conflicts, somatic complaints of head and back pain, and ongoing financial stress. She also complained that the medications that doctors prescribed for her somatic complaints and "*nervios*" (stress) didn't work. Furthermore, her daughters didn't listen to her, and she had to do everything around the house, despite her physical pain.

Course of Treatment

Reina was initially treated with CBT to reduce the depression and anxiety symptoms she reported. After three months in treatment, there was minimal improvement, due in part to her therapy-interfering behaviors (i.e., missing appointments, showing up late, not completing homework assignments, and constant chaos in her life). After Reina's therapist consulted with members of their team, it was suggested that Reina be evaluated for BPD.

Reina indeed met criteria for the disorder and was referred for DBT, although she did not engage in life-threatening behaviors or parasuicidal actions. As a result, DBT focused on reducing therapy-interfering behaviors, such as coming late to individual or group sessions and failing to complete homework assignments or diary cards, and level-three targets, like aiding Reina in skill use to regulate her emotions, aiding her in obtaining employment, reducing conflicts in interpersonal relationships, reducing isolation related to chronic pain and anxiety, reducing medication seeking from practitioners in Mexico, and reducing her (almost weekly) visits to urgent care, local hospitals, and primary medical care doctors. This goal was particularly challenging, as Reina reported feeling emotionally regulated after attending medical appointments and being prescribed a host of different medications from the various medical professionals from whom she sought care.

Cultural Enhancements in Treatment

Reina appeared to benefit from the Spanish DBT team's use of culturally congruent reinforcers. In particular, Reina appeared motivated by the use of *La Loteria Mexicana Tarjeta de Recompensa* in skills groups, and rapidly demonstrated completion of homework assignments, diary cards, and punctual attendance. Skills group leaders, as well as Reina's treating therapist, greeted and welcomed Reina to treatment by mindfully exercising the values of *personalismo, amabilidad, familismo,* and *respeto,* by saying, for example, "*Me alegro de verte, gracias por venir. Usted está en su casa aquí, pasele*" ("Good to see you, thank you for coming. Make yourself at home, come on in"). Reina appeared to enjoy the skills group, as she reported that it was a familiar and friendly place where she felt like she belonged. She explained that she felt safe and as if she were at home. She realized that, for the first time, she felt understood and validated. She adhered to individual therapy and the skills group structure after incorporating a few minutes of *platica* (e.g., "*¿Cómo está usted? El clima está frío, verdad?*" ["How are you? Isn't it cold outside?"]) at the beginning of sessions. While in individual and group sessions, *dichos* and *cuentos* were regularly incorporated to make relevant points. Reina was an animated and expressive person and would often joke and use *dichos* herself to explain certain topics and experiences she was having related to DBT skills. To illustrate her use of mindfulness skills, for example, Reina used the dicho "*El que mucho agarra poco aprieta. Yo uso la mente sabia y ejercicios de conciencia plena para hacer una cosa a la vez, si no me pongo ansiosa*" ("If you try to hold on to too much, your grip on things will be weak. I use wise mind and one mindfulness to do one thing at a time, if not, I get anxious"). Reina also chose to use the enhanced diary card with emotive pictures in place of words, and reported that it was easier for her to identify emotions by looking at the pictures because she was unable to read. She seemed to hand over her diary card in skills group with a sense of mastery in being able to complete it, despite being illiterate.

The value of *familismo* was also incorporated into Reina's treatment. When Reina was having problems with her 16-year-old daughter, who she reported was "acting up a lot," Reina's therapist was able to provide a referral to a child and adolescent mental health treatment clinic, where Reina's daughter was able to receive individual therapy. In the spirit of *familismo,* and in an effort to decrease poor communication patterns that lead to conflict between Reina and her daughter, Reina's therapist set up a session to meet with Reina, her daughter, and her daughter's therapist. Culturally sensitive mindfulness practices were also incorporated into Reina's skills group. For example, skills group leaders often read certain *cuentos* that elicited emotions and aided Reina in practicing "wise mind" skills.

Treatment Outcome

At the end of treatment, Reina reported a decrease in severity and frequency of symptoms and had achieved many of her behavioral goals, including experiencing fewer crying spells, less emotional dysregulation, fewer interpersonal conflicts, and less social isolation. She was also now working part-time. She also reduced the frequency of her medication-seeking behavior in Mexico and visits to urgent care clinics, hospitals, and general medical practitioners. Reina seemed proud of her gains, and for the first time in her life, she felt that she had the coping skills to manage her emotions and control her life.

Conclusion

DBT is a robust clinical intervention for BPD. It is not currently known through empirical avenues whether any adaptations to the treatment are needed for particular cultural groups. At the same time, in the spirit of the transactional model of the disorder, it is wise to consider enhancing the context of the individual to optimize treatment. This chapter focused on culturally sensitive enhancements to DBT for monolingual Spanish-speaking individuals. Several enhancements highlighted included *personalismo, amabilidad, familismo, respeto, platica,* and *formalismo.* Additionally, specific interventions including *dichos, cuentos,* and the game *Loteria* can be used to highlight specific skills and motivate compliance to treatment. The case presented illustrates the utility of culturally sensitive methods to enhance treatment outcomes.

References

American Psychiatric Association. (1994). *Diagnostic and Statistical Manual of Mental Disorders* (4th ed.). Washington, DC.

Comas-Diaz, L. (2011). *Multicultural care. A therapist's guide to cultural competence.* American Psychological Association.

Falicov, C. J. (1998). *Latino families in therapy: A guide to multicultural practice.* New York: Guilford Press.

Fuchs, C., Lee, J. K., Roemer, L. & Orsillo, S. M. (2013). Using mindfulness- and acceptance-based treatments with clients from nondominant cultural and/or marginalized backgrounds: Clinical considerations, meta-analysis findings, and introduction to the special series: Clinical considerations in using acceptance- and mindfulness-based treatments with diverse populations. *Cognitive and Behavioral Practice, 20*(1), 1–12.

Harley, R., Sprich, S., Safren, S., Jacobo, M., & Fava, M. (2008). Adaptation of dialectical behavior therapy skills training group for treatment-resistant depression. *Journal of Nervous and Mental Disease, 196*(2), 136–143.

Harned, M., Banawan, S., & Lynch, T. (2006). Dialectical behavior therapy: An emotion-focused treatment for borderline personality disorder. *Journal of Contemporary Psychotherapy, 36*(2), 67–75.

Koons, C. R., Robins, C. J., Tweed, J., Lynch, T. R., Gonzalez, A. M., Morse, J. Q. et al. (2001). Efficacy of dialectical behavior therapy in women veterans with borderline personality disorder. *Behavior Therapy, 32*(2), 371–390.

Linehan, M. M. (1993a). *Cognitive behavioral treatment of borderline personality disorder.* New York: Guilford Press.

Linehan, M. M. (1993b). *Skills training manual for treating borderline personality disorder.* New York: Guilford Press.

Linehan, M. M., Armstrong, H. E., Suarez, A., Allmon, D., & Heard, H. L. (1991). Cognitive-behavioral treatment of chronically parasuicidal borderline patients. *Archives of General Psychiatry, 48*(12), 1060–1064.

Linehan, M. M., Comtois, K. A., Murray, A. M., Brown, M. Z., Gallop, R. J., Heard, H. L. et al. (2006). Two-year randomized controlled trial and follow-up of dialectical behavior therapy vs. therapy by experts for suicidal behaviors and borderline personality disorder. *Archives of General Psychiatry, 63*(7), 757–766.

Lynch, T. R., Cheavens, J. S., Cukrowicz, K. C., Thorp, S. R., Bronner L., & Beyer, J. (2007). Treatment of older adults with co-morbid personality disorder and depression: A dialectical behavior therapy approach. *International Journal of Geriatric Psychiatry, 22*, 131–143.

Miranda, J., Bernal, G., Lau, A., Kohn, L., Hwang, W., & LaFromboise, T. (2005). State of the science on psychosocial interventions for ethnic minorities. *Annual Review of Clinical Psychology, 1*, 113–142.

O'Hearn, A., & Pollard, R. O. (2008). Modifying dialectical behavior therapy for deaf individuals. *Cognitive and Behavior Practice, 14*, 400–414.

Organista, K. C. (2006). Cognitive-behavioral therapy with Latinos and Latinas. In P. A. Hays, & Iwamasa, G. Y. (Eds.), *Culturally responsive cognitive-behavioral therapy* (pp. 73–95). Washington, DC: American Psychological Association.

Passel, J. S., & Cohn, D. V. (2008, February). *U.S. Population Projections: 2005–2050.* Washington, DC: Pew Research Center. http://www.pewhispanic.org/files/reports/85.pdf.

Pavlenko, A. (2006). *Bilingual minds: Emotional experience, expression, and representation.* Tonowanda, NY: Multilingual Matters Ltd.

Robins, C. J., & Chapman, A. L. (2004). Dialectical behavior therapy: current status, recent developments, and future directions. *Journal of Personality Disorders, 18*(1), 73–89.

Rosenfeld, B., Galietta, M., Ivanoff, A., Garcia-Mansilla, A., Martinez, R., Fava, J. et al. (2007). Dialectical behavior therapy for the treatment of stalking offenders. *The International Journal of Forensic Mental Health, 6*(2), 95–103.

Santiago-Rivera, A. L., Altarriba, J., Poll, N., Gonzalez-Miller, N., & Cragun, C. (2009). Therapists' views on working with bilingual Spanish-English-speaking clients: A qualitative investigation. *Professional Psychology: Research and Practice, 40*(5), 436–443.

Sobczak, L. T. R., & West, M. L. (2013). Clinical considerations in using mindfulness- and acceptance-based approaches with diverse populations: Addressing challenges in service delivery in diverse community settings. *Cognitive and Behavioral Practice, 20*, 13–22.

CHAPTER 5

Cultural Competency and Mindfulness-Based Cognitive Therapy for Depression

Eddie Erazo

Holly Hazlett-Stevens, Ph.D.
University of Nevada, Reno

Significant relationships between depression rates, socioeconomic status (SES), and ethnic minority groups in the United States have been well documented (Lorant et al., 2003), and stress disproportionately affects low SES individuals as well (Adler & Newman, 2002). Mindfulness-based cognitive therapy (MBCT) is an effective treatment for the prevention of depression relapse (Piet & Hougaard, 2011), yet much of the available research has not examined the effects of MBCT among socioeconomically and ethnically diverse samples. Thus, the demographic populations most in need of effective depression relapse prevention are the least represented in currently available MBCT research trials. This chapter will begin with a brief review of the research documenting the disproportionate rates of stress and depression found when demographic variables such as SES and ethnicity are taken into account. We will then present a brief overview of the promising clinical intervention known as MBCT for depression and the stress-reduction program (mindfulness-based stress reduction, or MBSR) on which it was based. Currently available MBCT outcome research trials will be reviewed with special attention to the demographic variables reported. Finally, additional research informing what modifications might be made to promote culturally competent delivery of these interventions will be discussed.

Diversity, Stress, and Depression

Much research has suggested that stress may play a causal role in depression, implicating factors such as the body's biological response to stress in the form of a corticotropin-releasing hormone (van Praag, 2004). If stress indeed can lead to depression, populations experiencing greater and more chronic levels of stress should demonstrate higher rates of depression as well. Not surprising, Wang (2005) reported an association between high levels of employee work stress and elevated risk of a major depressive episode. When evaluating the United States as a whole, rates of depression are significantly higher in Americans categorized as low SES (Lorant et al., 2003; Walsh, Levine, & Levav, 2012). Poverty is often considered to be linked to mental health through greater exposure to stressful environments (e.g., unemployment and violence) with less social and material resources (McLeod & Kessler, 1990). Living in poverty is disproportionately more common for ethnic minority groups than for White Americans (U.S. Department of Health and Human Services, 1999). Furthermore, factors such as low SES during childhood (Gilman, Kawachi, Fitzmaurice, & Buka, 2002), low SES of one's neighborhood (Galea et al., 2007), and low SES of one's parents (Ritsher, Warner, Johnson, & Dohrenwend, 2001) have all been shown to increase the risk of depression at least twofold when compared to high SES groups. To complicate things further, it appears that lower SES is associated with less improvement in response to some treatments for depression than is middle SES (Falconnier, 2009). In sum, the most socioeconomically disadvantaged populations also appear to be at greatest risk for depression. Therefore, the effectiveness of interventions for depression must be demonstrated across diverse samples of individuals, and the cultural competency of such interventions needs to be explored.

Mindfulness-Based Cognitive Therapy for Depression

MBCT was developed by Zindel V. Segal, J. Mark G. Williams, and John D. Teasdale specifically to prevent depressive relapse. In their first book, released in 2002, these psychologists described how they integrated cognitive therapy techniques with the present-moment, nonjudgmental awareness cultivated by the mindfulness meditation practices taught in mindfulness-based stress reduction (MBSR). MBSR was first developed in 1979 by Jon Kabat-Zinn at the University of Massachusetts Medical School. This eight-week public health course was established to assist medical patients with chronic conditions for which physicians could not offer any further help (Kabat-Zinn, 1990). The MBSR curriculum totals 30 hours of instruction, consisting of eight weekly group meetings lasting two and a half to three hours each plus one additional full-day session during the sixth week. During these classes, MBSR group participants formally practice a variety of mindfulness meditation practices, including breathing meditation, other sitting meditation practices, body scan meditation of bodily sensations, mindful movement based on hatha yoga postures, and walking meditation. MBSR class sessions include group discussion of experiences that arise from formal mindfulness meditation practice, educational information about the nature of stress and stress reactivity, and informal practices encouraging participants to apply mindfulness to everyday life and to stressful situations. MBSR group participants also are expected to complete 45 to 60 minutes of daily formal practice at home in between class sessions. Over the past 30 years, much research has documented the clinical benefits of MBSR for a variety of medical and psychological conditions (for meta-analytic reviews of this literature, see de Vibe, Bjørndal, Tipton, Hammerstrøm, & Kowalski, 2012; Fjorback, Arendt, Ørnbøl, Fink, & Walach, 2011; Hofmann, Sawyer, Witt, & Oh, 2010). Numerous ongoing clinical trials of MBSR are currently funded by the National Institutes of Health as well.

Segal and colleagues developed their depressive relapse prevention intervention from MBSR based on the notion that previously depressed individuals at risk for future depressive relapse may benefit from increased "mindfulness." Jon Kabat-Zinn (1994) defined this historically Buddhist term as "paying attention in a particular way: on purpose, in the present moment, and nonjudgmentally," reflecting that mindfulness refers to an ability to experience every internal and external phenomenon as it really is, rather than rejecting its existence (Gunaratana, 2002). A key element of mindfulness is a willingness to experience whatever is present in the current moment, whether pleasant or unpleasant, rather than increasing one's suffering by trying to escape it (Germer, 2005). In this way, thoughts, emotions, and sensations are simply experienced as they arise without engaging in judgment or reactivity.

MBCT therefore teaches mindfulness meditation practices to previously depressed individuals so that mindfulness skills can be used proactively during periods of remission to prevent future relapse. In the second edition of their seminal book, Segal, Williams, & Teasdale (2012) explained, that "the ultimate aim of the MBCT program is to help individuals make a radical shift in their relationship to the thoughts, feelings, and bodily sensations that contribute to depressive relapse" (p. 64). Due to the automatic reactivation of negative thinking patterns similar to previous depressive episodes that is characteristic of depression relapse, Segal and colleagues proposed that introducing new experiences to the mind and body was necessary to create an alternative view to the patient. In response to this realization, "the core skill that the MBCT program aims to teach is the ability, at times of potential relapse, to recognize and disengage from mind states charac-terized by self-perpetuating patterns of ruminative, negative thought" (Segal et al., 2012, p. 74). As a result, the patient is able to simply acknowledge a negative thought or feeling without resistance and either recognize it as just a thought or choose a specific strategy based on its ability to bring pleasure or mastery in the past. Patients eventu-ally become aware of unique warning signs of a depressive episode so that they might proactively develop a specific action plan in response.

Modeled after the MBSR curriculum, MBCT also consists of eight weekly sessions and one all-day session with an emphasis on recognizing and allowing thoughts and other internal experiences for the purpose of skillful responding. Although the format and mindful-ness meditation practices taught in MBCT greatly resemble MBSR, MBCT also includes specific presentation and group discussion of the role of interpretation in subsequent thoughts and feelings. Similar to many cognitive behavioral therapy protocols, MBCT participants learn to identify habitual patterns of thoughts, emotions, sensations, and behavior (Segal et al., 2012).

MBCT Efficacy Research

The first MBCT randomized controlled trial provided initial evidence that MBCT significantly reduced relapse in patients with three or more previous major depressive episodes compared to treatment as usual (TAU; Teasdale et al., 2000). In 2011, Piet and Hougaard identified six randomized controlled trials including 593 participants for their meta-analysis of MBCT effects. MBCT significantly reduced the risk of depression relapse with a risk ratio of 0.66 for MBCT in comparison to TAU or placebo controls, which corresponds to a relative risk reduction of 34%. This effect was most pronounced for patients with a history of three or more major depressive episodes, whereas no risk reduction was detected in patients with two episodes. Likewise, a separate meta-analysis including 16 studies conducted by Chiesa and Serretti (2011) showed that MBCT in addition to usual care was significantly more effective than usual care alone for the reduction of subsequent relapse in patients with three or more prior major depressive episodes.

Although MBCT was originally developed for the purpose of preventing major depressive relapse, MBCT also reduced residual depressive symptoms in patients diagnosed with major depressive disorder (see Chiesa & Serretti, 2011). Interestingly, both meta-analyses also found that MBCT was at least as effective as antidepressant medication (ADM) alone. In addition, MBCT displayed greater cost efficiency than ADM alone with regard to its efficacy in preventing depression relapse (Piet & Hougaard, 2011). Kuyken et al. (2008) examined a sample of participants that had been treated with ADM and randomly assigned each either to maintenance antidepressant medication (m-ADM) or to MBCT plus support to taper/discontinue ADM. The MBCT group demonstrated lower relapse rates over a 15-month follow-up and significantly reduced ADM usage, with 75% completely discontinuing ADM. In addition, enhanced mindfulness and self-compassion were found to mediate the effects of MBCT. Thus, MBCT may be more effective than ADM alone at reducing residual depressive symptoms, perhaps due in part to increased mindfulness and self-compassion.

MBCT and Diversity

Our examination of each MBCT investigation included in these meta-analyses revealed that the clinical samples included were predominantly female and Caucasian. No significant interactions were reported for gender between MBCT treatment and reduction in depressive relapse. Three investigations demonstrated that MBCT was more effective than TAU at preventing relapse within socioeconomically diverse samples (Godfrin & van Heeringen, 2010; Ma & Teasdale, 2004; Teasdale et al., 2000). In the current literature, few studies included clinical samples that appeared diverse with respect to both SES and ethnicity. However, two particular studies examined the effectiveness of MBCT within samples that were somewhat ethnically diverse. Segal et al. (2010) found that MBCT alone was as effective in preventing relapse as ADM within a clinical sample in which 20% of participants were "non-White." Thompson et al. (2010) reported that a distance delivery (phone or Internet) MBCT intervention effectively reduced depressive symptoms compared to a wait-list group among patients with epilepsy, 24% of whom were described as African American. Results comparing the effects of MBCT between ethnic groups were not conducted.

MBCT does appear effective for a variety of psychological conditions when administered in other countries using their native languages. For example, a study conducted in France found that MBCT was acceptable to outpatients diagnosed with bipolar disorder and that MBCT was associated with increased mindfulness skills (Mirabel-Sarron et al., 2009). Similarly, in Spain, Langer, Cangas, Salcedo, and Fuentes (2012) randomly assigned a group of patients suffering from psychosis to either MBCT or a wait-list condition. Upon completion of the treatment, the MBCT group scored significantly higher in their ability to respond mindfully to stressful internal events compared to the control group. Bondolfi et al. (2010) examined the relapse rates between unmedicated patients in remission from recurrent depression randomly assigned to MBCT and TAU or to TAU alone over a 60-week period, delivered in French in a French-speaking area of Switzerland. Although no difference in relapse rates between groups was found (MBCT + TAU = 33%, TAU = 36%), this may be due to the low relapse rate of the TAU condition in comparison to earlier studies (e.g., Ma & Teasdale, 2004, 66%; Teasdale et al., 2000, 78%). The relapse rate for the MBCT condition coincides with the current literature (Ma & Teasdale, 2004, 36%; Teasdale et al., 2000, 37%), and a significant difference was found in the time to relapse (MBCT + TAU = 29 weeks, TAU = 10 weeks; Bondolfi et al., 2010), also consistent with previous findings. In Iran, Kaviani, Javaheri, and Hatami (2011) delivered MBCT in Farsi. Nonclinical individuals were randomly assigned to MBCT or to a wait-list condition, and MBCT effectively reduced anxiety and depressive feelings before, during, and after the stressful event of an exam. Taken together, this preliminary evidence suggests that MBCT may be effective when delivered in other languages and countries. However, additional research targeting culturally diverse groups is needed before conclusions about the efficacy of MBCT can be generalized further.

Cultural Competency and Sensitivity

Although little research is currently available to inform culturally competent delivery of MBCT, the more widely studied MBSR intervention has been implemented within ethnically diverse and low-income urban areas. Two inner-city community health programs serving primarily minority and low SES patients have implemented MBSR. The first, known as the Worcester City Campus Program, is a satellite clinic of the original Stress Reduction Clinic at the University of Massachusetts Medical School. According to the UMass Center for Mindfulness website (http://www.umassmed.edu/cfm), MBSR has been delivered free of charge within two health centers serving the multicultural, multiethnic, impoverished inner-city population of Worcester since 1992. More than 500 patients have completed MBSR through this program, offered entirely in Spanish as well as in English. However, results from research conducted within this program have not yet been published.

The second inner-city MBSR program was developed in 1993 at the Community Health Center of Meriden, Connecticut. Modeled on the UMass Stress Reduction Clinic program, MBSR has been delivered to approximately 200 patients with heterogeneous medical and mental health conditions in either English or Spanish (Roth, 1997). The majority of patients served are Latino, 78% of whom receive public assistance. The cost of MBSR services are billed to patients' health insurance providers, uninsured patients pay a sliding-scale fee, and no patient is denied MBSR for financial reasons. The first research investigation in this setting demonstrated significant decreases in medical and psychological symptoms coupled with improved self-esteem (Roth & Creaser, 1997). Of the 79 patients included in this open trial, 51 (65%) received MBSR in Spanish and 28 (35%) in English. Roth and Creaser considered their completion rate of 60% to reflect a high level of acceptance of the MBSR intervention.

In a subsequent investigation, Roth and Robbins (2004) delivered MBSR to 48 Spanish-speaking and 20 English-speaking patients and included a comparison group of 18 Spanish-speaking patients who did not receive the intervention due to practical constraints. No differences in the number of medical and mental health diagnoses between the intervention and comparison groups or between the Spanish- or English-speaking intervention groups were found beforehand, and 66% of those who received MBSR completed the intervention. Of the 68 patients who completed the intervention and had complete data for analysis, the mean age was 51 years (ranging from 26 to 82 years) and 82% were women. Median monthly income was $531, and 50% reported receiving public assistance. The intervention group showed statistically significant improvement on five of eight general health and social functioning measures when compared to the no-intervention group. While preliminary, results from these studies suggest that MBSR can be delivered effectively within culturally diverse and low SES communities. More rigorous research utilizing randomized controlled designs is needed. Future research delivering MBCT could examine whether this alternative mindfulness-based intervention effectively reduces depression in inner-city settings as well.

Adaptations to Mindfulness-Based Interventions to Enhance Cultural Competency

Several adjustments have been reported in this clinical research literature to provide mindfulness-based interventions in an accessible, culturally competent, and sensitive manner.

Provide the intervention in patients' native language. To deliver the intervention in the patient's native language, instructors must be fluent in speaking that language, all audio and written material must be provided in that language, and reading material should be written at an appropriate reading level with accommodations for any patients who are not literate. As reviewed earlier, MBCT has been effectively delivered in French, Spanish, and Farsi, and MBSR offered in Spanish was effective when delivered in an inner-city urban setting in the United States.

Accommodate practical needs. Roth and Creaser (1997) reported common reasons for dropout included an inability to maintain the required time commitment, and the majority of patients who dropped out did so due to life circumstances beyond their control (e.g., illness, death or imprisonment of family member, securing employment, immigration problems). Lack of transportation and child care were additional reasons for dropout identified in the subsequent study (Roth & Robbins, 2004). As a result, Roth and Creaser (1997) emphasized the importance of accommodating the practical needs of culturally and/or socioeconomically diverse populations in several ways: (1) ensuring the intervention is affordable, (2) scheduling sessions at an optimal time of day, (3) providing transportation and child care whenever possible, and (4) reminder phone calls for the first few sessions. Indeed, the UMass Worcester City Campus Program provides MBSR in Spanish as well as English, free of charge, with on-site child care and free travel vouchers to maximize attendance.

Abercrombie, Zamora, and Korn (2007) conducted a small pilot study exploring the feasibility and acceptability of MBSR within a multiethnic low SES group of women with abnormal Pap smear results. Patients received MBSR in either Spanish or English at a San Francisco inner-city outpatient women's health clinic as part of a larger effort to improve adherence to abnormal Pap smear follow-up care. Patients completing MBSR reported reduced anxiety and rated MBSR classes very favorably. In their discussion, these authors highlighted the importance of sensitivity to patients' hectic schedules and unpredictable life events, providing support in the form of reminder phone calls, bus tokens, and taxi vouchers, as well as session refreshments and monetary incentives.

Implement the intervention within the community. Roth and Creaser (1997) further suggested that mindfulness-based programs be implemented within the existing infrastructure of the community, ideally at an agency or health care facility already utilized and trusted by patients. Mistrust is a major barrier for racial and ethnic minorities seeking mental health treatment (U.S. Department of Health and Human Services, 1999). Given the necessity that MBSR and MBCT instructors maintain their own mindfulness meditation and yoga practice to deliver these interventions, mental health staff members already inclined toward personal meditation practice would be ideal candidates to receive professional training in MBCT. One practical approach may be for institutions to provide staff members already engaged in personal meditation practice, and those who have the desire to begin one, with the training opportunities to facilitate their mindfulness practice and incorporate it into their professional lives by delivering MBCT. As a result, any current staff deemed competent of providing mental health care might enhance their own personal mindfulness practice and receive MBCT professional training, and effectively teach MBCT practices with an established trust, rapport, and ability to speak patients' native language.

Adaptations to improve cultural sensitivity. Roth and Creaser (1997) described several adaptations to the original MBSR protocol to improve its cultural sensitivity within Latino communities. Out of concern that the word *yoga* may hold negative connotations, mindful postures instead were referred to as "body movements" (*movimientos del cuerpo*, in Spanish). Roth and Creaser also offered opportunities for patients to speak about their meditation experiences in small groups and emphasized that patients were free to participate as they wished during the larger class discussions. The importance of instructor flexibility and adaptability to present the material in a sensitive and accessible way was underscored as well.

An interesting cultural consideration of mindfulness-based approaches is also relevant in mainstream American culture. The mindfulness meditation practices taught in these interventions originate from ancient Asian Buddhist traditions. Therefore individuals from a variety of Western cultures may hold attitudes or misconceptions about meditation that might serve as barriers. MBSR and MBCT are deliberately taught in a secular fashion, devoid of Sanskrit terms, references to Buddha or Buddhism, and any ritualistic acts such as bowing. Education and thorough secular explanation, in conjunction with offering practice modifications (e.g., walking or lying instead of sitting), appear key to dispelling misconceptions and fallacies in order to increase participation in meditation interventions (Williams, Ness, Dixon, & McCorckle, 2012).

A final cultural consideration may be more relevant to MBCT than to MBSR. Greater somatization associated with psychiatric diagnoses has been reported among ethnic minorities than among Caucasian individuals, including African Americans (Das, Olfson, McCurtis, & Weissman, 2006), Asian Americans (Farooq, Gahir, Okyere, Sheikh, & Oyebode, 1995), Hispanics (Hulme, 1996), and low-income urban adolescents (Reynolds, O'Koon, Papademetriou, Szczygiel, & Grant, 2001). With research suggesting that greater somatization leads to greater use of and preference for medical services over mental health ones (Escobar et al., 1987), it is critical that MBCT be presented in a culturally sensitive manner. As with MBSR (Roth & Robbins, 2004), MBCT might be advertised as an educational intervention to promote health rather than as psychotherapy or a treatment for mental illness, thereby preventing any stigma associated with seeking mental health care. Emphasizing the physical benefits of MBCT also may attract minorities that experience greater somatization and prefer holistic treatments without the mind-body separation typical of Western medicine (Robinson & Howard-Hamilton, 2000).

Summary and Conclusions

Although more research is needed, MBCT shows promise as a cost-efficient and potentially culturally competent intervention to address the elevated prevalence of depression in low SES and ethnic minority groups. MBCT was delivered effectively in French (Mirabel-Sarron et al., 2009; Bondolfi et al., 2010) and in Spanish (Langer et al., 2012) in European studies, as well as in Farsi in Iran (Kaviani et al., 2011). Although some degree of ethnic and socioeconomic diversity can be found in the currently available MBCT outcome research trials, the effectiveness of MBCT has not yet been examined within urban inner-city or other ethnically and socioeconomically diverse settings. MBSR—the stress-reduction intervention upon which MBCT was based—has been successfully delivered in Spanish in such settings, without significant differences in outcomes when compared to delivery in English (Roth & Robbins, 2004). Results from a few preliminary studies (Roth & Creaser, 1997; Roth & Robbins, 2004; Abercrombie et al., 2007) suggest that MBSR can be delivered in a culturally competent manner with several notable adaptations including (1) offering the intervention in the patients' native language, (2) accommodating practical needs, (3) implementing the intervention within the existing community infrastructure, and (4) presenting the material in a culturally sensitive manner. Given the stress burden associated with low socioeconomic status (e.g., poor living conditions, inferior education quality, poor employment opportunities, high levels of crime, violence, and incarceration), and the role of stress in depression risk, MBCT research needs to extend in this direction to address the cultural competency of this promising intervention.

References

Abercrombie, P. D., Zamora, A., & Korn, A. P., (2007). Providing a mindfulness-based stress-reduction program for low-income multiethnic women with abnormal Pap smears. *Holistic Nursing Practice, 21,* 26–34.

Adler, N. E., & Newman, K. (2002). Socioeconomic disparities in health: Pathways and policies—Inequality in education, income, and occupation exacerbates the gaps between the health "haves" and "have-nots." *Health Affair, 21*(2), 60–76.

Bondolfi, G., Jermann, F., Van der Linden, M., Gex-Fabry, M., Bizzini, L., Rouget, B. W. et al. (2010). Depression relapse prophylaxis with mindfulness-based cognitive therapy: Replication and extension in the Swiss health care system. *Journal of Affective Disorders, 122,* 224–231.

Chiesa, A., & Serretti, A. (2011). Mindfulness-based cognitive therapy for psychiatric disorders: A systematic review and meta-analysis. *Psychiatry Research, 187,* 441–453.

Das, A. K., Olfson, M., McCurtis, H. L., & Weissman, M. M. (2006). Depression in African Americans: Breaking barriers to detection and treatment. *The Journal of Family Practice, 55*(1), 30–39.

de Vibe, M., Bjørndal, A., Tipton, E., Hammerstrøm, K., & Kowalski, K. (2012). Mindfulness based stress reduction (MBSR) for improving health, quality of life, and social functioning in adults. *Campbell Systematic Reviews, 3,* 1–127.

Escobar, J. I., Golding, J. M., Hough, R. L., Karno, M., Burnam, M. A., & Wells, K. B. (1987). Somatization in the community: Relationships to disability and use of services. *American Journal of Public Health, 77*(7), 837–840.

Falconnier, L. (2009). Socioeconomic status in the treatment of depression. *The American Journal of Orthopsychiatry, 79*(2), 148–158.

Farooq, S., Gahir, M. S., Okyere, E., Sheikh, A. J., & Oyebode, F. (1995). Somatization: A transcultural study. *Journal of Psychosomatic Medicine, 39*(7), 883–888.

Fjorback, L. O., Arendt, M., Ørnbøl, E., Fink, P., & Walach, H. (2011). Mindfulness-based stress reduction and mindfulness-based cognitive therapy: A systematic review of randomized controlled trials. *Acta Psychiatrica Scandinavica, 124*(2), 102–119.

Galea, S., Ahern, J., Nandi, A., Tracy, M., Beard, J., & Vlahov, D. (2007). Urban neighborhood poverty and the incidence of depression in a population-based cohort study. *Annals of Epidemiology, 17*(3), 171–179.

Germer, C. K. (2005). Mindfulness: What is it? What does it matter? In Germer, C. K., Siegel, R. D., & Fulton, P. R. (Eds.), *Mindfulness and Psychotherapy* (pp. 3–27). New York: Guilford Press.

Gilman, S. E., Kawachi, I., Fitzmaurice, G. M., & Buka, S. L. (2002). Socioeconomic status in childhood and the lifetime risk of major depression. *International Journal of Epidemiology, 31,* 359–367.

Godfrin, K. A., & van Heeringen, C. (2010). The effects of mindfulness-based cognitive therapy on recurrence of depressive episodes, mental health and quality of life: A randomized controlled study. *Behaviour Research and Therapy, 48,* 738–746.

Gunaratana, B. (2002). *Mindfulness in plain English.* Somerville, MA: Wisdom Publications.

106

Hulme, P. A. (1996). Somatization of Hispanics. *Journal of Psychosocial Nursing and Health Services, 34*(3), 33–37.

Hofmann, S. G., Sawyer, A. T., Witt, A. A, & Oh, D. (2010). The effect of mindfulness-based therapy on anxiety and depression: A meta-analytic review. *Journal of Consulting and Clinical Psychology, 78*(2), 169–183.

Kabat-Zinn, J. (1990). *Full catastrophe living: Using the wisdom of your body and mind to face stress, pain, and illness.* New York: Dell.

Kabat-Zinn, J. (1994). *Wherever you go there you are: Mindfulness meditation in everyday life.* New York: Hyperion.

Kaviani, H., Javaheri, F., & Hatami, N. (2011). Mindfulness-based cognitive therapy (MBCT) reduces depression and anxiety induced by real stressful setting in non-clinical population. *International Journal of Psychology and Psychological Therapy, 11*(2), 285–296.

Kuyken, W., Byford, S., Taylor, R. S., Watkins, E., Holden, E., White, K. et al. (2008). Mindfulness-based cognitive therapy to prevent relapse in recurrent depression. *Journal of Consulting and Clinical Psychology, 76*, 966–978.

Langer, Á. I., Cangas, A. J., Salcedo, E., & Fuentes, B. (2012). Applying mindfulness therapy in a group of psychotic individuals: A controlled study. *Behavioural and Cognitive Psychotherapy, 40*, 105–109.

Lorant, V., Deliège, D., Eaton, W., Robert, A., Philippot, P., & Ansseau, M. (2003). Socioeconomic inequalities in depression: A meta-analysis. *American Journal of Epidemiology, 157*, 98–112.

Ma, S., & Teasdale, J. D. (2004). Mindfulness-based cognitive therapy for depression: Replication and exploration of differential relapse prevention effects. *Journal of Consulting and Clinical Psychology, 72*(1), 31–40.

McLeod, J. D., & Kessler, R. C. (1990). Socioeconomic status differences in vulnerability to undesirable life events. *Journal of Health and Social Behavior, 31*(2), 162–172.

Mirabel-Sarron, C., Dorocant, E. S., Sala, L., Bachelart, M., Guelfi, J.-D., & Rouillon, F. (2009). Mindfulness-based cognitive therapy (MBCT): A pilot study in bipolar patients. *Annales Médico-Psychologiques, 167*, 686–692.

Piet, J., & Hougaard, E. (2011). The effect of mindfulness-based cognitive therapy for prevention of relapse in recurrent major depressive disorder: A systematic review and meta-analysis. *Clinical Psychology Review, 31*, 1032–1040.

Reynolds, L. K., O'Koon, J. H., Papademetriou, E., Szczygiel, S., & Grant, K. E. (2001). Stress and somatic complaints in low-income urban adolescents. *Journal of Youth and Adolescence, 30*(4), 499–514.

Ritsher, J. E. B., Warner, V., Johnson, J. G., & Dohrenwend, B. P. (2001). Intergenerational longitudinal study of social class and depression: A test of social causation and social selection models. *The British Journal of Psychiatry, 178*, 84–90.

Robinson, T. L., & Howard-Hamilton, M. F. (2000). *The convergence of race, ethnicity, and gender: Multiple identities in counseling.* Upper Saddle River, NJ: Prentice-Hall.

Roth, B. (1997). Mindfulness-based stress reduction in the inner city. *Advances: The Journal of Mind-Body Health, 13,* 50–58.

Roth, B., & Creaser, T. (1997). Mindfulness meditation-based stress reduction: Experience with a bilingual inner-city program. *The Nurse Practitioner, 22*(3), 150–176.

Roth, B., & Robbins, D. (2004). Mindfulness-based stress reduction and health-related quality of life: Findings from a bilingual inner-city patient population. *Psychosomatic Medicine, 66,* 113–123.

Segal, Z. V., Bieling, P., Young, T., MacQueen, G., Cooke, R., Martin, L. et al. (2010). Antidepressant monotherapy vs. sequential pharmacotherapy and mindfulness-based cognitive therapy, or placebo, for relapse prophylaxis in recurrent depression. *Archives of General Psychiatry, 67*(12), 1256–1264.

Segal, Z. V., Williams, J. M. G., & Teasdale, J. D. (2012). *Mindfulness-based cognitive therapy for depression: A new approach to preventing relapse* (2nd ed.). New York: Guilford Press.

Teasdale, J. D., Segal, Z. V., Williams, J. M. G., Ridgeway, V. A., Soulsby, J. M., & Lau, M. A. (2000). Prevention of relapse/recurrence in major depression by mindfulness-based cognitive therapy. *Journal of Consulting and Clinical Psychology, 68*(4), 615–623.

Thompson, N. J., Walker, E. R., Obolensky, N., Winning, A., Barmon, C., Dilorio, C. et al. (2010). Distance delivery of mindfulness-based cognitive therapy for depression: Project UPLIFT. *Epilepsy and Behavior, 19,* 247–254.

University of Massachusetts Medical School: Center for Mindfulness in Medicine, Health Care, and Society (n.d.). Research: Major research findings. Retrieved March 9, 2013, from http://www.umassmed.edu/Content.aspx?id=42426.

U.S. Department of Health and Human Services. (1999). *Mental health: A report of the Surgeon General.* Rockville, MD.

van Praag, H. M. (2004). Can stress cause depression? *Progress in Neuro-Psychopharmacology and Biological Psychiatry, 28*(5), 891–907.

Walsh, S. D., Levine, S. Z., & Levav, I. (2012). The association between depression and parental ethnic affiliation and socioeconomic status: A 27-year longitudinal US community study. *Social Psychiatry and Psychiatric Epidemiology, 47,* 1153–1158.

Wang, J. (2005). Work stress as a risk factor for major depressive episode(s). *Psychological Medicine, 35*(6), 865–871.

Williams, A., Ness, P. V., Dixon, J., & McCorckle, R. (2012). Barriers to meditation by gender and age among cancer family caregivers. *Nursing Research, 61*(1), 22.

CHAPTER 6

Cultural Competency and Acceptance and Commitment Therapy

Rebecca M. Pasillas, Ph.D.

*Texas Tech University Health Sciences Center,
Paul L. Foster School of Medicine*

Akihiko Masuda, Ph.D.

Georgia State University

Acceptance and commitment therapy (ACT; Hayes, Strosahl, & Wilson, 1999, 2012) is a "new wave" cognitive behavioral therapy (CBT) that has been of great interest to practitioners and researchers in recent years. ACT is an *orientation* to psychotherapy, a therapeutic model of human struggle and its amelioration (Hayes, Luoma, Bond, Masuda, & Lillis, 2006). As such, it is important to note that ACT is not merely a set of specific techniques (e.g., "a man in a hole" metaphor, "values clarification" exercises). ACT is so labeled because of its intended functions: It targets core behavioral processes that are theorized to promote one's vital living and quality of life.

Recently, many practitioners and researchers have wondered whether ACT is culturally competent (Hall, Hong, Zane, & Meyer, 2011). Scholars also have pointed to the dearth of research investigating the effectiveness of ACT in diverse populations, particularly those with underserved backgrounds (Woidneck, Pratt, Gundy, Nelson, & Twohig, 2012). As discussed elsewhere (Sue, Zane, Hall, & Berger, 2009), failing to consider the intricate interaction between client and clinician as cultural beings in psychotherapy can be extremely countertherapeutic. ACT parallels this position with a focus on the idiographic, functional, and contextual nature of therapeutic work.

Why do some critics consider ACT to be culturally biased? This view seems to be dependent on the worldview held when trying to understand ACT, rather than the nature of ACT postulated by its originators. Specifically, Hayes and his colleagues (Hayes, Muto, & Masuda, 2011) stated that ACT, when understood merely in content and topography, is likely to be viewed as culturally biased. However, if ACT is viewed contextually and functionally, it should be very useful for and sensitive to a diverse body of clients. The purpose of this chapter is to outline an ACT perspective of cultural competency and issues related to clinicians' cultural competence while elucidating its philosophical and conceptual cores. First, we will present an overview of ACT, including its essential worldview (i.e., philosophical assumption) and theory. Then, we will discuss common issues related to cultural adaptation and cultural competence in the application of ACT.

110

Acceptance and Commitment Therapy: Overview

ACT is based on the philosophy of functional contextualism and relational frame theory (RFT), a contemporary behavioral theory of complex human behaviors (Hayes et al., 2006). In ACT, the term "behavior" refers to everything we do and say in a given context, including feeling, thinking, remembering, imagining, and overtly behaving. The theory and practice of ACT parallels many Eastern/ Western spiritual traditions (e.g., Buddhism) and Eastern psychotherapies (e.g., Morita therapy). Likewise, some ACT techniques are derived from other psychotherapy traditions, such as Gestalt therapy and humanistic/existential psychotherapy. However, ACT theory and practice have been formed independently from these through rigorous empirical verifications in a theoretically coherent manner (Hayes, Levin, Plumb-Vilardaga, Villatte, & Pistorello, 2013).

A detailed depiction of ACT's worldview and its basic guiding theory is beyond the scope of the present chapter. Nevertheless, a brief outline is necessary. From the perspective of functional contextualism (Hayes et al., 2013), an individual feels, thinks, and behaves the way she or he does in the "here and now" because of an ongoing history of interacting with internal and external environments (e.g., sociocultural contexts). Human beings are essentially contextual and historical beings. Without considering the sociocultural and life contexts in which a person's activities occur, we cannot fully understand that person. This functional and contextual perspective parallels a process model of clinicians' cultural competence proposed by López (1997).

The goal of ACT is the promotion of a client's vital living (Hayes et al., 2012). ACT views vital living as the ongoing process of flexibly choosing value-directed activities in a given context while being open to one's internal and external experiences. As such, ACT does not suggest specific *forms* of behaviors, feelings, or thoughts for the promotion of vital living. What characterizes vital living will vary for each individual, and it is understood in terms of the intricate interaction between the behavior of the person and the context in which the

111

behavior occurs. This function- and context-focused process account is crucial for understanding ACT.

Similar to conventional CBT models, RFT states that verbal processes (e.g., the so-called mind, thoughts, verbally labeled/evaluated emotions, memories, bodily sensations) play a central role in our living. Verbal processes can promote as well as hinder vital living. What may be unique to RFT is the assertion that the human mind (i.e., verbal process) does not inherently regulate our lives; it has its potency because we have learned to behave as though it has power to dictate actions. Additionally, RFT states that it is not the content of cognition that is problematic, but the function/impact it has over our activities. So-called problematic cognitions are not inherently problematic, and we do not have to make efforts to modify or eliminate them in form or frequency. On the contrary, RFT suggests that the most effective way to confront cognitions is to learn to *relate to* them differently. The processes of acceptance and mindfulness proposed in an ACT model are alternative behavioral choices in response to our private events, including problematic cognitions. Once again, ACT adheres to a function- and context-based process account.

ACT Treatment Approach

Clients seek psychotherapy because they have felt stuck in one way or another and their lives are less vital, at least in some areas (e.g., interpersonal relationships, work), than they would like. From an ACT perspective, many forms of psychological struggle and suffering can be viewed as verbally regulated processes of (1) excessive efforts to control unwanted private and verbal events, which are often futile and paradoxical; (2) the domination of cognitively based functions over those based in actual experience; and (3) a lack of clarity about one's core values and the ability to behave in accordance with them (Hayes et al., 2012). ACT is particularly suitable for clients whose vital activities have been suppressed by such excessive and paradoxical efforts (Luoma, Hayes, & Walser, 2007). To illustrate this point, consider someone who struggles with social anxiety. This individual is likely to attempt to suppress and change the feelings and thoughts associated with fears of negative evaluation. Unfortunately, this effort is often counterproductive and maintains struggles with these events in the long run. Further, the individual's life becomes narrowed as the person continues to make efforts to behave in accordance with this unworkable attempt.

To date, there are a number of ACT techniques and styles published elsewhere (Hayes et al., 2012; Luoma et al., 2007). In some ACT treatment manuals, ACT is grouped into specific therapeutic phases with specific exercises, homework assignments, and metaphors, and these phases are presented sequentially and additively (Eifert & Forsyth, 2005; Hayes & Wilson, 1994). These phases are as follows:

1. Shift in perspective (creative hopelessness)

2. Control as the problem, not the solution

3. Acceptance as an alternative agenda

4. A transcendent sense of self

5. Defusing language and cognition

6. Values

7. Willingness and commitment

Other ACT treatment protocols are not sequentially structured (Hayes et al., 2012; Luoma et al., 2007). Instead, they identify and target specific, but interrelated, core processes (Hayes et al., 2006) and present examples of therapeutic techniques to promote each of these processes. The ACT core behavioral processes to promote vital living are as follows:

- Acceptance

- Cognitive defusion

- Contact with the present moment

- Self-as-context

- Valued direction

- Committed action

It is not crucial in therapy to say or do exactly what is in the treatment protocol. Rather, therapists should adhere to ACT functionally and contextually to promote a client's vital living. What is considered to be an adequate form of ACT will vary across clients, clinicians, and the interactions between client and clinician. Procedures, techniques, and therapeutic styles delineated in ACT treatment manuals are examples, not absolute rules to be followed.

ACT Case Conceptualization

From an ACT perspective, case conceptualization is an ongoing and continuous intricate behavioral process between the clinician and the client throughout the course of therapy. While there are generic case conceptualization frameworks presented in ACT treatment manuals (Hayes et al., 2012; Luoma et al., 2007), understanding a given client is extremely idiographic. The purpose of case conceptualization is not only to understand the client and the client's presenting concerns and vital living, but also to elucidate plans for effective therapeutic actions. Regarding cultural competence, many forms of human struggles are attributed to one's fundamental view of the problems, causes, and solutions; therefore, it is important to fully incorporate the client's interpretation of the problem, etiology, and solution into the case conceptualization. When the client's cultural context is relevant to his or her struggle, consideration of cultural factors will be naturally integrated into a well-conducted case conceptualization.

ACT Therapeutic Style and Therapeutic Relationship

Stylistically, ACT is often said to be focused more on experiential learning and less on didactics (Hayes et al., 2012). With regard to the therapeutic relationship, the client and clinician are viewed as being in the "same soup"; the therapeutic relationship is less vertical. It is significant to note that therapeutic styles and relationships in ACT do not always have to be this way. The form of the therapeutic relationship is closely tied to its treatment goals. If a particular therapeutic style results in the promotion of the client's vital living, the therapeutic relationship is said to be a "right" one. What is important for an ACT clinician is not necessarily to choose the right therapeutic style at the outset, but to have the sensitivity to see which therapeutic style/relationship works for a given therapy case and to adjust it accordingly when necessary.

Working with a client functionally and contextually in session is at the heart of ACT. It is crucial for the clinician to become aware of the client's ongoing reactions to the therapeutic interaction with the clinician in session as well as the overall progress throughout the course of therapy. The clinician consequently chooses and adjusts the course of therapy based on this information. The clinician's own mindfulness and awareness training (e.g., slowing down) as well as videotape watching with a trained ACT supervisor may facilitate building sensitivity and effectiveness skills.

ACT Competency

"Is ACT an effective treatment?" This is a difficult question to answer because it can be scrutinized at different levels. A growing body of literature suggests that ACT is generally an effective treatment for a wide range of behavioral issues and that it achieves its effects through improving targeted core processes, such as psychological flexibility (Hayes et al., 2006). However, this does not necessarily mean that ACT is effective for each clinical case. Moreover, at a psychological and therapeutic level, the question "Is ACT an effective treatment?" is translated into "Is this collaborative human interaction between these two individuals effective?" The therapeutic competency in the context of a given psychotherapy case is inherently idiographic, and it depends on the client, the clinician, and their intricate interaction (Luoma et al., 2007).

ACT Account of Cultural Competency

"Is ACT culturally biased?" This question is also difficult to answer. ACT is not bias-free. This is not because ACT is a "bad" therapy, having a narrowly defined therapeutic goal and treatment style applicable to only a small group of individuals. Instead, it is because ACT follows a particular philosophical and conceptual perspective, as do other therapeutic approaches; following a particular worldview in and of itself is to have a biased view. Nevertheless, it is important to note that following a particular perspective is not necessarily toxic if the perspective is broadly effective. The goal of psychotherapy regarding cultural competence is not to be free from bias. We, as verbal and social beings, cannot escape from biases. Rather, it is to find a way to maximize the therapeutic effectiveness while making efforts to minimize the negative impact of biases brought to psychotherapy by the clinician and client.

Is ACT Culturally Competent?

Cultural competency is multifaceted, and it can be discussed at multiple levels with different foci (e.g., treatment level, agency level, systems level). In this section, we will focus on the behaviors of the clinician in the context of psychotherapy. Regarding a clinician's behavior (i.e., psychological level of analysis), Sue and colleagues (2009) view cultural competence as a multidimensional process of "scientific mindedness (i.e., forming and testing hypotheses), dynamic sizing (i.e., flexibility in generalizing and individualizing), and culture-specific resources (i.e., having knowledge and skills to work with other cultures) in response to different kinds of clients" (p. 529). We believe that these behavioral processes are crucial for effective psychotherapy. From a functional and contextual standpoint, ACT explicitly stresses the importance of treatment effectiveness in therapy and cultural competency. In ACT, the notions/skills of cultural competency should be closely linked to the individually tailored treatment goal (i.e., the promotion of vital living). As the behavioral presentations of vital living vary ideographically across clients, culturally competent therapeutic skills also vary contextually in practice.

Cultural Considerations for ACT

We will present some salient topics that are particularly relevant to the clinician's cultural competence in ACT in the following section. It is important to note that these topics are not specific to ACT but are important to all psychotherapies.

Perspective Taking and Empathy

To be an effective clinician, both culturally and ideographically, with a given client, the clinician must make efforts to wholeheartedly see and feel what it is like to be the client. This effort is related to, but distinct from, conducting a detailed factual assessment of the client. It is to fully get in touch with the client's experience as if the clinician contacts the world through the client's eyes, sees what the client sees, and feels what the client feels in given sociocultural contexts. The clinician is never able to know what the client goes through exactly; however, such efforts allow the clinician to better understand the client's struggle and to more fully craft a functional and contextual conceptual framework for developing effective actions.

ACT emphasizes the importance of working with a given client as a fellow human being (Luoma et al., 2007). This therapeutic stance is based on the goal of ACT linked to a clinician's value of *being a human being*. The experiential connection to self as being human as well as viewing a client as a fellow human promotes a balanced perspective on acceptance and change. Because being human essentially involves painful experiences, and personal growth is not linear or steady, progress in therapy can be slow. Letting go of struggles is hard, and moving toward a valued direction can be excruciating. As humans, we do not want to have any problems, and, yet, we do have problems. Embracing these human qualities promotes the kind of therapeutic sensitivity, compassion, and effectiveness tailored to a given therapeutic context.

Integration of Sociocultural Factors into Case Conceptualization

How does an ACT clinician take sociocultural factors into consideration? In essence, ACT views a given client and a client's clinical concerns in terms of the "act of a whole person in historical and situational contexts" (Hayes et al., 2012). From this worldview, sociocultural factors (e.g., historical background, current sociopolitical climate, socioeconomic status, community support, familial environment, language preferences and abilities, educational and literacy levels, acculturation levels, immigration history, religion and spirituality background) are not separate entities distinguished from the unit of understanding. Rather, they can be crucial parts of the client's "act-in-context" relevant to the client's presenting concerns and vital living. In case conceptualization, these factors are understood in terms of behavior patterns in given contexts. For example, cultural differences presented by an interracial couple can be understood as particular communication patterns or interactions in a given context. It is important to note that not all sociocultural factors are clinically relevant. A major goal of case conceptualization is to identify factors that are therapeutically relevant to a client's presenting concern. To understand whether and how given sociocultural factors impact an individual's presenting concern, a funnel approach is employed (Hawkins, 1979; Hayes & Toarmino, 1995). The goal of a funnel approach is to elucidate the contextual events that are particularly relevant to the promotion of vital living. In this process, it is imperative to explore the client's views toward sociocultural factors perceived to be relevant to the presenting concerns.

Awareness of One's Own Biases

Throughout the course of ACT treatment, clinicians must be cautious not to make assumptions or rely on biases about their clients' sociocultural context and factors impacting clinically relevant behavior. One's sociocultural background will impact a problem behavior in a manner that will differ from another client with a similar sociocultural background. It may present a significant disruption in the therapeutic relationship and the provision of treatment if a clinician makes a supposition concerning what a given client prefers based solely on knowledge about the sociocultural group to which the client belongs.

In ACT, a clinician's biases influence the provision of treatment. As noted in Hayes et al. (2012), it is especially important for a clinician to be aware of his or her own biases and to be flexible in disentangling the client's problematic behaviors in the context of the clinician's biases. Just as the client is learning to engage in vital and flexible living, the clinician utilizes flexibility and sensitivity to recognize his or her own biases within the therapeutic relationship. The clinician demonstrates moment-by-moment vital and flexible living in treatment by doing the following: "[A]cknowledge the issue (privately at first then to the client if that seems clinically useful); be more open with it psychologically; and focus on the values-based actions that can be taken in the service of the client" (p. 160). The ACT clinician using this framework shows the client *how* to take valued actions *while* experiencing a range of private experiences such as thoughts, emotions, and body sensations related to those biases.

The Role of Language

A key issue of language in ACT is not necessarily whether the language ability of the clinician matches the language ability of the client. Instead, it is whether and how language (i.e.., verbal processing) plays a role in the client's vital living and problematic behavior. In ACT, verbal processes, which regulate and maintain clinically relevant behaviors, are viewed as the central force behind human suffering (Hayes et al., 2012). In language, what is crucial is its learned function of regulating other behaviors and emotions. Language of a particular form influences how emotions are expressed in any setting, including in treatment. For example, the expressiveness and intensity of emotions in bilingual individuals are based on the language spoken by the individuals *and* on the language preference (not language proficiency) of the individuals (Marian & Kaushanskaya, 2008). As bilingual individuals tend to express intense emotions and recall additional specific information in one language, but not in the other, knowing which language of a particular form occurs under what psychosocial context is crucial to identify the verbal processes targeted in session.

Promotion of awareness provides an opportunity for the clinician and client to be aware of the verbal process occurring in the present moment. Suppose a bilingual client has difficulty identifying internal experiences (e.g., emotions, thoughts, and memories). She also states that she typically experiences her sense of self in her second language. In ACT, the clinician should elucidate clients' language abilities (e.g., being bilingual), language choice, and their relevance to the presenting concerns on a functional and contextual basis. A clinician should pay close attention to the context in which a spoken language shifts (e.g., changing from one language to a second language during a conversation). Language switching may be irrelevant to the presenting concerns, or it may be the manifestation of *avoiding* emotionally charged aversive internal experiences such as thoughts, feelings, and memories. Alternatively, language switching may function as a way to purposefully *experience* avoided internal experiences. If the bilingual client continues to refer to a word in another language to describe herself, then the clinician (whether familiar with the client's second language or not) may want to deconstruct the history of the word as a way to understand the verbal relation between the word and the client's sense of self. In short, understanding the role of a particular language will inform the clinician on how to intervene in treatment.

In addition to understanding the role of language in a client's clinically relevant behaviors, providers must also be cognizant of the client's literacy levels because this may determine the form in which the intervention is delivered to the client. Certain exercises or other intervention techniques may need to be tweaked or adapted to accommodate the client's literacy level (Fuchs, Lee, Roemer, & Orsillo, 2013). For example, if the client has never learned to read fluently, the clinician may need to consider whether any experiential exercises, metaphors, and handouts will need to be modified. By meeting the literacy needs of the client, the clinician's actions may also function to strengthen the therapeutic relationship, as it demonstrates respect and flexibility on the clinician's part.

Modification of Metaphors, Activities, and Sessions

Structural modifications are always expected in ACT, and they depend on the client's clinically relevant behaviors and their sociocultural context. Some modifications may include modifying the content of mindfulness exercises, metaphors, and activities; modifying the length of metaphors, exercises, and session activities (e.g., brief and precise); or modifying the session formats (e.g., including "key brokers" in sessions—see the following section). These modifications will always be in the service of the client and his or her treatment goals, as ACT is a client-centered treatment.

One area of caution for ACT clinicians to consider is the content of metaphors. ACT clinicians may have a tendency to become caught up with the *content* of ACT metaphors. Beginning ACT therapists especially may make efforts to deliver metaphors exactly as written in the ACT treatment manual rather than considering the utility of a metaphor for a given treatment purpose. Unfortunately, this narrow approach overlooks the intended function of the metaphor, which is to help the client become aware of certain psychological processes for behavior change. A topographical adherence may cloud the actual influence of the metaphor on the client and may unintentionally result in negative consequences. The chessboard metaphor, for example (Hayes et al., 2012, pp. 231–233), illustrates the experience of self as an observer differentiated from the experiences actually observed. This can be a powerful metaphor in treatment if it appropriately reflects the client's life. The chessboard metaphor can elicit unintended negative reactions because some may perceive it as the presentation of an implicit bias toward a particular group of people. Specifically, the black chess pieces are sometimes presented as the "bad" thoughts (or feelings, memories, physical sensations, etc.), and the white chess pieces are the "good" thoughts (or feelings, memories, physical sensations, etc.). By utilizing the chessboard metaphor exactly as it is written in the treatment manual, the clinician may unintentionally anger or upset the client because the client is attending to the content of the metaphor. Rather than harnessing the message of this metaphor, the metaphor's function is reduced or lost because of the implicitly biased content. For that reason, ACT clinicians must carefully choose their words, examples, and metaphors, or the intended treatment function may be lost. What is imperative is the functional and contextual adherence to ACT with sensitivity to the client's ongoing reactions to the therapeutic interaction. Modifying the content of ACT metaphors to reflect the client's sociocultural context, if such adaptation is likely to promote vital living, is expected.

The Role of "Key Brokers"

The modality of ACT (e.g., individual therapy, group therapy, workshop, online) varies across intervention settings. In working with some clients, the involvement of "key brokers" could be another sociocultural consideration. Key brokers may include immediate or extended family members, friends, or community members (e.g., clergy, spiritualists, etc.) who are a significant part of the client's context. At times, involving a key broker in treatment may be helpful and vital for the client and his or her treatment goals. Working with key brokers may set the context for the client to create change and develop effective living. In practice, clinicians may want to ask: What is the social and familial context of the client? What is the clinical utility and appropriateness of bringing the key broker into session with the client? Will the key broker assist with the client's pursuit of living a valued life? Is the client willing to engage the involvement of a key broker? If the key brokers are involved in therapy, clinicians should follow proper ethical procedures, such as obtaining consent from the client to involve the key broker and consent from the key broker to be involved in the client's treatment. The level of involvement of key brokers in therapy sessions should be determined on a case-by-case basis, while taking the client's preference into consideration.

The Role of Religion and Spirituality

Historically, there have been tensions between religion and the field of psychotherapy, with psychotherapy sometimes disregarding the religious and spiritual domains of a client's life. However, religion and spirituality can serve as important aspects of a client's vital living; ACT clinicians should not ignore the power and importance of this influence in a client's life. From an ACT perspective, the issue of spirituality and religion in psychotherapy is not necessarily an ontological one, but a psychological and functional one. For some clients, spiritual and religious practice is an essential part of a vital life. Ignoring or shying away from these subjects can be countertherapeutic in these cases. Spiritual and religious practice may be most relevant for religious/spiritual clients when such clients are connecting with compassion, humanity, and the genuine aspects of self and others. At a minimum, assessing the role of a client's religious and spiritual background provides clinicians with baseline information regarding the client's psychological flexibility processes. If the client notes that religion and spirituality play a major role in his or her life, the clinician's responsibility is to determine how religion and spirituality reflect the client's vital living. For many clients, spirituality and religion may facilitate their connection to their own values, their experience of the here and now, and compassion toward self and others. For the ACT therapist, exploring the client's spirituality and religiosity may be an excellent opportunity to get in touch with the client's greater openness, honesty, and vulnerability. Finally, as noted earlier in this chapter, clinicians must take note of any biases regarding religion and spirituality and how their biases are behaviorally impacting psychotherapy (e.g., ignoring the importance of clients' religious and spiritual backgrounds).

Conclusion

From the beginning of ACT's development, issues reflecting the importance of cultural competence have been part of the discussion. As ACT has been expanded to a broad range of clinical contexts serving diverse bodies of clients in recent years, cultural competency and cultural adaptation have become imperative topics to pursue. We hope this chapter evokes awareness and thoughtful investigation and promotes the cultural competency of ACT to better serve our clients.

References

Eifert, G. H., & Forsyth, J. P. (2005). *Acceptance and commitment therapy for anxiety disorders: A practitioner's treatment guide to using mindfulness, acceptance, and values-based behavior change strategies.* Oakland, CA: New Harbinger Publications.

Fuchs, C., Lee, J. K., Roemer, L., & Orsillo, S. M. (2013). Using mindfulness- and acceptance-based treatments with clients from nondominant cultural and/or marginalized backgrounds: Clinical considerations, meta-analysis findings, and introduction to the special series: Clinical considerations in using acceptance- and mindfulness-based treatments with diverse populations. *Cognitive and Behavioral Practice, 20*(1), 1–12. doi: 10.1016/j.cbpra.2011.12.004.

Hall, G. C. N., Hong, J. J., Zane, N. W. S., & Meyer, O. L. (2011). Culturally competent treatments for Asian Americans: The relevance of mindfulness- and acceptance-based psychotherapies. *Clinical Psychology: Science and Practice, 18*(3), 215–231. doi: 10.1111/j.1468-2850.2011.01253.x.

Hawkins, R. P. (1979). The functions of assessment: Implications for selection and development of devices for assessing repertoires in clinical, educational, and other settings. *Journal of Applied Behavior Analysis, 12*(4), 501–516. doi: 10.1901/jaba.1979.12-501.

Hayes, S. C., Levin, M. E., Plumb-Vilardaga, J., Villatte, J. L., & Pistorello, J. (2013). Acceptance and commitment therapy and contextual behavioral science: Examining the progress of a distinctive model of behavioral and cognitive therapy. *Behavior Therapy, 44*(2): 180–198. doi: 10.1016/j.beth.2009.08.002.

Hayes, S. C., Luoma, J. B., Bond, F. W., Masuda, A., & Lillis, J. (2006). Acceptance and commitment therapy: Model, processes and outcomes. *Behaviour Research and Therapy, 44*(1), 1–25. doi: 10.1016/j.brat.2005.06.006.

Hayes, S. C., Muto, T., & Masuda, A. (2011). Seeking cultural competence from the ground up. *Clinical Psychology: Science & Practice, 18*(3), 232–237. doi: 10.1111/j.1468-2850.2011.01254.x.

Hayes, S. C., Strosahl, K. D., & Wilson, K. G. (1999). *Acceptance and commitment therapy: An experiential approach to behavior change.* New York: Guilford Press.

Hayes, S. C., Strosahl, K. D., & Wilson, K. G. (2012). *Acceptance and commitment therapy: The process and practice of mindful change* (2nd ed.). New York: Guilford Press.

Hayes, S. C., & Toarmino, D. (1995). If behavioral principles are generally applicable, why is it necessary to understand cultural diversity? *The Behavior Therapist, 18*, 21–23.

Hayes, S. C., & Wilson, K. G. (1994). Acceptance and commitment therapy: Altering the verbal support for experiential avoidance. *The Behavior Analyst, 17*(2), 289–303.

López, S. R. (1997). Cultural competence in psychotherapy: A guide for clinicians and their supervisors. In C. E. Watkins Jr. (Ed.), *Handbook of psychotherapy supervision* (pp. 570–588). Hoboken, NJ: John Wiley & Sons.

Luoma, J. B., Hayes, S. C., & Walser, R. D. (2007). *Learning ACT: An acceptance and commitment therapy skills-training manual for therapists.* Oakland, CA: New Harbinger Publications.

Marian, V., & Kaushanskaya, M. (2008). Words, feelings, and bilingualism: Cross-linguistic differences in emotionality of autobiographical memories. *The Mental Lexicon, 3*(1), 72–90. doi: 10.1075/ml.3.1.06mar.

Sue, S., Zane, N., Hall, G. C. N., & Berger, L. K. (2009). The case for cultural competency in psychotherapeutic interventions. *Annual Review of Psychology, 60*, 525–548. doi: 10.1146/annurev.psych.60.110707.163651.

Woidneck, M. R., Pratt, K. M., Gundy, J. M., Nelson, C. R., & Twohig, M. P. (2012). Exploring cultural competence in acceptance and commitment therapy outcomes. *Professional Psychology: Research and Practice, 43*(3), 227–233. doi: 10.1037/a0026235.

PART III

Application of Acceptance- and Mindfulness-Based Approaches to Diversity Issues

CHAPTER 7

Functional Adaptation of Acceptance- and Mindfulness-Based Therapies: An Ethical Imperative

Claudia Drossel, Ph.D.

Veterans Affairs South Central Mental Illness Research, Education, and Clinical Center and University of Arkansas for Medical Sciences

Claudia McCausland, Ph.D.

Memphis Veterans Affairs Medical Center

Norbert Schneider, Dipl. Psych., Dipl.-Soz.-Päd

Private Practice in Fürth, Germany

Roberto Cattivelli, Ph.D.

University of Parma

Interest in acceptance- and mindfulness-based therapies has swept across the psychological community worldwide. We—two native German speakers who trained and practice in the United States (Claudia Drossel [CD] and Claudia McCaisland [CM]), one native English speaker who trained and practices in German (Norbert Schneider [NS]), and one native Italian speaker who trained and practices in Italian (Roberto Cattivelli [RC])—were asked to write this chapter to help facilitate the implementation of acceptance- and mindfulness-based treatments across sociocultural and linguistic contexts. While treatment manuals for these therapies have been translated into many different languages, most translations follow the original U.S. English texts quite literally. There is little room to accommodate special aspects of the sociocultural and linguistic contexts, as by virtue of their occupation translators do not have license for flexibility. Often, we have heard practitioners say, "This part of the manual sounds awkward and cobbled together when I use it in session." Naturally practitioners are concerned about adherence to the treatment manual and the fidelity to the therapy of their choice.

Fidelity, however, can be understood in two ways: (1) fidelity to the *topographical aspects* of the treatment (i.e., following the original version by the letter—for example, starting acceptance and commitment therapy [ACT] with a translation of the "person in the hole" metaphor) and (2) fidelity with regard to the *functional aspects* of the treatment. Bilingual speakers are familiar with the difference between topography and function. For example, "making mountains out of molehills" is an English idiom that concisely points out exaggeration. A topographical (i.e., literal) translation into German might confuse the German-speaking listener. A German-speaking listener, however, immediately would relate to "making an elephant out of a mosquito" as the functional equivalent.

In general, the functional-contextual approach considers the meaning of what is said as a dynamic process that emerges in the interplay between speaker and listener and not as a "thing" that can be passed on from speaker to listener (Skinner, 1974). Instead, "meaning" arises out of the history of the verbal community (e.g., the social convention for saying "It is cold"), the individual histories of speaker and listener (e.g., living in a hot climate may have shifted one's relative judgment of "cold"), and—last but not least—the actual impact on the listener. In terms of impact, the phrase "I am cold" may be a simple description, but socially it may *function* as a request. This function is discovered through observation. For instance, if Sally tends to change the thermostat setting after hearing Joe say, "I am cold," an utterance that looks like a description actually functions as a social demand. Thus, for any interpersonal relationship, this functional approach to language has implications for therapy: topography denotes appearance, while function characterizes the actual impact of what is said (or of a treatment technique used) on both client and therapist.

Treatment manuals, regardless of the language in which they have been developed, emphasize topographical aspects of delivery, and mindfulness- and acceptance-based therapies are no exception. Practitioners face the challenge of achieving the functional meaning of the treatment without getting stuck on a particular topography of delivery. Developing functional equivalents of treatment requires skill, resourcefulness, creativity, and sensitivity to context. Indeed, as we describe in the following pages, *each* implementation of a therapy can be viewed as a unique opportunity for adaptation, in a novel context, with *your* specific client. With ACT, widely translated and described in detail in the current volume, we will show how a functional approach to the treatment itself can facilitate a culturally responsive application that is tailored to each client. A *functional* application of ACT may not *look like* and, in fact, may appear to deviate from the original treatment manual (Hayes, Strosahl, & Wilson, 1999, p. 16). Yet, it is exactly such an application that replicates the manual's therapeutic impact given your unique therapeutic situation with your particular client.

Acceptance and Commitment Therapy: A Functional Overview

ACT clearly defines both its philosophical and its scientific base (Waltz & Hayes, 2010). It emerged from a functional-contextual school of psychology that reaches back to the 1930s. Careful study of what is now called "act-in-context" characterizes this functional-contextual school. Its underlying worldview has four major tenets (Chiesa, 1994):

TENET 1: Human beings are conceptualized as unique dynamic focal points of ongoing and historical biological, psychosocial, and cultural relations.

These relations are reciprocal with human behavior—we change our world and are also being changed (Skinner, 1957/1992), as if we were part and parcel with one ongoing M. C. Escher–like *Drawing of Hands* that lasts our lifetime. For this reason, the subject matter of psychology is not a person encapsulated in his or her skin and cut off from the world but the entire dynamic person-and-context relation. Understanding and nudging this relation is at the heart of the therapeutic process. By virtue of its nature, this lived process requires engagement: the courage to try something, to observe what happens, and to engage and try again, one step at a time. Here, in being active—observing, reengaging—is where mindfulness resides (Hayes et al., 1999, p. 62).

This functional-contextual view of person-and-context relations provides the therapist with the opportunity to be genuinely curious and come to know aspects of the client's personal, political, and economic context. In addition to individual history, sociocultural factors influence clients' reasons for therapy, their understanding of and engagement in the process, and expectations for therapy in general and of the therapist in particular (Hays, 2008). Among these are:

- age and generational influences

- developmental disabilities

- chronic illnesses or disabilities acquired later in life

- religion/spiritual orientation, or absence thereof

- ethnicity (i.e., communally shared values, customs, beliefs, norms)

- racial identity (i.e., consequences of the social construction of "race" for that particular person, in terms of privilege and discrimination)

- socioeconomics (related to occupation, income, education, marital status, gender, ethnicity, community, family history)

- sexual orientation

- indigenous heritage

- national origin

- gender

Within the functional-contextual perspective, the ethical imperative to study the act-in-context cannot be dissociated from respect for the dignity of the individual. While we, as human beings, are never able to feel exactly what somebody else feels, compassion for ourselves and others arises out of our understanding of individual and sociocultural histories as well as current circumstances and the knowledge that similar histories and circumstances would put us into similar situations.

TENET 2: The relationship among thoughts, feelings, and behavior is viewed as interchangeable.

While lay people as well as countless cohorts of introductory psychology students learn to recognize "cognition" and "emotion" as "good reasons" for behavior, anybody can reverse the flow of causation: Intervene to change behavior and, voilà, cognitions and emotions will follow suit. We learn to observe our own behavior in context (Bem, 1972), and we likewise learn to observe our thoughts and feelings in theirs. In a functional-contextual worldview, thoughts, feelings, and behavior conceptually coexist on an "even keel." Neither receives privileged status as an explanation for the other. Consequently, ACT—in contrast to traditional CBT, which expects cognition to change before behavior does—teaches clients that thoughts and feelings do not have to change as a prerequisite for behavior to change. Intervening on behavior without altering thoughts or feelings first is termed "acceptance." Acceptance lies in the therapist's and the client's skill to let difficult sensations, percep-tions, cognitions, memories, and emotions be, and take them as an inevitable part of being human that tends to distract us from build-ing a meaningful life.

TENET 3: Human language is our greatest asset and our greatest liability.

The functional-contextual worldview draws attention to the circumstance that our social-verbal community shapes our language and thus our explicit and implicit beliefs, evaluations, and judgments of self, others, and the world (Deutscher, 2010). Our narratives, heuristics, and rationalizations, evolved over centuries, are necessarily insufficient and flawed (e.g., we still refer to the sun setting and rising). Our lives are spent in an intricate balance of following transmitted narratives to our tremendous benefit ("Don't cross the street unless the light is green"), seeking shelter in their deceptive certainty and safety ("I am …," "I can't …"), and giving ourselves and others the benefit of incredulity ("In the past I told myself and others that I could not tolerate the sight of blood, but am I sufficiently sure to let that keep me from applying to medical school?"). The functional-contextual approach assumes that language *can* get in the way of living one's life and *can* become a source of suffering. Whether and how language gets in the way, however, is for each of us to discover—by being active, observing, and engaging in the world (see Tenet 1).

TENET 4: Tenets 1 to 3 apply to everybody.

Neither scientist nor therapist is excluded. Thus, the examination of the person-and-context relations, the question as to what we assume to be necessary and sufficient explanations for our and others' behavior, and the assessment of how much our language abilities (particularly judging, evaluating, and rationalizing) contribute to our and others' suffering are relevant to all human beings across contexts. These tenets are much like the process of weaving, and each individual's context determines fabric, colors, and patterns.

Four Tenets Lost in Translation

The first attempts to disseminate and translate these four tenets to a broad audience failed (Rachlin, 1980; Skinner, 1953, 1974). Author-scientists spoke their laboratory language of precision and procedures; for example, they still relied on the terms "stimulus" and "response." While the tone seemed technical and distant from experience, and thereby irrelevant to the general public, the publications' implications met with criticism, defensiveness, and even outrage by academicians at the time (e.g., Krutch, 1953/1970). As a result, a body of academic literature emerged that discussed the peculiarities—and awkwardness—of speaking about reciprocal person-context relations (for a review, see Chiesa, 1994).

While the US dissemination of these tenets through early functional-contextual literature was met with indifference at best, the ubiquity of psychological jargon and a historical association of the words "stimulus" and "response" with "stimulus→response"–psychology hampered a translation of the literature. Metzger (1996, p. 30) found close to 600 mistakes in the German translation of Skinner's *About Behaviorism, Was ist Behaviorismus?* (Skinner, 1978). The rigid application of the unidirectional S→R framework to operate contingencies led to the quite nonsensical circumstance that, within the German translation, the impact (i.e., the "stimulus," or consequence in the Skinnerian account) *preceded* the behavior that produced it.

Whole sentences that did not fit the S→R framework were omitted. As emphasized in Tenets 3 and 4, translators also have no special protection from the treacherous aspects of language—noted by the Italian caveat "*traduttore-traditore*," translator-traitor. For this reason, contextual science encourages the study of its underlying philosophy to make our assumptions about human behavior explicit and to designate Tenets 1 through 4 as the guideposts for our flexible application of treatment to our clients' unique circumstances.

In the 1980s contextual science began to systematically study how language interacted with behavior and contributed to people's struggling with change (for a brief review, see Hayes et al., 1999). Findings showed that, when people had a specific rule, they followed it even when circumstances had changed. For example, being told that rapidly pushing a button would win points, study participants maintained their high rate even when conditions changed and only slowness paid off. This effect diminished when rules were vague and ambiguous (e.g., pushing the button fast or slow will produce points). Individuals were more likely to attend to circumstances. Importantly, attention to context was also reduced when specific rules were *self*-generated. Our long history of following rules given to us by other people ("Take your coat when it's cold outside") increases the risk that we adhere to rules that we make up for ourselves, and that a rule itself will make us less sensitive to noticing person-and-context relations: "To a hammer, everything looks like a nail."

Using ACT Functionally

With failed dissemination of functional-contextual approaches in recent history, ACT developers adopted a dissemination strategy that aimed at protecting therapists and clients alike from the pitfalls of language (Tenet 3). In addition to traditional written explanations of philosophy and science, developers relied on lived exercises and metaphors to generate vague rules, thereby hoping to maintain or increase the sensitivity of the therapist's and the client's behavior to context (McCurry & Hayes, 1992). Explicit in this therapy training approach was the expectation that, once the functions of exercises and metaphors are abstracted from workshops and repeated practice with the manual, therapists will flexibly obtain similar functions with new content, adjusted to each individual therapeutic situation (Hayes et al., 1999, p. 16).

The Trouble with Words

Therapists who use ACT in a non-Anglo-American linguistic context may notice difficulties with ACT-specific terms right away. Words that have become the buzzwords of the therapy or even make up its label may not have equivalent translations. "Commitment," for example, is a term that does not have direct German or Italian translations. It requires us to shift from topography to function, as the literal translation does not produce the intended impact. In ACT, "commitment" denotes a tight correspondence between "saying" and "doing." It refers to the "stick to it–ness" needed to move from the mere verbal profession of a long-term value to its consistent manifestation in a person's life through actions in the short term: If maintaining my health throughout my lifespan matters to me, people who know me should be able to recognize this value via my daily nutritional choices and adherence to exercise. Commitment does not imply obligation toward a third party but an authentic life through actions in accordance with one's values. This has been called "engagement" by Sartre (1945/2007).

Engagement (*sich engagieren* as a verb in German) means "to actively work for a good cause." In ACT, clients are invited to engage in activities that champion and stand for what clients perceive matters in their lives. However, engagement on one's own behalf is a concept that runs counter to the collectivist aspects of many cultures that traditionally discourage all forms of perceived egotism and self-promotion. If a specific term's connotations distract from the function of therapy, it is our job to circumvent it. As one of the authors' (RC's) Italian clients said upon hearing the English word "commitment": "Ah, I don't know this word, but it sounds bad!" The removal of barriers to actions that are meaningful to the client in the long term is the bread and butter of therapy. For example, clients who feel taken aback by a call for "engagement" may be more open to the rationale that all barriers in the way of a correspondence between saying/ valuing and doing ("authenticity") are grist for the therapeutic mill.

It is possible (and often necessary) to practice ACT without using its specific therapeutic jargon. First, we do not want to introduce clients to a new vocabulary that they ultimately can share only with their therapists, especially when it is not clear whether this eagerness to connect with the therapist via a shared vocabulary translates into effective behavior outside the therapy session. Second, we would like for skills to generalize to the client's context, where jargon may have counterproductive colloquial meanings (e.g., "acceptance" as "surrender," "mindfulness meditation" as "emptying one's mind," "compassion" as "pity" in Italian). Third, therapy aims to expose clients to behavior-context relations within their own frame of reference. ACT (perhaps more appropriately written "Act!") has as its goal an actively engaged client who samples what behavior patterns might bring him or her closer to long-term dreams and overarching values. As the client begins to engage in his or her own life effectively (i.e., as defined by the client), the therapist becomes superfluous.

The Trouble with Metaphors

Just as it is not necessary to use therapy-specific terms, it is possible to practice ACT completely without the metaphors or exercises that are described in the manuals. Indeed, clients who think concretely might not be able to move beyond the literal content of metaphors. One of the authors' (CD's and CM's) clients responded to each illustration with a discussion of literal content: Hearing "values are like constellations that guided sailors across the seas," he excitedly spoke of his recent cruise. Here, metaphors did not support the generation of vague rules but introduced new literal content. Sociocultural histories also affect the interpretation of metaphors, as with the image of "soldiers on parade" in countries with a history of militarism (e.g.,

Germany). In addition, the content of metaphors can evoke clients' personal histories, including trauma. For example, a client, originally from South Asia, was forced to sit on a bucket while holding on to ropes wound on a windlass. Thus, her parent could lower her into a well, where she spent hours for perceived misbehavior. The use of the "person in the hole" metaphor, to normalize our general human tendency to get stuck, conjured up her individual history, a situation of sheer hanging on, in which not even digging was an option. This client, now a U.S. citizen with an advanced college degree, lived her life in terror of "the well," paralyzed by the thought of a misstep. Given her history, "keeping distance from the well," instead of "digging out of a hole," became shorthand for behavior patterns that decreased her anxiety yet prevented active engagement in life. This client was able to move from the content of the past events to an abstract level of behavioral-context relations.

McCurry and Hayes (1992) suggested that figurative speech should:

1. match the developmental level of the client (i.e., the client's cognitive ability to move from concrete content to abstract meaning);

2. originate in everyday, commonsense events;

3. kindle a rich perceptual and imaginative response; and

4. fit the scope of the problem (i.e., unambiguous examples for specific problems and room for multiple interpretations if problems are vague).

We would add that, for a therapeutically effective use of figurative illustrations of person-and-context relations, they also must be part of the clients' sociocultural contexts. For example, U.S. Americans tend to be quite fluent in movie or TV quotes, such as George Costanza's "opposite day" from *Seinfeld*, as shorthand for complex person-context relations. Effective therapists learn their clients' language and constantly engage in cross-checks to ascertain the desired impact. The toolbox for illustrations is endless: clients' personal stories, culture-specific idioms and adages, fairy tales or legends, nursery rhymes, songs, fiction, TV shows, movies, visual arts, cartoons, anime, and so on all provide raw material for shared meaning. Maffini and colleagues are currently studying a symbol-based system ("mateMatrix"; personal communication with RC) to convey therapeutic strategies functionally.

The Function of Selected ACT Components

Below we will walk through selected ACT components, outlined in chapter 6. We will clarify the main function of each component without ACT-specific terms or common metaphors to facilitate cross-checking for functional fidelity to the therapy.

Creative Hopelessness. ACT views all human actions as a function of ongoing and historical biological, social, and cultural relations (Tenet 1). It follows that we always behave exactly as we ought—that is, perfectly, given our historical and ongoing contexts, and their continuous reciprocal interplay with our behavior, in line with Suzuki's remark, "You are perfect just as you are *and* you could use a little improvement" (cited in Chödrön, 2006, p. 31). Any illustration reflects that the client behaved as he or she ought—perfectly.

"Ought" refers to the reasonableness of the clients' current actions, considering their context as well as the general human propensity to get stuck. Any illustrations you develop with the client should convey to the client a sense that it is safe to relax with the present situation, including all thoughts and feelings it brings about. Chödrön (1997, p. 46) describes the function of hopelessness as creating a "beginning of the beginning," a space in which a person feels understood as being stuck; where the client's overwhelming experience of not finding a solution is not invalidated by the therapist's quick jump to problem-solving; where uncertainty is modeled. As a powerful relationship-building tool, "creative hopelessness" produces a sigh of relief: "Suffering is part of life, and we don't have to feel it's happening because we personally made the wrong move" (p. 49). Your job is to get the client to breathe that sigh of relief without receiving a solution to his or her problems.

For creative hopelessness to occur, you must be comfortable with letting the client's narratives, including his or her descriptions of attempts to change, unfold without flexing your "expert" or "fix-it" muscles. At any time in the therapeutic process, creative hopelessness calls for your genuine interest and curiosity in person-and-context relations. Clients' expectations of what should have worked to get them "unstuck" and reduce their suffering, and what actually did work, may differ greatly by aspects of interpersonal and sociocultural histories and current environments.

Control is the problem. Therapeutic activities subsumed under this heading challenge clients' assumptions that a change in their private events (i.e., sensations and perceptions, memories, thoughts, or feelings) must be the prerequisite for behavior change (Tenet 2). From a functional-contextual perspective, our language ability leads to our inadvertent application of general social rules about the public expression of private events (e.g., "You should control your emotions") to the events themselves ("I shouldn't feel what I'm feeling"). As a result, we focus our lives on fairly futile attempts to feel or think differently. ACT holds up a magnifying glass to the indiscriminate influence of social rules, conventions, and expectations on clients, especially regarding clients' attitudes toward their own private events. An assessment of each client's individual sociocultural context fosters the client's detection of potential sociocultural sources that support clinging to futile, introspective change strategies. The case conceptualization, formulated with the client, views the client's allocation of time and effort to private events as a major barrier to action: In accordance with Tenet 2, illustrations and exercises point out that preoccupation with introspection as well as ongoing attempts to change the content of thoughts and feelings keep clients from fully living their lives.

The therapeutic task is to find a shared language that illustrates Tenet 2 in ways that speak to the client. Western culture is replete with examples of such "paralysis by analysis." Watzlawick (1983/1993) dedicated a book to this pursuit of unhappiness, giving poignant everyday vignettes of getting trapped by the very process of "languaging" about private events.

Defusing language. As pointed out earlier (Tenet 3), language can be a gift and a burden. If we truly believed each thought that crossed our minds and acted on it, our behavior would be markedly ineffective, not to mention erratic. The function of defusion is to decouple the perceived causal links among cognition, emotion, and behavior. It fosters the skill to recognize when our language abilities, such as reasoning and analyzing, work for us and when they are best ignored.

> Für die Fähigkeit, denken zu können, zahlen wir den übermäßig hohen Preis, auch denken zu müssen. (*Our ability to think comes with the exorbitantly high price of also having to think*; Laub, 1984, p. 22)

One way to cope with this high price of language is to change its impact on our behavior: From a functional-contextual perspective, "languaging" is the brain's steady hum, akin to a heartbeat. Exercises facilitate your clients' recognition of this hum and their ability to step back from it and notice its patterns. Delays between having a thought or a feeling and acting upon it open up a larger contextual perspective that clients can use to their advantage. This larger perspective increases the likelihood that clients can orient toward outcomes that are valued in the long term, rather than impulsive short-term ones (Rachlin, 2000).

Defusing self. The limits of language also apply to the self-concept, in that a client's self-descriptions may have become barriers to engagement (e.g., "I am not the type of person who…"; "that's just not like me…"). The function of a therapeutic intervention is to reframe the self, according to Tenet 1, as a location or intersection of dynamic behavior-context relations. The self as such a spot for the unique interplay of person-world is distinguished from our narratives about the self, part of the steady hum of the brain's heartbeat (Tenet 3). Illustrations work to enhance this distinction and enable the client to treat self-statements as no different in kind from other thoughts. The therapist's task is to facilitate noticing whether and when rigid self-statements get in the way of living an authentic life. Flexibility in the conceptualization of the self is the goal, to promote change when situations call for it.

Values. In accordance with its conceptualization of self as a locus for the interplay of person-world, life is viewed as a series of enterprises and each person as "the sum, organization, and aggregate of the relations that constitute such enterprises" (Sartre, 1945/2007, p. 38). Based on the notion that "you are [...] your life" (p. 38), clients choose specific, overarching values designed to give direction and personal meaning to activities within a large number of life domains. This is a process in which meaning making comes to the forefront as one of the advantages of our language ability. Many people have never thought about what truly matters to them and for what they would be ready to stand up. In-session exercises and illustrations facilitate this process and tease out the impact of social demand from individual ideals of conduct. Defining and prioritizing values becomes part of the process of being active, observing, and reengaging.

Putting ACT into ACTion. Throughout the duration of therapy, client and therapist take a stance of curiosity and genuine interest to implement Tenets 1 through 4. They ask, "What happens when I do x in the service of my long-term value y?" ACT supports an experimental approach to life. The therapist's role is to ask, "How is it working?" and "What got in the way?" to help further distinguish between verbal-emotional and external barriers specific to each client's sociocultural context.

Conclusion

Functional fidelity requires letting go of the topographical agenda, in which manual-based metaphors and exercises are expected to produce predetermined, ad hoc, and anticipated outcomes. Cultural competency (i.e., genuine interest in and adoption of the client's frame of reference) creates space for the client's narratives, abstractions, elaborations, and understanding. Again and again, client and therapist engage in the cycle of being active together, observing, describing, and reengaging.

Striving for the function of treatment demands our full attention, to monitor our impact on the client and the client's impact on us, to listen attentively, and to adapt our behavior accordingly—without buying into our own thoughts as to what "should" work for this particular client. Because we do not know the client's behavior in advance, we intervene from a stance of uncertainty yet philosophical consistency with Tenets 1 through 4. The client's increasing engagement in his or her life over time is our dynamic gauge of what works.

Functional approaches are more difficult to teach and disseminate and potentially less liked by therapists, as it takes time to assess the impact of the intervention; however, we encourage you to try. Learning to use ACT functionally is somewhat like learning to play the piano: Initially, your actions are guided by instructions and rules, bound to teaching tools like the exercises and the metaphors outlined in ACT manuals, and supplemented by workshop participation. However, with a lot of study and practice, the music itself comes to guide the behavior; notes on the sheet are crutches and lose their necessity. There is a continuous effort to notice even the slightest variation in tone and to adjust accordingly. The practitioner learns to identify interactions that have the intended impact on the client, as well as problem areas for further practice. Skillful and artful therapists make the most complex interactions seem smooth and easy. They rely on the license to vary their behavior and repeat what works for this particular client: Try using the client's words, observe what happens, and engage and try again, a step at a time, in the service of the client's overarching life goals and values.

References

Bem, D. J. (1972). Self-perception theory. *Advances in experimental social psychology, 6*, 1–62.

Chiesa, M. (1994). *Radical behaviorism: The philosophy and the science.* Boston, MA: Authors Cooperative, Inc.

Chödrön, P. (1997). *When things fall apart: Heart advice for difficult times.* Boston, MA: Shambhala Publications, Inc.

Chödrön, P. (2006). *Practicing peace in times of war.* Boston, MA: Shambhala Publications, Inc.

Deutscher, G. (2010). *Through the looking glass: Why the world looks different in other languages.* New York: Picador.

Hayes, S. C., Strosahl, K. D., & Wilson, K. G. (1999). *Acceptance and commitment therapy: An experiential approach to behavior change.* New York: Guilford Press.

Hays, P. (2008). *Addressing cultural complexities in practice: Assessment, diagnosis, and therapy* (2nd ed.). Washington, DC: American Psychological Association.

Krutch, J. W. (1953/1970). *The measure of man.* New York: Grosset & Dunlap.

Laub, G. (1984). *Denken verdirbt den Charakter. Alle Aphorismen.* Munich, Germany: Carl Hanser Verlag GmbH & Co KG.

McCurry, S. M., & Hayes, S. C. (1992). Clinical and experimental perspectives on metaphorical talk. *Clinical Psychology Review, 12*, 763–785.

Metzger, R. (1996). *Die Skinner'sche Analyse des Verhaltens: Ein integrativer Ansatz für die klinische Psychologie.* Pfaffenweiler, Germany: Centaurus-Verlagsgesellschaft.

Rachlin, H. (1980). *Behaviorism in everyday life.* Englewood Cliffs, NJ: Prentice-Hall.

Rachlin, H. (2000). *The science of self-control.* Cambridge, MA: Harvard University Press.

Sartre, J.-P. (1945/2007). *Existentialism is a humanism* (C. Macomber, Trans.). New Haven, CT: Yale University Press.

Skinner, B. F. (1953). *Science and human behavior.* New York: The Macmillan Company.

Skinner, B. F. (1957/1992). *Verbal behavior.* Acton, MA: Copley Publishing Group.

Skinner, B. F. (1974). *About behaviorism.* New York: Vintage Books.

Skinner, B. F. (1978). *Was ist Behaviorismus?* (K. Laermann, Trans.). Reinbek, Germany: Rowohlt Verlag.

Waltz, T. J., & Hayes, S. C. (2010). Acceptance and commitment therapy. In N. Kazantzis, M. A. Reinecke, & A. Freeman (Eds.), *Cognitive and behavioral theories in clinical practice* (pp. 148–192). New York: Guilford Press.

Watzlawick, P. (1983/1993). *The situation is hopeless, but not serious: The pursuit of unhappiness.* New York: W. W. Norton & Company.

CHAPTER 8

Promoting the Multicultural Competency of Psychological Professionals through Acceptance- and Mindfulness-Based Methods

Michael P. Twohig, Ph.D.

Melanie M. Domenech Rodríguez, Ph.D.

Angela M. Enno, M.S.

Utah State University

The *Guidelines on Multicultural Education, Training, Research, Practice, and Organizational Change for Psychologists* (American Psychological Association [APA], 2003) charges educators and practitioners to infuse diversity into clinical work, research, teaching, and graduate training. In addition to increasing knowledge and skills training on multicultural issues, mental health professionals are asked to recognize that "they may hold attitudes and beliefs that can detrimentally influence perceptions of and interactions with individuals who are ethnically and racially different than themselves" (APA, 2003, p. 382). Even though much has been written about the importance of multicultural competency, little is known about the effectiveness of models to develop cultural competence (Mollen, Ridley, & Hill, 2003). For example, Worthington, Soth-McNett, and Moreno (2007) found that of the 75 published articles on multicultural competency, only eight (10.7%) were multicultural counseling training interventions. The dearth of evidence to support training practices is highly problematic given ethical (APA, 2010) and professional (APA, 2006) calls for competent service delivery. In this chapter, we offer some guidance on the training of multicultural competency using techniques from acceptance and commitment therapy (ACT; Hayes, Strosahl, & Wilson, 2012) to promote greater engagement with more traditional multicultural competency issues.

Cultural Competence

Cultural competence is a specific professional competence that concerns itself with cultural background as a relevant context for a client's presenting concern and treatment. Despite its importance, limited progress has been made in translating aspirational principles into concrete guidance for improved competence. The limited progress may be in part due to the lack of consensus among multicultural experts on what constitutes cultural competence (Ridley & Kleiner, 2003). Nonetheless, there is considerable agreement that cultural competence requires self-awareness, knowledge, and specific skills.

This has come to be known as the tripartite model of cultural competence.

This tripartite model was presented by Stanley Sue (1998) in the context of a different tripartite model. His original conceptualization specified scientific mindedness, dynamic sizing, and culture-specific elements as the three necessary ingredients for cultural competence. According to Sue, therapists who are scientifically minded are those who "form hypotheses rather than make premature conclusions about the status of culturally different clients, who develop creative ways to test hypotheses, and who act on the basis of acquired data" (p. 445). Dynamic sizing refers to the therapists' specific "skills in knowing when to generalize and be inclusive and when to individualize and be exclusive" (p. 446).

It is in the last category, culture-specific elements, that Sue presented self-awareness, knowledge, and skills. He specified that self-awareness is the clinician's understanding of the self as a cultural being (e.g., has worldviews), of the specific knowledge about the cultural other, and of skills in the realm of intervention techniques that are specifically useful with the cultural group with which the clinician is working. Notably, Sue (1998) stated that skilled professionals "have the ability to translate interventions into culturally consistent strategies" (p. 446), suggesting that psychotherapists could act as translators of mainstream knowledge to culturally diverse clients.

The Role of Internal Experiences

Available evidence also suggests that multicultural issues are emotionally charged (Pope-Davis, Liu, Toporek, & Brittan-Powell, 2001), and critical incidents in supervision and training around developing cultural competence can be either growth promoting or fear provoking (Toporek, Ortega-Villalobos, & Pope-Davis, 2004). Multicultural training, therefore, needs to address some of the psychological issues that may act as barriers to developing multicultural competence in addition to knowledge deficits.

For supervisors and trainees, changing clinical practice requires much more than knowledge (Addis, Wade, & Hatgis, 1999). Barriers for White American students, for example, often involve trainees' fears of failing and making mistakes, offending someone, or appearing racist. These barriers can get in the way of genuinely engaging with multicultural issues to improve cultural competence (Suinn & Borrayo, 2008). Emotions also play a role. Liu, Sheu, and Williams (2004) found that multicultural competence was positively related to the amount of anxiety students felt about conducting multicultural research, indicating that greater training and knowledge are related to increased anxiety around the topic. Another study found that support for diversity initiatives was somewhat unrelated to implementation (Rogers, 2006), suggesting that a value for diversity may not be sufficient to implement changes and pointing to the need to address psychological barriers as a necessary component of cultural competency training. Written differently, to know "what" to do is necessary but not sufficient for cultural competence when trainees have difficulty recognizing, accepting, and addressing the reactions they have to engaging with multicultural issues.

Acceptance and Commitment Therapy

ACT may represent a promising solution to the problem of addressing barriers to multicultural competence development in that it directly targets the way people relate to their inner experiences, enabling them to modulate the impact of thoughts and emotions on their actions. ACT generally targets two major areas: (1) acceptance and mindfulness processes, and (2) personal values and behavior change processes. In the acceptance and mindfulness phase, ACT teaches openly noticing and considering inner experiences as events rather than as descriptions of the person experiencing them. The values and behavioral commitment phase focuses on choosing the directions one wants to move in life and making commitments to moving in those directions.

There is little concern in ACT for the form or frequency of any particular inner experience; instead, ACT targets what the person does when the thought is present. For example, having a thought, such as "I know nothing about working with Latina clients," while working with Latina clients in practice is not itself problematic. However, the way that the therapist responds to that thought can have a broad and deep impact. That is, if avoidance of useful training and consultation occurs in response to this thought and associated inner experience (e.g., fear of the unknown), then the therapist is not working in a culturally competent manner. If, in response to that thought, the therapist seeks consultation and training on working with Latina clients, which may involve emotional discomfort, he or she is likely behaving in a culturally competent manner.

Supporting Data

Preliminary findings suggest that ACT may be effective at facilitating the pursuit of novel and value-consistent actions (e.g., learning cultural competence) in the presence of difficult inner experiences (e.g., feelings of fear, uncertainty). For example, a one-day ACT promoted substance abuse counselors' adaptation of best pharmacological practices more so than training in best practices alone (Varra, Hayes, Roget, & Fisher, 2008). Consistent with an ACT theory, these outcomes were mediated by changes in the power of thoughts about use of these medications rather than in the content of the thoughts. Similarly, greater adoption of the practices taught was found when ACT components were added to a traditional education workshop on group drug counseling (Luoma et al., 2007). Finally, using a counterbalanced design, the researchers found that ACT resulted in positive changes in intentions to engage in culturally competent actions (Lillis & Hayes, 2007). In summary, these findings suggest that ACT can meaningfully increase behavior change and adoption of novel and value-consistent behavior in behavioral health professionals.

Tested Protocol

In this section we will describe the unpublished findings from a test of ACT to facilitate multicultural competency. The workshop was tested with 6 faculty members and 25 graduate students ($N = 31$) in a combined clinical/counseling/school psychology PhD program in the western United States. Students' years in the program ranged from 1 to 6 with a mean of 2.72 years ($SD = 1.6$). Faculty reported having been on the faculty for 7 to 22 years with a mean of 12.5 years ($SD = 6.06$). Females constituted 65% ($n = 20$) of participants. The ethnic composition of the sample was primarily White American ($n = 23$, 74%). The remainder included three (10%) Native American or biracial Native American/White American, three (10%) Asian American or biracial Asian American/White American, and two (6%) Latino/a participants.

The intervention consisted of a 4.5-hour workshop format of ACT and took place on a college campus. The training was facilitated by the three authors of this chapter. This training specifically focused on decreasing the impact of fears and feelings of incompetency that inter-fere with pursuing learning opportunities to increase skills in cultural competence. While all six processes in ACT were targeted (see Hayes et al., 2012, for the six processes: acceptance, defusion, present moment, self-as-context, values, and behavioral commitments), the training most heavily focused on acceptance, defusion, values, and a behavioral commitment. To assess the effects of the training, a brief assessment packet was completed at three points in time: one week prior to the training, one week after the training, and six months after the training.

Introduction. The training began with a brief introduction to ACT, its focus of intervention, and the data supporting its general use and use specific to pursuing values while experiencing fear or discomfort. Participants were then told that the training focused on finding a new way to interact with thoughts, feelings, and bodily sensations that could occur while pursuing greater multicultural competency. Participants were also informed that the training involved discussion about individual experiences and that very little training on specific skills would occur. As this type of discussion might lead to more discomfort than a didactic training, participants could choose how much they participated in the group discussion.

Defusion. The training began with a defusion exercise to set the context for our focus on the ways people interact with their inner experiences when dealing with difficult situations. This particular exercise is designed to promote one's awareness of the inevitability and automatic nature of social categorization without justifying it or pathologizing it. In this exercise the participants were initially asked to look at one person and state what came to mind about that person. It is important to note that this exercise typically works best if participants focus on a person who is not well known to them. One of the faculty facilitators (White American, male) volunteered as an object, and the participants brainstormed preconceptions toward him. Responses included "hard working," "smart," and "a little boring." As the participants did not know the facilitator well prior to the workshop, they were then asked to become aware of and process the automatic and indirect nature of those evaluative statements (e.g., "most evaluations were not based on real interactions with the individual but assumptions and stereotypes"). Once the descriptors were set, the participants were asked to note (1) how much they would like to work with, (2) eat lunch with, and (3) do a favor for the presenter. Subsequently, participants were invited to ask personal questions of the male facilitator (e.g., "Do you have a family?" "How many hours do you work a week?"), which he answered. Once again, they were asked to notice the changes in their perceptions of the facilitator as he answered these personal questions. Participants reported that the facilitator became less intimidating and more interesting, and they had greater interest in and willingness to interact with him. The facilitators reiterated the automatic nature of stereotyping and judging that occurs and suggested paying attention to this process and the ways it affects our behaviors. The facilitators also suggested that better understanding the automatic nature of judgments, categorizations, and stereotypes would then strengthen their willingness to allow automatic judgments and categorizations to occur when they occur, while pursuing anxiety-provoking and yet personally important actions, perhaps, pursuing the opportunities for learning and refining cultural competency.

Following this exercise, participants were asked to privately note situations when they would have liked to pursue multicultural competency but did not do so due to fear or another internal experience. Examples included taking on more diverse clients, implementing multicultural skills they had learned with diverse clients, engaging in certain research topics, or simply pursuing training on multicultural topics. There was a consistent report from participants that they held back in these areas based on fear of incompetence, not actual skill or knowledge deficits. The presenters suggested that ACT skills might be applied to thoughts, feelings, and bodily sensations that hold them back, as well as other areas of multicultural competency that they might be avoiding. For example, someone might fear looking ignorant or uneducated when seeking consultation in an area where he or she needs guidance. Participants were asked to see that fear for what it was—as a thought and a feeling.

Creative hopelessness. To further facilitate acceptance, or allowing one's internal events to occur without interfering with personal values, a common ACT module called "creative hopelessness" (Hayes, Strosahl, & Wilson, 1999, p. 87) was covered. The purpose of this exercise is to help the participants become oriented toward the possibility that direct attempts to change the form or frequency of unwanted inner experience might prevent them from accomplishing the things that are important to them. Participants were asked to mentally note or share one multiculturally competent action they wanted to engage in but did not do so because of fear, anxiety, or another internal experience. They were then asked to write down (1) the ways they tried to manage or control these experiences, (2) how successful they were in the short term, (3) how successful those attempts have been in the long term, and (4) whether these attempts moved them closer or farther away from the things they value. Participants reported that they could avoid the thought in the short term but that it continued to be a concern over the long term. Participants also expressed that such efforts prevented them from following what was ultimately important to them.

Control is the problem. Some inner experiences are not easily controlled, and attempts to do so may actually interfere with successful functioning. The phase of ACT focusing on the futility of control attempts is called "control is the problem" (Hayes et al., 1999, p. 115). In this phase, the participants' efforts to control unwanted internal events were first validated and normalized. While making such efforts to control external events is often effective, attempting to do so with internal events is often much less successful in the long term. In order to facilitate experiential awareness of the futility of control effort, participants were asked about their ability to not get anxious in front of a crowd, or to not think some thought of importance. It was highlighted that this struggle is similar to efforts to control fear and the sense of uncertainty within the context of multicultural trainings and opportunities. Once participants experienced the difficulty inherent in ridding themselves of their fears and concerns surrounding multicultural competencies, the facilitators presented acceptance as an alternative way of responding to those particular internal experiences.

Acceptance. In ACT, the term "willingness" is often used over the term "acceptance" because it seems to carry fewer additional meanings. There was training on allowing one's inner experiences to occur without needing to regulate or control them. In the present training, participants were encouraged to engage in diversity-affirming actions *with* their fears and uncertainty, instead of controlling or regulating these unwanted experiences *prior to* engaging in multicultural actions. For example, if someone wants to be a competent therapist for Native American clients, she can either wait until the fear of looking ignorant has subsided before pursuing the training, or take that fear with her and continue to pursue the training.

The "two scales" metaphor (Hayes et al., 1999, pp. 133–134) was used to teach willingness. In this metaphor, "fear" is presented as the first scale, which is hard to regulate, and "willingness to have fear" is presented as the second scale. As being willing is a behavior that one can choose more or less freely, it is presented as something that one can regulate. The participants were then introduced to the idea that when one is willing, not only is it possible to work on things that are important to the participant, but it allows the fear scale to move freely. In contrast, as seen in the earlier phases of the training, attempts to control or regulate the fear are often unsuccessful and prevent movement in important directions for the participants.

As each individual enacts willingness in a unique manner, participants were asked to think about what willingness might look like for them in the specific multicultural instances where they struggle. One example of willingness involved a student engaging in research in a feared area and bringing the fear with him while starting the project. Another example was noticing the anxiety-provoking thoughts about being the numerical minority at a cultural event and attending anyway so that experiential knowledge of that culture could be gained. Finally, we discussed bringing the fear of appearing ignorant into a multicultural competency consultation on a difficult case. The facilitators stressed the importance of practicing willingness by highlighting that the more participants practiced being willing to experience internal events, the more proficient they would become and the easier it would be.

Mindfulness. While there are many versions of exercises that teach being present or mindful, the exercise used in this training was "leaves on a stream" (similar to the "soldiers in the parade" exercise; Hayes et al., 1999, pp. 158–162). In this exercise participants were taught to close their eyes and observe their inner experiences as if each were a leaf on a stream. The goal was not to eliminate thoughts but rather to be able to simply observe the thoughts away from one's mind. These types of exercises promote mindfulness as well as help participants see thoughts simply as thoughts. We suggested that participants practice this type of exercise on a regular basis to disengage from thoughts that were pulling for fusion. It was also suggested that they could practice mindfulness prior to entering into the situations where fears would likely interfere with value-congruent action.

Values. Finally, a discussion about values as they related to pursuing cultural competency occurred. It was noted that values are personally chosen and pursued but never achieved. This conceptualization is consistent with the pursuit of multicultural competence, which is understood as a "lifelong developmental process" (Buckley & Foldy, 2010, p. 691). Participants were encouraged to identify which part of cultural competence was personally relevant. Although perhaps an individualistic orientation, this approach helps facilitate motivation. This approach also allows each therapist to take his or her level of competence into account and build from his or her interests and passions. Thus, for some people, pursuing cultural competence might be about being a more successful therapist, for others it might be about being a more helpful instructor, some may have an interest in working with one particular group, and so on. The goal in addressing values is to find meaning for engagement. Rather than identifying the largest, most perfect value, we are looking for something that would keep the participant engaged outside of the training.

Values are pursued but never achieved. Goals can be achieved, but they are generally considered expressions of a particular value. So, for example, reading a novel that takes place in another cultural context (e.g., *Reading Lolita in Tehran*; Nafisi, 2003) might be a step toward improving knowledge about an "other" cultural group and enhance the therapist's culture-specific skills. Similarly, writing a book on cultural competency may be another step in that direction. Neither of these events accomplishes the *goal* of being a culturally competent therapist but can move therapists forward across developmental and professional levels in their values. Seeing these types of situations as values helps maintain engagement, whereas a goal can be accomplished and progress can stop.

In this training, participants clarified their values and then made small behavioral commitments to engage in a particular action to pursue that value. Behavioral commitments are usually smaller steps toward a value that is clear and can be accomplished. Achievable examples of behavioral commitment are reading an article or book, attending an event or training, or receiving consultation. Participants were encouraged to continue to make small behavioral commitments to pursue their values. They were informed that if they continued to follow their values, the goals would change and the values might also grow. Participants were prepared to welcome these changes and to attend specifically to whether their actions were guided by values rather than being guided by a goal to regulate fear.

Findings from a Feasibility Test

All assessments occurred in the same academic year. The following measures were completed: (1) "face-valid ratings" of knowledge of multicultural counseling and training in multicultural counseling, and (2) the Multicultural Counseling Knowledge and Awareness Scale (Ponterotto, Gretchen, Utsey, Rieger, & Austin, 2002). There was minimal missing data, which was handled conservatively by using related observations that assumed no change. Results are displayed in Table 1.

Taken together, these findings suggest that multicultural competency may be improved by a brief training in ACT. It was worth noting that these findings occurred for faculty and students, although it is unclear how much actual behavior change occurred as a result. Approximately two weeks after the trainings, a process group was formed to discuss the ideas brought up in the training and the participants' reactions to the training. Anecdotal data from the process group suggested that at least some participants further engaged with multicultural skills outside the formal training.

Table 1

Means and Standard Deviations on Self-Ratings
of Knowledge and Training and Multicultural Counseling
Knowledge and Awareness Scale (MCKAS)

Scale	Subscales	Pre M (SD)	Post M (SD)	6 Month follow-up M (SD)
Self-Rating	Knowledge	4.10 (1.32)	4.52 (1.09)	4.77 (1.06)
	Training	3.48 (1.18)	4.19 (1.22)	4.32 (1.05)
MCKAS	Knowledge	99.55 (16.73)	106.10 (11.37)	109.23 (11.31)
	Awareness	72.84 (7.22)	74.76 (7.14)	74.23 (7.52)
Total		172.39 (23.95)	180.86 (18.51)	183.46 (18.83)

Considerations for Diverse Audiences

Much of the literature on cultural competence training focuses, either explicitly or implicitly, on training White Americans to work with ethnic minorities. That is, very little is known about how ethnic minorities respond to cultural competence training. However, extant qualitative published works including qualitative findings (D. W. Sue et al., 2011) and critical incidents (Domenech Rodríguez & Bates, 2012) suggest that trainers must proceed with caution when a group is culturally diverse. There are also documented instances of ethnic minority trainees seeking and establishing their own support communities that serve to increase cultural competence (e.g., Watts-Jones, Ali, Alfaro, & Frederick, 2007), suggesting that connecting away from White Americans may be an important component of multicultural competence training for ethnic and cultural minorities.

Our anecdotal data from ethnic minority participants suggest the importance of being cognizant to the interpersonal and intrapersonal dynamics played out among diverse participants from various sociocultural backgrounds. For example, they perceived that sharing personal experiences and reactions during the training unfairly placed them in a vulnerable position relative to White American students as being underrepresented in the group. Ethnic minority participants also reported disagreeing with an underlying assumption of the training that all participants had a choice whether to engage in multicultural dialogues and activities in their work and personal lives: This assumption, for some participants, was more consistent with an individualistic worldview and with privileged statuses in society. Although ethnic minority individuals may experience some degree of choice regarding multicultural engagement, there are times when they cannot disengage even if they wish to do so. As one participant poignantly observed, when an African American student walks into a room of all White American students, he cannot control that others perceive him as a cultural "other."

Similarly when a participant made a comment that reflects ignorance or a lack of sensitivity to diversity issues, the ethnic minority individual perceived it as a microaggression (D. W. Sue et al., 2007). As such, participating in multicultural training can represent a risk of exposing oneself to unsolicited psychological assaults for ethnic minority participants.

Finally, ethnic minority participants reported that topics throughout the training brought up difficult personal memories. In addition to this heightened sense of vulnerability, some trainees reported that the training did not push their own growth but rather made them feel in a position of educating others about multicultural issues.

These anecdotal findings suggested that it may have helped to do some preparation and debriefing for minority students about the nature of training in order to ensure that their perspectives were included and addressed, and that every effort would be made to create a sense of cultural safety within the training. It may also be that this training is most appropriate for trainees at a particular stage of self-awareness regarding their ethnic identity development and personal values and beliefs, as well as awareness of power and privilege.

Conclusions

The work presented in this chapter is based on the assumption that, in developing cultural competence, professionals experience multiple interfering inner experiences in the realm of self-awareness, and that knowledge or skill alone is not sufficient to produce a culturally competent professional. For example, high content knowledge about multicultural topics, but an unwillingness to implement this knowledge, may result in incompetent behavior. Similarly, a lack of knowledge of how to behave in a multiculturally competent way, but a high willingness to try, may also be problematic.

This chapter and related research suggests that therapists who are pursuing or expanding their multicultural competency should expect some level of emotional or cognitive discomfort. The approach outlined here suggests that the issue is not the level of the discomfort that occurs, but the way one responds to it. The authors suggest mindfully noticing thoughts and feelings, and continuing on in one's valued direction. Trainers of multicultural competence might benefit from increasing the time spent addressing the emotional and cognitive reactions that occur within and outside of the training context while pursuing multicultural competence.

References

Addis, M. E., Wade, W. A., & Hatgis, C. (1999). Barriers to dissemination of evidence-based practices: Addressing practitioners' concerns about manual-based psychotherapies. *Clinical Psychology: Science and Practice, 6,* 430–441.

American Psychological Association (APA). (2003). Guidelines on multicultural education, training, research, practice, and organizational change for psychologists. *American Psychologist, 58,* 377–402.

American Psychological Association (APA). (2006). Evidence-based practice in psychology. *American Psychologist, 61*, 271–285.

American Psychological Association (APA). (2010) Report of the ethics committee, 2009. *American Psychologist, 65*(5), 483–492.

Buckley, T. R., & Foldy, E. G. (2010). A pedagogical model for increasing race-related multicultural counseling competency. *The Counseling Psychologist, 38*, 691–713. doi: 10.1177/0011000009360917.

Domenech Rodríguez, M.M., & Bates, S.C. (2012). Aspirations meet in the classroom: Ethics and diversity move teaching forward and upward. In R. E. Landrum & M. A. McCarthy (Eds.), *Teaching ethically: Challenges and opportunities* (pp. 101–111). Washington, DC: APA Press. doi: 10.1037/13496-000.

Hayes, S. C., Strosahl, K. D., & Wilson, K. G. (1999). *Acceptance and commitment therapy: An experiential approach to behavior change.* New York: Guilford Press.

Hayes, S. C., Strosahl, K. D., & Wilson, K. G. (2012). *Acceptance and commitment therapy: The process and practice of mindful change* (2nd ed.). New York: Guilford Press.

Lillis, J., & Hayes, S. C. (2007). Applying acceptance, mindfulness, and values to the reduction of prejudice: A pilot study. *Behavior Modification, 31*, 389–411.

Liu, W. M., Sheu, H. B., & Williams, K. (2004). Multicultural competency in research: Examining the relationships among multicultural competencies, research training and self-efficacy, and the multicultural environment. *Cultural Diversity and Ethnic Minority Psychology, 10*, 324–339.

Luoma, J. B., Hayes, S. C., Twohig, M. P., Roget, N., Fisher, G., Padilla, M., et al. (2007). Augmenting continuing education with psychologically focused group consultation: Effects on adoption of group drug counseling. *Psychotherapy: Theory, Research, Practice, Training, 44*, 463–469.

Mollen, D., Ridley, C. R., & Hill, C. L. (2003). Models of multicultural competence: A critical evaluation. In D. B. Pope-Davis, H. L. K. Coleman, W. M. Liu, and R. L. Toporek (Eds.). *Handbook of multicultural competencies: In counseling & psychology.* Thousand Oaks, CA: Sage.

Nafisi, A. A. (2003). *Reading Lolita in Tehran.* New York: Random House.

Ponterotto, J. G., Gretchen, D., Utsey, S. O., Rieger, B. P., & Austin, R. (2002). A revision of the Multicultural Counseling Awareness Scale. *Journal of Multicultural Counseling and Development, 30*, 153–180.

Pope-Davis, D. B., Liu, W. M., Toporek, R. L., & Brittan-Powell, C. S. (2001). What's missing from multicultural competency research: Review, introspection, and recommendations. *Cultural Diversity and Ethnic Minority Psychology, 7*, 121–138.

Ridley, C. R., & Kleiner, A. J. (2003). Multicultural counseling competence: History, themes, and issues. In D. B. Pope-Davis, H. K. Coleman, W. Liu, R. L. Toporek (Eds.), *Handbook of multicultural competencies: In counseling & psychology* (pp. 3–20). Thousand Oaks, CA: Sage. doi: 10.4135/9781452231693. n1.

Rogers, M. R. (2006). Exemplary multicultural training in school psychology programs. *Cultural Diversity and Ethnic Minority Psychology, 12*, 115–133.

Sue, D. W., Capodilupo, C. M., Torino, G. C., Bucceri, J. M., Holder, A. M. B., Nadal, K. L., & Esquilin, M. E. (2007). Racial microaggressions in everyday life: Implications for clinical practice. *American Psychologist, 62*, 271–286. doi: 10.1037/0003-066X.62.4.271.

Sue, D. W., Rivera, D. P., Watkins, N. L., Kim, R. H., Kim, S., & Williams, C. D. (2011). Racial dialogues: Challenges faculty of color face in the classroom. *Cultural Diversity and Ethnic Minority Psychology, 17*, 331–340. doi: 10.1037/a0024190.

Sue, S. (1998). In search of cultural competence in psychotherapy and counseling. *American Psychologist, 53*, 440–448.

Suinn, R. M., & Borrayo, E. A. (2008). The ethnicity gap: The past, present, and future. *Professional Psychology: Research and Practice, 39*, 646–651.

Toporek, R. L., Ortega-Villalobos, L., & Pope-Davis, D. N. B. (2004). Critical incidents in multicultural supervision: Exploring supervisees' and supervisors' experiences. *Journal of Multicultural Counseling and Development, 32*, 66–83.

Varra, A. A., Hayes, S. C., Roget, N., & Fisher, G. (2008). A randomized control trial examining the effect of acceptance and commitment training on clinician willingness to use evidence-based pharmacotherapy. *Journal of Consulting and Clinical Psychology, 76*, 449–458.

Watts-Jones, D., Ali, R., Alfaro, J., & Frederick, A. (2007). The role of a mentoring group for family therapy trainees and therapists of color. *Family Process, 46*, 437–450. doi: 10.1111/j.1545-5300.2007.00224.x.

Worthington, R. L., Soth-McNett, A. M., & Moreno, M. V. (2007). Multicultural counseling competencies research: A 20-year content analysis. *Journal of Counseling Psychology, 54*, 351–361.

CHAPTER 9

Acceptance, Mindfulness, and Spirituality

Amy R. Murrell, Ph.D.

Jonathan E. Schmalz, M.S.

Aditi Sinha, M.S.

University of North Texas

As acceptance- and mindfulness-based treatments become increasingly utilized in diverse clinical settings, it is of utmost importance to consider the relevance and applicability of these models with diverse client groups. In this chapter, through the use of clinical examples, we will address religion and spirituality as culturally relevant variables. We will also cover the similarities between acceptance- and mindfulness-based psychotherapy and religious and spiritual traditions, and discuss how to handle difficulties within a functional framework when working with clients who are struggling with religious and/or spiritual issues.

Defining Religion and Spirituality

In contemporary discussions of religion and spirituality, the two terms are becoming increasingly separated from one another. Religion, most often, refers to the rites, rituals, and traditions handed down by religious institutions as ways of approaching the sacred (Wulff, 1996). Spirituality, on the other hand, refers to the personal experiences of the sacred. Each of these definitions relies on experience. As examples, religious behavior consists of experiences like prayer or mosque attendance. Spiritual behaviors might include a person's reported closeness to a higher power or feelings of faith. It is important to recognize that there are racial and ethnic differences, as well as individual preferences, that likely occur with respect to these variables. For example, African Americans report being more religious than European Americans, and they are less likely to say that they are spiritual and not religious (Taylor & Chatters, 2010).

Religion and Spirituality in Psychotherapy

Religion and spirituality have a tendency to become the metaphorical elephant in the therapy room. However, approximately 92% of the general U.S. population identifies with an organized religion, and clients often rate religion and spirituality as more important in their lives than mental health practitioners recognize (Bergin, 1991). Studies suggest that 55% to 81% of clients prefer to discuss spiritual issues in therapy, while less than 20% specifically wish not to discuss such matters (Rose, Westefeld, & Ansley, 2001). Clinicians are less likely to place importance on religion and spirituality in their own lives than are the majority of clients (Bergin & Jensen, 1990). Research indicates that such discrepancies are meaningful; differences between client and therapist in religious values impact therapy outcomes differently than other values (Worthington, 1988). Indeed, a body of research has found that efforts to tailor treatment to clients' religious and spiritual beliefs improve treatment outcome (Worthington, Hook, Davis, & McDaniel, 2011).

Appreciating the Differences: Culturally Relevant Factors

Discrepancies between client and therapist in religious and spiritual values can be more pronounced with clients from underrepresented cultural groups, or when there is a mismatch between client and clinician. African Americans, Asian Americans, and Hispanic Americans tend to be more collectivist than European-Americans. And White clinicians may see collectivist clients as weak or overly dependent. White clinicians may overpathologize clients with different values about self-disclosure, insight, expressiveness, and the like—which are all relevant in the realm of the sacred. Thus, it is not particularly surprising that many individuals from racial and ethnic minority groups seek help for psychological distress in their places of worship (and in primary care facilities) more frequently than they see mental health professionals (US Department of Health and Human Services, 2001).

One way to improve culturally competent practice with diverse clients is to focus on the relationship. Appreciating the differences (or perceived differences) between a client's tradition and the therapist's is paramount to creating a genuine relationship. Recently, the first author (Amy Murrell) was called by a mother seeking services for her child. The mother stated that she had "heard excellent things" about Amy's clinical skills but had concerns about seeking secular therapeutic services. Then she proceeded to ask her, "Are you a Christian?" Amy had a brief moment when she felt a sinking feeling, and said, "No, I am not. I am Jewish." There was silence for several seconds. Amy felt like the mother wanted more information from her. She said, "I am religious and spiritual, and I am very willing to discuss religion in session—with you, with your child—in whatever form that takes. I feel like I know a lot about Christianity, but that isn't the same as being Christian, so if you aren't comfortable coming here for services, I completely understand." Again, there was silence for quite a while. This time, Amy chose not to speak. It felt different the second time; it is difficult to be present and aware on the phone, but Amy was committed to being useful, so she attempted. It worked out. After about a minute, the client said she was praying about it and felt confident that it was best to bring her child. She specifically stated that Amy's willingness to listen to her concerns without being critical of religion, without getting defensive, and her own value of religion and spirituality (even though it wasn't "exactly the same") mattered greatly to her.

Acceptance- and Mindfulness-Based Treatments

Acceptance- and mindfulness-based treatments (e.g., ACT, DBT, functional analytic psychotherapy (FAP), MBCT, and MBSR) can be characterized in a variety of ways, and there is some variability in the degree of emphasis of core concepts among models; however, there are treatment features relevant to religion and spirituality that unite much of the acceptance and mindfulness work: an open and nonjudgmental stance toward experience, focus on distancing from thoughts and/or language, a highlight on values and actions consistent with important ideals, and emphasis on interpersonal connectedness. One advantage that these approaches have in terms of addressing diversity is the importance of moment-to-moment awareness in terms of ideographic analysis (Murrell, Rogers, & Johnson, 2009).

As with any treatment, effective acceptance- and mindfulness-based practitioners attend with sensitivity and openness to the diverse beliefs of clients, recognizing their own biases and clients' potential perceptions of bias. In some ways, bias is addressed through the connectedness perspective that acceptance and mindfulness traditions often include. In fact, that perspective is one of many commonalities that acceptance- and mindfulness-based treatments have with religious and spiritual traditions. Thus, these models provide a unique perspective in helping clients to explore and enrich their experience of the sacred.

Similarities in Religion & Spirituality and Acceptance & Mindfulness Therapies

A number of ancient traditions emphasize the holistic nature of being, our connectedness to each other, and the present moment. One Hindu belief is that misery occurs when human beings are unable to realize and accept the only great Truth—that each form of life contains the pure Universal Energy and thus is itself the immortal Universe (Vivekananda, 1948); falsely believing that one is separate from others and the Universe is considered the greatest cause of suffering. Other religious traditions address the ubiquitous nature of human suffering. The Bible directly addresses this topic with the story of Adam and Eve, considered to represent the loss of human innocence and the beginning of suffering for humankind (S. C. Hayes, Strosahl, & Wilson, 1999).

In several religious traditions, God is described as everything and nothing at once. Viewing God as omnipresent, eternal, and perfect is common in Eastern and Western faiths. It is typical to hear God described not as a "thing" but as "love" or a spiritual "place" of whole and complete acceptance (S. C. Hayes, 1984). Assisting clients in contacting a perspective of self that is accepting of, and unaffected by, the content of the mind is similar to this way of describing God's love.

169

For example, the first author (Amy) worked with a client with bipolar I disorder who struggled with melding her symptoms and her Catholic faith. Through guided meditations eliciting beginner's mind and observer self, she understood herself as "God's perfect reflection."

As a response to suffering, many faiths emphasize compassion for self and others. Such calls to common humanity are consistent with acceptance- and mindfulness-based treatments. Facilitating mindful awareness of suffering, and discouraging overidentification with it, allows for the experience of common humanity. Consequently, feeling connectedness with others who suffer, instead of feeling alone in one's problems, is part of both religious and psychotherapeutic approaches.

In session with the client with bipolar, Amy discussed this connection, compassion, and related responsibility through the following metaphor: Suppose an artist has a fixed amount of liquid gold to pour into a mold to make a perfect work of art. The art will cast light that shines throughout the world, but the mold cracks and the gold flecks leak out and float away. The only way to complete the artwork is to gather the flecks and put them together. Unfortunately, the flecks continue to split and drift until each is tiny and spread afar, covered in dust. Therefore, the only way to complete the art is to get help from others, and to help others.

This particular metaphor is from a Kabbalistic tradition (Cooper, 1997). The basic premise is that there is a spark of holiness in all life and that it is our responsibility to connect the flecks. On a spiritual or metaphysical level, this is about light and connection to its source. On a psychological level, it is about behavior. It is about choosing what is important in your life and acting consistently with that. It begs the questions: How am I living my life? How do my actions affect who I am, who I have been, and who I will be? In a more global sense, we might even ask, "To what extent is the world balanced on my next action?" This client answered by saying that she was going to start a local mental health foundation, and she did. Values that work with clients could be thought of as holiness in action—ongoing, in context. Through mindfulness work in session, Amy and the client slowly cleared off the dust (i.e., verbal behavior, ego) so that the client saw the gold.

Defining Religion and Spirituality Functionally

A functional-contextual approach to clinical work uses moment-to-moment principles of behavior analysis as relevant to clients' direct and indirect learning histories in order to predict and influence behavior. Functional assessment allows the practitioner to identify and describe problem behavior along with contextual antecedents and consequences that maintain it, while recognizing that the clinician and client are inseparable from current and historical contexts. As a way to illustrate this process, consider the following example: One of the authors (Aditi Sinha) had a client who was a middle-aged African American minister. He reported that he had problems with depression, anxiety, and alcohol use. He did not make eye contact, he kept his head low, and his body posture was slouched. These nonverbal cues suggested he experienced feelings of shame as he revealed these issues; in fact, it felt to Aditi almost as if he were in a confessional. She validated his courage to come to therapy and speak about such private matters. Immediately after Aditi spoke, he popped straight up in his chair, straightened out his jacket, and looked her in the eye: "I have been a leader in my church for the last 20 years and I've given my life to God. What is your religion…is it Islam?" For a moment, Aditi was taken aback by his sudden change in behavior and switch in content. His tone was condescending; he appeared much "bigger" than before. She was mindful of her own anxiety. Aditi quickly assessed the sequence of events that occurred—nonverbal cues of shame, an expression of warmth from an authority figure, a reactive statement of religious expertise, a personal question directed toward her, and her resultant feelings of intimidation.

At this point, the functional analysis suggested a shift in balance of power. Aditi's response was important in that it could either build or damage rapport early on in the therapeutic relationship, and she also recognized that her religious beliefs might truly matter to him. Aditi knew that a carefully worded response would allow her to understand if this interaction was primarily about power and control or genuine religious concerns. She said that she was not a Muslim but could understand why her religious affiliation (or lack thereof) would matter to him in light of his chosen profession. Aditi then asked him, as someone who was versed in this domain, what he might suggest to help someone at his church who was trying to navigate a relationship with someone with different religious or spiritual beliefs. He subsequently relaxed in his chair, made gentle eye contact, and became more conversational. Aditi told him that she hoped that they could create that kind of space in their relationship and that he would likely have to help her with such matters as they continued to work together. The client was satisfied with this response and spontaneously brought in new personal information. Indeed, the function of asking about Aditi's religion was not because he felt it necessary that they have the same beliefs but that the question centered on a topic that allowed him to be an expert and regain control. If this were not the case, the client would have likely continued to express concern about their religious differences.

From a functional-contextual perspective, there is recognition that all behaviors are initiated and maintained for one or more purposes, and these transactional relationships are always changing. So, behaviors that might have effectively served one or more purposes in the past, in certain contexts, may no longer work effectively. The minister's "playing big" may be necessary and effective with some people, but in therapy the behavior was not maintained. Such behaviors are simply part of a person's learning history and should not be viewed as bad. Working from a functional-contextual perspective, a clinician can see that, using Frankl's (1992) phrase from *Man's Search for Meaning*, "An abnormal reaction to an abnormal situation is normal behavior" (p. 32). We like to say that when an accepting and open posture is used with clients—when they are viewed as "whole, complete, and perfect"—they are less likely to be defensive, aggressive, avoidant, and the like.

Conceptualizing religion and spirituality in terms of their function in the therapeutic context provides the therapist a means of understanding religious and spiritual behavior with increased precision in prediction and influence. From an acceptance and mindfulness perspective, religion/spirituality, like other valued domains (e.g., relationships, work), is most powerful and adaptive when it occurs in a flexible, values-driven manner.

Religion and Spirituality as Valuing

Meta-valuing is a way to flexibly live out multiple values simultaneously and synergistically. It refers to the process of caring about values. The ACT therapist, specifically, wants to know the struggles and strengths as they occur in the context of a person with deeply held values (Wilson & Murrell, 2004). Many individuals come to therapy with inflexible ideas about the "correct" ways to be religious and to engage in religious practice. It is not uncommon for individuals to have rigidly set rules about what practices should be done as well as how, when, and where such behaviors are appropriate. At times, clients may experience an unsettling sense of mismatch between their religious and spiritual values and their perceptions of mindfulness work in therapeutic practice. One man that Jonathan Schmalz, one of the authors, worked with expressed his concerns about doing "that Oriental stuff" prior to an initial group mindfulness exercise. Jonathan asked him to share what his concerns were, validated them, and then presented him with a brief and honest synopsis of the history of mindfulness practice in Eastern spiritual traditions and how the practice has been found to be useful in clinical practice. The client expressed no further concerns, so Jonathan thanked him for sharing and conducted the exercise. That same man, following the mindfulness exercise, expressed how it was a spiritual experience for him.

Although it has origin in Eastern and other meditative traditions, the present authors typically discuss mindfulness as a way to get in touch with oneself so that decisions can be less automatic or habit driven and more consistent with deeply held values. If clients appear to need a more didactic explanation (which may be related to a need for control), the authors note that mindfulness can help one accept things as they are, and they ask clients if that is a problem they have. Alternatively, clients may not be familiar with mindfulness practice and simply may be confused about what the practice entails. In this case, it may be more appropriate (with permission) to move directly into a short mindfulness exercise, such as identifying the smallest sound, in order to demystify the experience. As with any clarification in therapy, descriptions or demonstrations of mindfulness are most effective when they are specifically tailored to client concerns.

A variety of values measures and exercises can be used to clarify the role of religion and spirituality in clients' lives. Cards such as "ACT Conversations" (L. Hayes & Coyne, 2012) can be helpful in the clarification process. Cards with words such as "Belonging," as well as phrases such as "Being compassionate" and "Finding peace," and questions like "What do you think is your main purpose in life?" can start dialogues about value expression and related behavior. In instances when clients' histories have not provided adequate reinforcement for self-determination, forced choice options can initially shape the act of choosing and might be especially relevant to the abstract, complex ideas associated with religion and spirituality. Amy once conducted therapy with an 11-year-old who had recently lost his mother to cancer. To disrupt some of the client's attachment to the burdensomeness of his values struggles, she made choosing a game. A prompt at the top of a two-sided folder with windows read, "In a world where you could choose, no matter what anyone else said or did, would you rather...?" The client was asked to open each window and look at phrases or pictures that represented two sides of a choice and then place a token over which he or she chose in that moment. For the "Prayer" item, the first choices were "pray" and "don't pray" and then later became "pray at home" vs. "pray at church," for example.

Clinical Considerations

Sometimes the content of a client's religious or spiritual sentiments (e.g., "You have to give it up to God.") may sound flexible and accepting but may actually serve avoidant functions. At base, in conversing with clients, we have understood the intention of these statements as something equivalent to the acceptance aspect of the serenity prayer. However, it sometimes functions as an avoidant equivalent of thought stopping. In these instances, it can be helpful to encourage clients to contact other potential contingencies. In ACT, we refer to this as defusion. One might encourage the client to become aware, in the present moment, of this particular bit of mind activity. We have also found it helpful to share similar sentiments that involve action along-side acceptance. "Pray as if everything depended on God, and act as if everything depended on you," is an example. The intention here is not to get involved in a theological debate or model for the client that you, the therapist, are attached to that sentiment. In fact, the words do not really matter—you could otherwise model a flexible, aware, and de-literalized stance. A last response, which can be helpful, is humor. Share a joke with the client about the man who, while drowning in the ocean, praying for help from God, declines assistance from a diver, a ship, and a helicopter. The man drowns and upon meeting God in the afterlife asks why God did not answer his prayer. God responds, "I sent you a diver, a ship, and a helicopter!" Humor can be an excellent therapeutic tool for encouraging flexibility.

When Religion and Spirituality Help Keep Clients Stuck

The emphasis on a whole life, meta-valuing perspective within acceptance- and mindfulness-based treatments leads to a tendency to explore with clients how their religious and spiritual values fit in with their other values. Jonathan worked with a young man who had experienced extensive traumas during military combat. He found his religious worldview shaken by the loss and destruction he experienced. He was simultaneously angry at God and convinced that God must not exist. He initially reported that he had stopped attending church regularly, and that, when he did go, he felt irritated with the naiveté of the devotees around him. Jonathan and the client had previously established that he deeply valued his relationship with his infant son. He had already spoken with several ministers about his struggle to

175

reconcile what he had experienced with his previous understanding of God. He was looking for logical answers to his dilemma and, following some open-ended exploration of the matter, he directly solicited Jonathan for a possible solution. In that moment Jonathan felt more than just unease associated with potentially imposing his worldview upon his client. Jonathan was also aware that his client was fighting with his own memories and becoming increasingly entangled in that struggle. Jonathan reflected back to him the mental gymnastics he observed him performing and reiterated how important this must be for him to commit so much energy to it. Then Jonathan simply told him with empathy in his voice, "You may never find the answer, at least not one that comes with words." He expressed a sort of confusion by this statement, but it clearly resonated with him. Three sessions later the client told Jonathan he had not made any progress in finding an answer but that he had started going to church again because it was important to him that his son be raised with faith.

The intervention in this example was simple. Rather than help him to overengage in the struggle—or even with a struggle of how to stop struggling—Jonathan selectively ignored the verbal struggle and suggested that he may be using a hammer on a screw, in a sense. With a different client, with a different history, Jonathan may have specifically encouraged him to consider the various ways he had tried to solve the dilemma and identify how effective that method had (not) been. He may have also included a metaphor about letting go of the struggle, if that would be helpful. The crux, in the end, is recognizing the function of the behavior.

Struggling with One's Faith Is Not Necessarily Avoidant or Unhelpful

It is worth mentioning that struggling with one's faith is not necessarily avoidant or unhelpful. For the man just discussed it was, but willingness to struggle with difficult aspects of one's faith that may be incongruent with other values one holds dearly is actually an indication of flexibility or, at the very least, the inverse of dogmatism. Clients overly burdened by rule-governed religious behavior, experiencing dissatisfaction in other valued domains of their life as a result, may benefit from interventions that encourage the willingness to struggle with the rules of their faith.

Knowing when to encourage religious struggle or disrupt it can become a fine line to walk. Understanding the function of the behavior in relation to other aspects of the client's life is paramount. With the emphasis on flexibility within an acceptance- and mindfulness-based treatment, clinicians might find themselves struggling with the apparent rigidity of a client's religious beliefs and feel unduly inclined to encourage struggle. If the clinician becomes rigid about the pursuit of flexibility, at the expense of a client's religious values, real damage to the therapeutic relationship can result. For example, Jonathan once had to apologize to a client whom he pushed a bit too fast to consider disentanglement from rule governance about "Christian values" and decide for herself whether she wanted to stay married.

Interventions are particularly useful when they influence present-moment contingencies affecting client behavior. Aditi introduced a defusion exercise in therapy after recognizing that a client's discussion of a spiritual struggle functioned to help him avoid feelings of anxiety about being the author of his own life. The middle-aged client presented for therapy to decrease PTSD symptoms related to a high school car accident in which he observed two friends die. From the client's perspective, God had "chosen" him to witness, rather than experience, the accident. He often told Aditi that there "had to be a purpose" in his survival, but he did not know exactly what God wanted for him. Simultaneously, the client experienced overwhelming anger and guilt for "causing" the accident. He believed that the girls were angry with him (in their afterlife). While themes of responsibility, control, and forgiveness were pervasive throughout treatment, and tied with the client's religious and spiritual beliefs, he continually returned to his struggle about fulfilling his obligations to God and his two deceased friends. The client felt that he owed them and could only make up this debt by giving his own life; however, his religious beliefs prevented him from committing suicide. Consequently, he spent more than thirty years engaging in various self-punishing behaviors. One day, he described the struggle of his spirituality as "perpetually folding in on itself." Aditi asked him to visualize the struggle as an object and describe its size, shape, color, and other formal properties. She asked him what it felt like (physically and emotionally), in that moment, to carry this with him all the time. He sat in silence and, slowly, his shoulders started to sag. Then she saw him connect with the weight of the pain that he carried. He sobbed, quietly, for several minutes. Aditi asked the client if they could work together to find out what he wanted out of life, while the object continued to fold in on itself in his palm. The client lifted up his head, made eye contact, and said, "That is a big deal." In the following weeks, Aditi asked him to visualize the object in his palm during session as they focused on exploring his deeply held personal values. Not only did this exercise help the client understand that his entire behavioral repertoire had become related to undoing the trauma, he started to see himself as separate from, and bigger than, this spiritual struggle. From this point, he was able to contact feelings of grief about the time he had lost and his fear about moving forward with his life.

Conclusion

Acceptance- and mindfulness-based therapies are uniquely poised to address issues of religion and spirituality with clients. As with any approach, multicultural appreciation and sensitivity create the foundation for effective client-therapist trust and collaboration. Understanding, validating, and encouraging discussion about concerns regarding mismatch or perceived mismatch between a client's and therapist's religious and spiritual values are central to an effective course of therapy. From that center point, acceptance- and mindfulness-based therapies share a number of similarities with various religious and spiritual traditions. With a respectful attitude and commonalities, the acceptance- and mindfulness-based clinician is also able to engage clients with their values of religion and spirituality in a unique manner. Understanding the function of religious and spiritual experiences as reported by clients allows clinicians to predict and disrupt aspects of that experience that are driven less by deeply felt, meaningful values and more by following the rules and expectations of others. Simultaneously, acceptance- and mindfulness-based work can allow clients to experience their religious and spiritual values as symbiotic and synergistic with the other values they hold dearly. Furthermore, the existing values-driven, appetitive functions of a client's religious and spiritual values can be powerful in affecting change in many areas of the client's life. Religion and spirituality have long been powerful forces affecting human behavior. Acceptance- and mindfulness-based approaches can allow clients to recover lost vitality in their religious and spiritual practice, discover what a powerful motivation it can be for them, and/or come to see how their religious and spiritual values can meaningfully interact with the other values in their lives.

References

Bergin, A. E. (1991). Values and religious issues in psychotherapy and mental health. *American Psychologist, 46*(4), 394–403.

Bergin, A. E., & Jensen, J. P. (1990). Religiosity of psychotherapists: A national survey. *Psychotherapy, 27,* 3–7.

Cooper, D. A. (1997). *God is a verb: Kabbalah and the practice of mystical Judaism.* New York: Riverhead Books.

Frankl, V. E. (1992). *Man's search for meaning: An introduction to logotherapy.* Boston: Beacon Press.

Hayes, L., & Coyne, L. W. (2012). ACT Conversations Values Cards. Retrived from http://bondlifeone.files.wordpress.com/2012/03/values-cards-with-questions-15-yrs-hayes-coyne.pdf.

Hayes, S. C. (1984). Making sense of spirituality. *Behaviorism, 12*(2), 99–110.

Hayes, S. C., Strosahl, K. D., & Wilson, K. G. (1999). *Acceptance and commitment therapy: An experiential approach to behavior change.* New York: Guilford Press.

Murrell, A. R., Rogers, L. J., & Johnson, L. (2009). From shy lamb to roaring lion: An Acceptance and Commitment Therapy (ACT) case study. *Behavior and Social Issues, 18*(1), 1–18.

Rose, E. M., Westefeld, J. S., & Ansely, T. N. (2001). Spiritual issues in counseling: Clients' beliefs and preferences. *Journal of Counseling Psychology, 48*(1), 61–71.

Taylor, R., & Chatters, L. M. (2010). Importance of religion and spirituality in the lives of African Americans, Caribbean Blacks, and non-Hispanic Whites. *Journal of Negro Education, 79,* 280–294.

U. S. Department of Health and Human Services. (2001). *Mental health: Culture, race, and ethnicity—a supplement to mental health: A report of the surgeon general.* Rockville, MD: U.S. Department of Health and Human Services, Substance Abuse and Mental Health Services Administration, Center for Mental Health Services. Pulled from the Internet on December 9, 2012. http://www.ncbi.nlm .nih.gov/books/NBK44243.

Vivekananda, S. (1948). *Teachings of Swami Vivekananda.* Kolkota, India: Advaita Ashrama.

Wilson, K. G., & Murrell, A. R. (2004). Values work in acceptance and commitment therapy: Setting a course for behavioral treatment. In S. C. Hayes, V. M. Follette, M. M. Linehan (Eds.), *Mindfulness and acceptance: Expanding the cognitive-behavioral tradition* (pp. 120–151). New York: Guilford Press.

Worthington, E. L. Jr. (1988). Understanding the values of religious clients: A model and its application to counseling. *Journal of Counseling Psychology, 35,* 166–174.

Worthington, E. L. Jr., Hook, J. N., Davis, D. E., & McDaniel, M. A. (2011). Religion and spirituality. *Journal of Clinical Psychology: In Session, 67,* 204–214.

Wulff, D. M. (1996). The psychology of religion: An overview. In E. P. Shafranske (Ed.), *Religion and the clinical practice of psychology* (pp. 43–70). Washington, DC: American Psychological Association.

CHAPTER 10

Acceptance and Mindfulness for Undermining Prejudice

Jason Lillis, Ph.D.
Brown University

Michael Levin, Ph.D.
Utah State University

Prejudice toward individuals based on their group memberships is a major source of human misery. Extreme manifestations of prejudice include many of the most horrific, large-scale acts of violence such as genocide, racial wars, and terrorism. Discrimination based on group status can be observed in central domains of society including employment, housing, education, health care, judicial systems, and financial systems (e.g., Pager & Shepherd, 2008). In addition to the direct consequences of such discrimination, these experiences negatively impact the physical and mental health of those who are discriminated against (Pascoe & Richman, 2009). Prejudice is an important target for reducing human suffering and improving the quality of life of people belonging to marginalized groups.

The Psychological Flexibility Model of Prejudice

The psychological flexibility model (Hayes, Luoma, Bond, Masuda, & Lillis, 2006) identifies prejudice as a generalized verbal process that involves normal and useful language abilities gone awry. Thus, prejudicial thoughts can be difficult to change directly. Promoting psychological flexibility via cognitive defusion, acceptance, mindfulness, and values-based processes should reduce the impact of prejudice without having to directly change automatic thought content and subsequently decrease discriminatory behavior while promoting more pro-social behavior.

Prejudice as a generalized verbal process. We define prejudice as the objectification and dehumanization of people as a result of their participation in evaluative verbal categories. This expansive definition includes bias and discrimination directed at any group that can be identified by a verbal label, such as "Black," "White," "gay," "Muslim," or "woman," as well as "poor," "psychotic," "addict," "handicapped," "obese," and so on. This definition also highlights the role of language processes that make acts of bias and discrimination possible.

There has been a number of studies demonstrating that prejudiced attitudes toward various groups tend to co-occur and comprise a single latent variable (e.g., Bäckström & Björklund, 2007). Individuals who are biased against African Americans are likely to be prejudiced toward other ethnic minority groups, women, sexual minorities, and so on. This suggests that prejudice may involve a general process of having biases and engaging in discrimination toward individuals based on their group status in verbal evaluative categories, rather than being constrained to biases toward any one specific group. If this is the case, then interventions may be more efficacious if they can target the verbal processes that underlie prejudice, as opposed to focusing on the content of beliefs and biases toward specific groups.

Prejudice is the result of normal language abilities. The same verbal processes involved in prejudice (categorization, association, evaluation) are useful and reinforced in everyday life. The ability to socially categorize and arbitrarily relate verbal categories is learned early in childhood (Berens & Hayes, 2007; Kohlenberg, Hayes, & Hayes, 1991), and there is nothing to prevent irrelevant and potentially harmful distinctions of all kinds from entering into verbally defined and evaluated groupings. The evaluation of verbal categories is a central verbal skill, key to both problem solving *and* prejudice (Barnes-Holmes, Hayes, Barnes-Holmes, & Roche, 2001). In other words, the same process that allows you to evaluate that your "car" is "broken or undesirable," which can result in behaviors that attempt to get it running again, can also lead to evaluating a "gay" person as "broken or undesirable," which can result in discriminatory behavior. In addition, stereotyping reduces the cognitive burden of understanding a complex social environment, making it useful despite obvious costs (Macrae, Milne, & Bodenhausen, 1994).

These normal language processes (i.e., categorizing, associating, evaluating) can occur relatively automatically and without conscious awareness. Unfortunately, this also applies to prejudice. Research on implicit cognition during the past few decades shows that many individuals, including those who deny prejudiced attitudes, maintain implicit (i.e., automatic, unconscious) racial biases (Greenwald,

Poehlman, Uhlmann, & Banaji, 2009). These implicit biases are important, as they can subtly influence discriminatory actions in a variety of ways even if one is unaware of them (Dasgupta, 2004).

Prejudice is rigid and resistant to change particularly in form. New ideas are resisted if they conflict with old ways of thinking (Moxon, Keenan, & Hine, 1993), suppressing unwanted thoughts can increase their frequency and intensity (Wenzlaff & Wegner, 2000), and implicit cognition occurs automatically and potentially outside of one's awareness (Greenwald & Banaji, 1995). Given this, some researchers have questioned the feasibility of directly changing prejudicial thoughts (Bargh, 1999; Lillis & Hayes, 2007).

An alternative approach is to reduce the impact of prejudice without having to directly modify prejudicial thought or emotional content. Such a focus could decrease discriminatory behavior effectively, while promoting more prosocial behavior via the use of values-based processes.

Emerging Trends in Prejudice-Reduction Efforts

There have been substantial efforts across a range of fields to combat prejudice (Paluck & Green, 2009). Within this vast literature, there are emerging trends that highlight the relevance of psychological flexibility processes for reducing prejudice. This chapter will review a selection of this research in the context of the psychological flexibility model. We will then describe a psychological flexibility intervention approach to reducing prejudice.

Discouraging social pressure and thought suppression. A common prejudice-reduction approach is to leverage social influence processes. Examples include social norms messages (e.g., Stangor, Sechrist, & Jost, 2001), expert opinions (e.g., Levy, Stroessner, & Dweck, 1998), and the variety of direct and indirect societal messages stating racism is bad and one should not be racist. Although there is a commonsense appeal to these approaches, research indicates that when regulating prejudice is driven by such external motivators (i.e., social pressure), there can be a paradoxical *increase* in prejudice attitudes and behavior (e.g., Legault, Gutsell, & Inzlicht, 2011).

External motivation alone may lead to increases in prejudice in part because it can motivate ineffective suppression strategies (Hausmann & Ryan, 2004). When there is social pressure to not appear prejudiced and it is "wrong" to have prejudiced thoughts, it makes sense that individuals would turn to trying to push prejudiced thoughts out of their mind. Such suppression efforts produce a subsequent increase in prejudiced thoughts as well as discriminatory behaviors toward the target group (e.g., Galinsky & Moskowitz, 2000; Wenzlaff & Wegner, 2000). Thus, interventions focusing on external social pressure and suppressing prejudiced thoughts can increase prejudice, suggesting that psychological flexibility interventions emphasizing personal values relevant to prejudice reduction, as well as acceptance and defusing from prejudiced thoughts, may be a more effective alternative.

Enhancing internal motivation. A recent trend has been examining the benefits of increasing internal or self-determined motivation for regulating prejudice (i.e., motivators based on personal relevance and importance as well as a sense of autonomy and choice). Research has shown that higher internal motivation is related to more effective prejudice regulation, even when one's self-control resources are depleted (Legault, Green-Demers, & Eadie, 2009), and that interventions emphasizing internal motivation for regulating prejudice can reduce both explicit and implicit prejudice (Legault et al., 2011). Another related study found that highlighting one's most important values eliminated racial discrimination in a job candidate rating task (Fein & Spencer, 1997). These studies suggest that enhancing motivation linked to chosen, personally relevant goals and values is a promising avenue for prejudice reduction.

Increasing awareness of automatic prejudices. More common, subtle forms of contemporary prejudice (i.e., modern racism) share a common characteristic in which individuals deny explicit prejudice beliefs but nonetheless demonstrate implicit biases (Todd, Bodenhausen, Richeson, & Galinsky, 2011). This disconnection between explicit and implicit beliefs may be due to a lack of awareness of or willingness to admit one's prejudice biases. An important step in targeting this form of prejudice is to raise awareness of one's prejudiced reactions and biases so that their influence on one's behavior can be modulated (Monteith & Mark, 2005). In line with this approach, one study found that actively encouraging awareness of moments when one was prejudiced as part of a larger prejudice-reduction intervention reduced discriminatory behavior among individuals with low explicit and high implicit prejudice (Son Hing, Li, & Zanna, 2002).

Promoting cognitive flexibility and perspective taking. A number of studies have found empirical support for prejudice-reduction interventions that seek to alter the process of favoring perceived in-groups over out-groups by targeting the salience of particular group statuses (Paluck & Green, 2009). These contextual interventions expand and elaborate on perceived group statuses, reducing the emphasis on "us" vs. "them." Studies have also found that perspective-taking manipulations such as writing about or imagining what someone belonging to a minority group might be thinking and feeling can reduce explicit and implicit prejudice as well as increase empathy and positive interactions with individuals belonging to minority groups (e.g., Shih, Wang, Bucher, & Stotzer, 2009; Todd et al., 2011; Galinsky & Moskowitz, 2000).

Increasing contact. Increasing contact with individuals belonging to marginalized groups is one of the most well-known approaches to prejudice reduction. A meta-analysis of 515 studies found strong empirical support for the impact of increased contact on reducing prejudice (Pettigrew & Tropp, 2006). Effects were particularly strong when contact occurred under ideal conditions including equality, cooperation, authority support, and a shared goal (Pettigrew & Tropp, 2006). Research suggests that increased liking, empathy, and self-disclosure as well as decreased intergroup anxiety may account for how intergroup contact reduces prejudice (e.g., Pettigrew & Tropp, 2006; Turner, Hewstone, & Voci, 2007). In addition, personal importance of contact is a key variable in predicting whether increased contact leads to prejudice reduction (Van Dick et al., 2004).

Summary. This selective review highlights emerging trends consistent with a psychological flexibility approach to prejudice reduction, which we will present in the following section. Within the prejudice-reduction field, researchers are exploring methods focused on how to deal with prejudiced thoughts, motivation, and intergroup behaviors. Researchers have begun to develop and evaluate approaches consistent with psychological flexibility sensibilies: teaching awareness and flexibility with prejudiced thoughts, discouraging thought-suppression strategies, emphasizing internal motivation for prejudice reduction rather than external motivation, promoting perspective taking, and encouraging intergroup interactions situated within a cooperative, prosocial context. We now turn to a discussion of how the psychological flexibility model brings these features together into an integrated mindfulness-, acceptance-, and values-based approach to prejudice reduction.

A Psychological Flexibility Intervention for Reducing Prejudice

The psychological flexibility approach uses acceptance and mindfulness processes to reduce the impact of prejudicial thoughts, beliefs, and attitudes; it also uses values and behavior change processes to promote behavior more consistent with chosen ideals. The approach is experiential in nature, utilizing metaphors and exercises to create a context promoting psychological flexibility. We will walk through each component and provide rationale, exercises, and a discussion of relevant issues. These strategies come from a study that tested a brief prejudice-reduction intervention for college students (Lillis & Hayes, 2007).

Reducing the impact of prejudicial thoughts and stereotypes. The psychological flexibility model assumes that prejudice is the result of normal language processes (categorization, association, evaluation), making them hard to change directly. Thus, an important component of this approach is to undermine the literal *impact* of thoughts, without trying to change the form or frequency of thoughts. This approach is nontraditional and could be seen as controversial. However, we are not saying that *behaving* in prejudiced and discriminatory ways is acceptable. Rather we are saying that there is substantial evidence to support targeting the process of thinking as opposed to the content of thoughts in order to produce behavior change.

An important first step is illustrating the automatic and additive nature of thoughts through experiential exercises. For example, you can tell participants that it is important to remember the answer to this question (playing it up for dramatic and irreverent effect). The question: "What should I plant?" The answer: "Carrots and peas." Have them repeat that answer to your question a few times playfully. Discuss that, with just a few moments of mere exposure to these words and this association, they now might have "carrots and peas" as a recurring thought for some time. You can continue by asking them to simply forget "carrots and peas" or have the answer to the question "What should I plant?" be something else entirely. This will be hard to do, illustrating the point that verbal relations work more by addition as opposed to subtraction.

This can be followed by simply asking participants to complete common phrases, such as "There's no place like...[home]" or "Only the good die...[young]." After running through a number of these, discuss the nature of "programming," automatic thoughts our minds give us that can be prompted by context. Thoughts are a product of our history. We have been exposed to massive amounts of words from parents, family members, peers, teachers, media, the Internet, and so on. Although it often feels like our thoughts are important and true, they are also automatic and historical, like "carrots and peas."

The next step would be to have participants observe these processes in relation to prejudicial stimuli. For example, participants can be asked to "notice their programming" by completing statements in writing, such as "Most Black people tend to…" or "People who live in this country and don't speak the language are…" or "Being gay is…" It is important to create a safe space where participants can simply be aware of and watch these verbal processes without having to suppress or censor what shows up in order to promote awareness of the automatic nature of thoughts. The ensuing discussion should validate the normality of whatever thought content showed up, while continuously pointing to the historical and automatic nature of the thoughts themselves. If thoughts are arbitrary and historical, perhaps treating them as true and important is not warranted.

Additional exercises can be used to provide multiple examples for undermining the literal nature of thoughts. For example, have participants repeat a word out loud until only the sound remains, a technique known to reduce the believability and distressing impact of thoughts (e.g., Masuda, Hayes, Sackett, & Twohig, 2004). It may also be useful to have participants imagine their thoughts coming from a "biased radio" that constantly generates prejudicial thoughts. Teaching the distinction between "noticing" and "buying into" a thought can also be helpful. Each of these exercises is designed to promote mindful awareness of the process of thinking and create psychological distance from thought content, thus undermining the literal nature and impact of biased thoughts.

Mindfulness and acceptance of unwanted emotions. Humans have a strong tendency to try to reduce, eliminate, or change unwanted emotions, often referred to as experiential avoidance (Hayes et al., 2006). Experiential avoidance can reinforce prejudice. Consider the following example: A Caucasian teenager is taught that it is wrong to discriminate against people of a different race or ethnicity, and subsequently that "nervous" feeling around African Americans is evidence of prejudicial attitudes. In this scenario, it would not be surprising if the next time the teenager was in the presence of African American peers the feelings of anxiety *and now* guilt were present. The easiest way to avoid those feelings would be to avoid contact with African Americans altogether. This avoidance would function to reduce the unwanted feelings; however, it would have the effect of limiting contact with people of different racial and ethnic backgrounds. This reduced contact could serve to reinforce stereotypes and bias, as the teenager becomes less connected to the individual qualities and characteristics of each person, leaving only the verbal products of history to operate.

The psychological flexibility model promotes mindful awareness and acceptance of emotional experiences as they are and without struggle. The goal is to undermine experiential avoidance in the service of behaving consistently with chosen ideals. In our previous example, teaching the teenager acceptance skills could allow him to become aware of his emotions, reduce any struggle with emotions, and engage in desired behavior in the presence of anxiety and guilt, thus allowing him to build new behavioral patterns with respect to peers from different racial or ethnic backgrounds.

A first step is to promote mindful awareness of emotional experiences through guided imagery. You can present a series of scenarios and ask participants to notice any emotional reactions or changes in their body. For example:

> Imagine you are applying for a desirable job. You've been out of work, money is tight. You think you're the best candidate, your résumé is great, you interviewed well. Just get present with that… Then you find out that you're not getting the job, that the job went to another candidate, and that that candidate was a different race. Notice what happens with your body, and try to sit with it, without fighting or changing it… Check in with yourself, what did you feel? What race did you picture the other person to be?

It can be hard to notice unwanted emotional reactions. However it is important to point out the cost of avoidance. Suppressing emotions makes it difficult to remain in the present moment, harming one's ability to experience and connect with another person. As described earlier, it also creates a difficult standard that could inhibit diversity-seeking and prosocial behavior. The latter problem can be illustrated using a metaphor:

Imagine you are strapped to a chair above a shark tank with the world's most sensitive arousal detector, and you are told that all you have to do is stay completely relaxed, completely calm. If the detector registers any arousal in you, the seat will go out like a dunk tank at a carnival and you will be plunged into the water with the sharks. It is pretty obvious what would happen, no? Yet we often do this to ourselves. "I can't feel anxious at work!" Or "I can't feel uncomfortable around gay people!"

In processing the metaphor it can be useful to point out that while emotions may not be controllable, at least not all of the time, behavior is. For example, if we are asked to sing or else we would fall into the shark tank, we could do it. This distinction is key for building the foundation of the psychological flexibility approach to reducing prejudice. Instead of trying to control our own cognitive and emotional reactions to people and situations, focus on our behavior.

The alternative to suppression and avoidance is acceptance. Acceptance is making room for the full range of human emotions, allowing them to come and go without struggle. Acceptance is like holding emotions gently in our hands as we move about. From an accepting stance, behavior can be more flexible, as opposed to directing effort toward suppression and avoidance, which could take the form of prejudice.

A number of experiential exercises can promote acceptance. Unwanted emotions can be imagined as objects with physical characteristics. Mindfulness-based exposure exercises can be used to track bodily sensations associated with different emotional experiences, breaking them down piece by piece. Or alternatively, emotions can be contacted and metaphorically "breathed into."

An important distinction is that acceptance is not about treating reactions as true or valid in a verbal sense. For example, if one feels anxious around White people, acceptance does *not* mean the anxiety is "true," that it is "right" to be anxious around White people. Acceptance means that in this moment anxiety is present, and one can be willing to experience anxiety in the service of behaving consistently with chosen ideals.

Promoting empathy via perspective-taking skills. Promoting empathy through perspective-taking exercises is another key component of the psychological flexibility approach. Perspective taking can help break down the dominance of categorical language functions and transform the experience of "us vs. them" to more of a "we." Often participants experience a sense of common humanity while simultaneously becoming more in contact with the varied individual characteristics of people. Virtually anything that facilitates taking the perspective of the "other" can be useful here. A sequence of exercises is described below.

Participants can be asked to identify an emotion they struggle with from time to time and try to remember the first time the emotion was experienced. Participants then write down the emotion, fold the piece of paper, and hold it in a closed-handed fist. Everyone is then asked to raise his or her hand and keep it raised as the facilitator verbally states increasing time periods (1 week, 1 month, 1 year, etc.). Participants put their hands down when the time period exceeded how old the emotion is. Typically most hands remain in the air for long time periods that extend into early childhood. The ensuing discussion highlights the ubiquity of human suffering.

In the next step, participants are asked to write their emotion on a name tag and place it on their chest. When all have completed, participants are guided through an observer exercise and asked to notice what it is like to wear their emotion "badge," with specific attention paid to the experience of noticing. The goal is contact with a stable sense of self, the noticing self. Participants are then asked to notice other participants' badges, to "climb behind the eyes" of each person, noticing what he or she might be thinking or feeling. A further iteration asks participants to notice the other person noticing them. As the exercise progresses, awareness is expanded and perspectives are shifted. For example, participants may be asked to notice what it was like to experience their badge as a young child, or conversely what it would have been like for another participant to experience their badge as a young child, and so on.

Clarifying values. Behavior change is the primary goal of psychological flexibility: both the reduction of discriminatory behavior and an increase in prosocial and humanitarian action. Thus, clarifying values is another key component of the psychological flexibility model. As one becomes more free from the dominance of literal language (stereotypes, judgments, beliefs) and the pull to avoid unwanted cognitive and emotional experiences, values can become the guide for behavior.

A useful way to discuss values is to describe them like guides. For example, sailors used to use the stars as guides at night to let them know in which direction they were headed. Similarly, we can use our values as a "compass," letting us know that we are on track. At any point we can check in to see if we are moving "east" and orient back if we have strayed.

Values are not feelings. If one values being a loving person only when feelings of love are present, behavior will be inconsistent at best and harmful at worst. Therefore it is useful to discuss that values are a choice and that thoughts and emotions will do whatever they do as we pursue our values. Values should not be used as an attempt to make us feel or think a certain way.

Uncovering core values can be difficult. In dealing with prejudice, an appeal to relationship values can be helpful. One exercise asks participants to imagine being at their eighty-fifth birthday party and have each important person in their life speak about them and have them say what they would most want him or her to say. The goal is to imagine an ideal, if you were exactly the person you wanted to be in relation to the people you care about. Common themes include being a loving person, treating people with respect, being close and connected to others, being honest and open, and learning from others. Once these core values are present, they can be organized into values statements and broadened out to include a wider range of people: coworkers, members of one's town, state, country, and so on.

Behavioral commitments. The final piece of a psychological flexibility intervention for prejudice is making behavioral commitments: any activity designed to get participants exposed to new experiences and people can fit here, with specific attention to being mindful, defused, and accepting, while orienting to behavior consistent with chosen values. For example, college students could be prompted to attend a social club or party in which they would be a minority member. Coworkers could be asked to work on committees together, and so on. This component is consistent with the vast literature supporting contact as an effective strategy for reducing prejudice. The psychological flexibility model, however, provides acceptance, mindfulness, and values skills that can increase the likelihood of positive contact experiences, as well as the motivation to engage in contact.

Evaluation. Research on the effect of psychological flexibility–based intervention for reducing prejudice is still in the early stages. However, a preliminary study revealed the favorable effects of this psychological flexibility–based intervention on increasing prosocial behavioral intentions at post and one-week follow-up, while improving defusion, mindfulness, and acceptance of prejudicial thoughts and biases (Lillis & Hayes, 2007).

Conclusion

Prejudice is widespread and difficult to impact due to the verbal processes involved. The psychological flexibility model presents an alternative to attempting to directly change prejudicial thoughts in form. Promoting mindful awareness, cognitive defusion, acceptance, and values-based processes can reduce the impact of prejudicial thought content and emotional reactions while orienting to prosocial values as a means for navigating behavior. Although evidence is still limited, extant conceptual and empirical works suggest this approach warrants further study.

References

Bäckström, M., & Björklund, F. (2007). Structural modeling of generalized prejudice: The role of social dominance, authoritarianism, and empathy. *Journal of Individual Differences, 28*, 10–17.

Bargh, J. A. (1999). The cognitive monster: The case against the controllability of automatic stereotype effects. In S. Chaiken & Y. Trope (Eds.), *Dual Process Theories in Social Psychology* (pp. 361–382). New York: Guilford Press.

Barnes-Holmes, Y., Hayes, S. C., Barnes-Holmes, D., & Roche, B. (2001). Relational frame theory: A post-Skinnerian account of human language and cognition. *Advances in Child Development and Behavior, 28*, 101–138.

Berens, N. M., & Hayes, S. C. (2007). Arbitrarily applicable comparative relations: Experimental evidence for a relational operant. *Journal of Applied Behavior Analysis, 40*(1), 45–71.

Dasgupta, N. (2004). Implicit ingroup favoritism, outgroup favoritism, and their behavioral manifestations. *Social Justice Research, 17*, 143–169.

Fein, S., & Spencer, S. J. (1997). Prejudice as self-image maintenance: Affirming the self through derogating others. *Journal of Personality and Social Psychology, 73*, 31–44.

Galinsky, A. D., & Moskowitz, G. B. (2000). Perspective-taking: Decreasing stereotype expression, stereotype accessibility, and ingroup favoritism. *Journal of Personality and Social Psychology, 78*, 708–724.

Greenwald, A. G., & Banaji, M. R. (1995). Implicit social cognition: Attitudes, self-esteem, and stereotypes. *Psychological Review, 102*, 4–27.

Greenwald, A. G., Poehlman, T. A., Uhlmann, E. L., & Banaji, M. R. (2009). Understanding and using the Implicit Association Test: III. Meta-analysis of predictive validity. *Journal of Personality and Social Psychology, 97*, 17–41.

Hausmann, L. R. M., & Ryan, C. S. (2004). Effects of external and internal motivation to control prejudice on implicit prejudice: The mediating role of efforts to control prejudiced responses. *Basic and Applied Social Psychology, 26*, 215–225.

Hayes, S. C., Luoma, J. B., Bond, F. W., Masuda, A., & Lillis, J. (2006). Acceptance and commitment therapy: Model, processes and outcomes. *Behaviour Research and Therapy, 44*(1), 1–25. doi: 10.1016/j.brat.2005.06.006.

Kohlenberg, B. S., Hayes, S. C., & Hayes, L. J. (1991). The transfer of contextual control over equivalence classes through equivalence classes: A possible model of social stereotyping. *Journal of the Experimental Analysis of Behavior, 56*, 505–518.

Legault, L., Green-Demers, I., & Eadie, A. L. (2009). When internalization leads to automatization: The role of self-determination in automatic stereotype suppression and implicit prejudice regulation. *Motivation and Emotion, 33*, 10–24.

Legault, L., Gutsell, J. N., & Inzlicht, M. (2011). Ironic effects of antiprejudice messages: How motivational interventions can reduce (but also increase) prejudice. *Psychological Science, 22*, 1472–1477.

Levy, S. R., Stroessner, S., & Dweck, C. S. (1998). Stereotype formation and endorsement: The role of implicit theories. *Journal of Personality and Social Psychology, 74*, 421–436.

Lillis, J., & Hayes, S. C. (2007). Applying acceptance, mindfulness, and values to the reduction of prejudice: A pilot study. *Behavior Modification, 31,* 389–411.

Macrae, C. N., Milne, A. B., & Bodenhausen, G. V. (1994). Stereotypes as energy-saving devices: A peek inside the cognitive toolbox. *Journal of Personality and Social Psychology, 66,* 37–47.

Masuda, A., Hayes, S. C., Sackett, C. F., & Twohig, M. P. (2004). Cognitive defusion and self-relevant negative thoughts: Examining the impact of a ninety-year-old technique. *Behaviour Research and Therapy, 42,* 477–485.

Monteith, M. J., & Mark, A. Y. (2005). Changing one's prejudice ways: Awareness, affect, and self-regulation. *European Review of Social Psychology, 16,* 113–154.

Moxon, P. D., Keenan, M., & Hine, L. (1993). Gender-role stereotyping and stimulus equivalence. *Psychological Record, 43,* 381–394.

Pager, D., & Shepherd, H. (2008). The sociology of discrimination: Racial discrimination in employment, housing, credit, and consumer markets. *Annual Review of Sociology, 34,* 181–209.

Paluck, E. L., & Green, D. P. (2009). Prejudice reduction: What works? A critical look at evidence from the field and the laboratory. *Annual Review of Psychology, 60,* 339–367.

Pascoe, E. A., & Richman, L. S. (2009). Perceived discrimination and health: A meta-analytic review. *Psychological Bulletin, 135,* 531–554.

Pettigrew, T. F., & Tropp, L. R. (2006). A meta-analytic test of intergroup contact theory. *Journal of Personality and Social Psychology, 90,* 751–783.

Shih, M., Wang, E., Bucher, A. T., & Stotzer, R. (2009). Perspective taking: Reducing prejudice towards general outgroups and specific individuals. *Group Processes & Intergroup Relations, 12,* 565–577.

Son Hing, L. S., Li, W., & Zanna, M. P. (2002). Inducing hypocrisy to reduce prejudicial responses among aversive racists. *Journal of Experimental Social Psychology, 381,* 71–78.

Stangor, C., Sechrist, G. B., & Jost, J. T. (2001). Changing racial beliefs by providing consensus information. *Personality and Social Psychology Bulletin, 27,* 484–494.

Todd, A. R., Bodenhausen, G. V., Richeson, J. A., & Galinsky, A. D. (2011). Perspective taking combats automatic expressions of racial bias. *Journal of Personality and Social Psychology, 100,* 1027–1042.

Turner, R. N., Hewstone, M., & Voci, A. (2007). Reducing explicit and implicit outgroup prejudice via direct and extended contact: The mediating role of self-disclosure and intergroup anxiety. *Journal of Personality and Social Psychology, 93,* 369–388.

Van Dick, R., Wagner, U., Pettigrew, T. F., Christ, O., Wolf, C., Petzel, T. et al. (2004). The role of perceived importance in intergroup contact. *Journal of Personality and Social Psychology, 87,* 211–227.

Wenzlaff, R. M., & Wegner, D. M. (2000). Thought suppression. *Annual Review of Psychology, 51,* 59–91.

CHAPTER 11

Acceptance and Mindfulness for Undermining Stigma

Jason B. Luoma, Ph.D.

Portland Psychotherapy Clinic, Research, and Training Center

The term "stigma" originally referred to a practice among the ancient Greeks of literally marking or branding people who were slaves, criminals, or traitors. It has since come to refer to a mark or indicator that a person is devalued or has a lower social status. The content of stigma varies across time and cultures, but the stigmatization process occurs across all human societies.

For those who are stigmatized, stigma results in many negative social and health consequences. Among those labeled as mentally ill, stigma is associated with unemployment, lower quality of life (QOL), poorer treatment adherence, higher symptom severity, and constricted social networks (Livingston & Boyd, 2010). Stigma toward those with addictions results in interpersonal rejection, discrimination, and barriers to employment (Luoma & Kohlenberg, 2012). Stigma toward obesity is associated with depression, isolation, and reduced QOL (Puhl & Heuer, 2009). Similar findings have been documented for HIV stigma (Gonzalez, Solomon, Zvolensky, & Miller, 2009), sexual minority stigma (Yadavaia & Hayes, 2012), and many other conditions. Cross-sectional studies suggest that stigma may also harm the mental health of the stigmatizer (Masuda & Latzman, 2011).

Stigma can occur at structural or individual levels. At the structural level stigma takes the form of laws, physical structures, or institutional practices that systematically disenfranchise or devalue certain groups of individuals. At the individual level, stigma takes two forms: public stigma and self-stigma. Public stigma refers to the reaction that out-group members have toward the stigmatized group (Corrigan, 2007). Self-stigma reflects difficult thoughts and feelings (e.g., shame, negative self-evaluative thoughts, fear of being stigmatized) that emerge from identification with a stigmatized group, resulting in negative behavioral effects (Luoma, Kohlenberg, Hayes, & Fletcher, 2012).

In this chapter, we focus mostly on the individual level of analysis, though these ideas can be scaled to influence stigma at a structural level. Specifically, we outline an account of stigma that is based on a psychological flexibility model of healthy personal and interpersonal functioning. Emerging from work on acceptance and commitment therapy (ACT) and a modern behavior analytic theory of language and cognition called relational frame theory (Hayes, Niccolls, Masuda, & Rye, 2002), a central tenant of this model of stigma is that the objectification of human beings occurs because of a pervasive tendency to behave toward people in terms of their participation in verbal categories. This behavior dominates over other ways of responding, resulting in insensitivity to other aspects of the context, including the situationally variable human beings.

The chapter begins with a brief conceptual overview of public and self-stigma, followed by a review of mainstream models of stigma intervention. An alternative psychological flexibility model of stigma as a way to target stigma reduction is proposed. Finally, data from ACT interventions for stigma reduction are reviewed.

Stigma Models

Models of stigma span different levels of analysis and disciplines. Attempts have been made to specify overarching, general models of stigma (Pescosolido, Martin, Lang, & Olafsdottir, 2008). Still other models have focused on stigma at the individual level of analysis or one part of the stigmatization process, such as stereotyping (Macrae, Milne, & Bodenhausen, 1994), implicit attitudes (Greenwald & Banaji, 1995), or perspective taking (Galinsky & Moskowitz, 2000). Common to these models is the idea that stigmatization is fundamentally social and language based. Through our interactions with others, we are taught the common stereotypes associated with significant social groups (Devine, 1989). We automatically classify people into social group categories and use these labels to predict the behaviors of those around us and to provide guidance about how to respond to them. This stereotyping process is a normal part of human behavior, as it reduces the cognitive burden of responding to complex social situations (Macrae et al., 1994). Public stigma occurs when we assign a devalued or constricted social category to others.

Likewise, we also learn to place ourselves in various social categories. This process of conceptualizing the self reflects everyday learning processes in which the individual learns to generate coherent stories that seem to describe who they are as an individual and explain one's actions (Luoma & Kohlenberg, 2012). The nature of the conceptualized self is fluid with various aspects of self-content triggered contextually. Some of these identities may be more central and have consistent effects across many situations, while others are more situationally bounded. Self-stigma occurs when a person is attached to a conceptualized self that includes the identification with a marginalized and devalued group, and the person may come to devalue herself, experiencing shame, self-doubt, and feelings of helplessness and powerlessness. Additionally, people may come to fear being a target of stigma, and then avoid seeking treatment, employment, or relationships.

Mainstream Models of Stigma Intervention

Mainstream methods for changing public stigma can be categorized into one or more of the following: education, contact, or protest (Corrigan et al., 2001). In educational approaches, new information is provided in an attempt to dispel negative stereotypes. Some educational interventions show short-term improvements (Corrigan et al., 2001; Penn, Kommana, Mansfield, & Link, 1999), but gains are generally not maintained (Corrigan et al., 2002) or limited to those with lower levels of prejudice to begin with. Other educational interventions may have paradoxical effects. For example, an increasingly promoted educational strategy to reduce stigma at the highest levels of mental health care is to refer to mental disorders as "brain diseases" with biological or genetic causes. However, this strategy has been shown to be ineffective at best, and in some cases may actually increase both public and self-stigma (Rüsch, Todd, Bodenhausen, & Corrigan, 2010; Walker & Read, 2002).

Protest interventions generally attempt to suppress stigmatizing attitudes through disputing the morality of holding and expressing such views. This strategy, while extremely common, is found to be largely ineffective (Corrigan et al., 2001) with notable paradoxical effects. For example, demanding correct behaviors can increase physical avoidance of stigmatized persons (Langer, Fiske, Taylor, & Chanowitz, 1976) and increase implicit prejudice (Legault, Gutsell, & Inzlicht, 2011).

The final group of stigma-reduction strategies involves arranging positive social contact between members of the stigmatized group and the public. Contact-based interventions are the most consistently successful strategies in reducing stigma in the short term, with some studies showing change maintained over time and changes in overt behavior (Corrigan et al., 2001, 2002). Unfortunately, this method can be hard to implement because of numerous variables that need to be managed in real-world applications (Corrigan, 2007).

Acceptance and Mindfulness Models of Stigma Reduction

While research exists on interventions for reducing stigma, little of this research is translational (i.e., emerges from basic experimental research). The present psychological flexibility model is informed by basic research on complex human behavior, including cognitive rigidity, stereotyping, and perspective taking, and the intervention model involves helping people to approach stigma-relevant situations in a more conscious and aware manner. Rather than making efforts to change the form, frequency, or content of stereotypes and attitudes, the model largely focuses on secondary change with regard to cognitive content. On the other hand, first-order change is applied to overt behavior, wherein people are helped to behave in a way that is more flexible and values-consistent in the presence of stereotype-eliciting situations. Psychological flexibility is composed of six psychological processes. The first four processes directly target mindfulness and acceptance, while the last two provide a guide for more flexible behaviors that emerge from mindfulness and acceptance.

Mindfulness and automaticity. Stigma-related biases emerge very rapidly in response to stigma-related stimuli, and they often go unnoticed (Greenwald, Poehlman, Uhlmann, & Banaji, 2009). These biases, even when denied overtly, can be measured implicitly and predict negative social interactions with members of target groups (e.g., McConnell & Leibold, 2001). While evidence is still limited, some data suggest that conscious and mindful awareness of the present moment may mitigate some of the influence of these biases. For example, a brief mindfulness intervention has been shown to reduce the effects of priming age-related stereotypes on subsequent stereotype-activated behavior (Djikic, Langer, & Stapleton, 2008). The preliminary data suggest that greater mindfulness may attenuate effects of implicit biases on action.

The psychological flexibility model teaches mindfulness in the presence of stigma in a variety of ways. Individuals may build awareness of biases and the automatic process of stereotyping through meditative exercises and daily self-monitoring. Mindfulness may be further increased by voluntary contact with stigma-eliciting situations. For example, as a homework assignment, the participant might be asked to interact with a stranger and notice the stereotypes his or her mind generates as he or she spends time getting to know that person. The goal of these mindfulness exercises is to increase participants' ongoing present-moment awareness of events as they unfold in stigma-relevant contexts.

Acceptance, suppression, and avoidance. Suppression and avoidance of stigmatizing attitudes may lead to negative effects among both in- and out-group members. When people fear being devalued in a given social context based on a certain identity, they often expend energy searching for and defending against the perceived threat. This behavioral effort results in reduced performance, which can persist even after they leave the stereotype-relevant situation (Inzlicht & Kang, 2010). People with HIV/AIDS who cope with stigma through disengagement have higher levels of anxiety and depression than those who less frequently disengage (Gonzalez et al., 2009). Among overweight individuals, experiential avoidance has been shown to partially mediate the relationship between body-mass index (an indicator of obesity) and quality of life (Lillis, Levin, & Hayes, 2011).

Together, the promotion of acceptance may be helpful to ameliorate the problematic effects of suppression and avoidance in the context of self-stigma.

The effects of suppressing stereotypes related to public stigma are still less clear. However, newer research suggests that the effects of stereotype suppression may have more to do with the motivation behind suppression. That is, people who are motivated to suppress stereotypes because they value reducing their prejudice may be more successful than those who are told by others to do so (Legault et al., 2011).

The psychological flexibility model teaches experiential acceptance in the context of stigma in a variety of ways. Typically, a safe intervention context is created at first so that unhealthy efforts to suppress evaluative thoughts and stereotypes are less likely to occur. Common ACT exercises (e.g., the polygraph metaphor or the quicksand metaphor; Hayes, Strosahl, & Wilson, 1999) build awareness of the paradoxical processes involved in avoiding cognitive content, including stigma and stereotypes. Additionally, participants might engage in expressive writing about stigma-related content without trying to suppress or control their emotional reactions. During the course of intervention, individuals are instructed that what is important is not necessarily whether one has stigmatizing beliefs or not, but how one acts when they occur. Given the paradoxical effects of suppressing stigmatizing beliefs, the goal is to develop a more open and compassionate stance toward these psychological experiences without acting on them.

Cognitive change versus defusion. The process of "us" and "them" is an inextricable feature of social interaction. The process of putting others and self into social groups is massively useful for the individual and highly reinforced. Stereotypes, once formed, tend to maintain themselves (Hayes et al., 2002), while stereotype-disconforming information tends to be forgotten (Hilton & von Hippel, 1996). Stereotype-congruent behaviors of self and others are inferred to dispositional causes, while stereotype-incongruent behaviors are inferred to situational causes (Hewstone, 1990), thus supporting stereotypes.

Cognitive defusion is a more effective path to decreasing the *influence* of rigid and inflexible stereotypes, rather than attempting to directly change their form or frequency. In cognitive defusion exercises, people are taught to notice the ongoing process of thinking, to see thoughts as thoughts rather than what they seem to be (e.g., a truth about self or others). One study found that defusion from stigmatizing attitudes mediated the effects of an acceptance- and mindfulness-based intervention on public stigma (Hayes et al., 2004).

In cognitive defusion, people are taught to notice stigmatizing thoughts as they arise so that behavior is less tied to or controlled by these thoughts. Such awareness permits one's action to come under other sources of influence, such as *direct experience* (with others) or *personal values* such as compassion, openness, or fairness. Classic ACT techniques may be used to help people to notice the tendency of the mind to construct the world while being unaware of this process. The technique of word repetition might be applied to a stigmatizing thought. In such an exercise, the word "loser" might be repeated out loud for thirty to sixty seconds while participants are coached to notice what happens. Typically the word loses its meaning and gains additional psychological functions beyond its literal meaning. "Physicalizing" exercises where stigma-related thoughts or feelings are imagined to have a physical form can also be used to aide in cognitive defusion. For example, participants may act out a tug-of-war with the group leader who plays the "shame monster" in which the participant is encouraged to notice the workability (or unworkability) of his or her struggle with trying to get rid of shame (Luoma et al., 2012). Highlighting the distinction between thoughts/feelings and behaviors, participants may also be encouraged to carry a card on which stigma-related judgments they have about themselves or others are written while noticing that having those thoughts does not need to interfere with or dictate one's actions (LeJeune, Luoma, Terry, & Glaser, 2012).

Flexible perspective-taking versus rigid self- (and other) processes. Through language and social training, we learn to tell coherent stories about ourselves and others (i.e., conceptualized self/other). When we observe people behaving, we learn to explain this behavior in terms of dispositional causes (e.g., "He did that because he's lazy") and in terms of group membership (e.g., "That's because he's schizophrenic"). In addition, these basic processes of social classification that underlie stigma are maintained because they favor one's in-group and justify mistreatment of out-groups (Tajfel, 1982). These in- and out-group effects may be reduced through fostering identification with an over-arching category that places both individuals in "the same in-group." Examples of this strategy are compassion-focused interventions designed to foster the sense of commonality in suffering as fellow human beings. These methods have been shown to increase feelings of connectedness with others and better interpersonal functioning (Fredrickson, Cohn, Coffey, Pek, & Finkel, 2008). Compassion-focused interventions seem to work, at least partially, by increasing self–other overlap, whereby the other is seen as more similar on a salient dimension (Galinsky, Ku, & Wang, 2005).

Mimicking the movements of another is an additional perspective-taking exercise that appears to reduce prejudice toward a perceived out-group (e.g., Inzlicht, Gutsell, & Legault, 2012). Other perspective-taking exercises involve imagining being in someone else's place—for example, through writing a first-person narrative, or meditative exercises that promote contact with a sense of self as a conscious, transcendent observer of experience. These exercises are theorized to loosen the attachment to a sense of self as being separate and distinct from others and to build a more interconnected and interdependent sense of self.

Helping individuals gain a sense of "common humanity" may compete with an "us-them" perspective, a defining feature of stigma. The "cross-cutting categories exercise" is an exercise in a group-based ACT stigma-reduction intervention used for this purpose (Luoma et al., 2012). This exercise involves volunteers responding to a series of personal questions in front of other members; when done effectively, it elicits a sense of vulnerability in the volunteers and a sense of empathy and compassion in the observers. Concurrently, the audience members notice how quickly their minds generate assumptions about the volunteers based on very little information; they also observe how these judgments tend to disappear as the sense of a shared human experience is gained. Other exercises might utilize visualization techniques with which a person imagines that a loved one has developed a stigmatizing condition or the participant writes a story in which she lives a day in another person's life while experiencing the stigma of the target group (LeJeune et al., 2012). These exercises are designed to promote a positive sense of connection and empathy in relation to the target group (e.g., the "mentally ill"). Taken together, the goal of these exercises is to lead people through a variety of psychological perspectives so that they may relate to the stories about self and other from a more distanced and compassionate perspective.

Values and intrinsic motivation. Finally, the psychological flexibility model focuses on values. Values are defined as "freely chosen, verbally constructed consequences of ongoing, dynamic, evolving patterns of activity, which are intrinsic in nature" (Dahl, Plumb, Stewart, & Lundgren, 2009). The freely chosen and intrinsic nature of value is the most relevant to the topic of stigma, as interventions aimed at helping people to contact their own motivations to reduce prejudice tend to result in lower levels of prejudice (Phills, Kawakami, Tabi, Nadolny, & Inzlicht 2011; Legault et al., 2011). In ACT for stigma reduction, people are guided through expressing their own chosen valued directions in relation to out-groups or stigma-related domains of living. While acceptance and mindfulness processes reduce the dominance of more habitual stereotype-based responses to self and other, values provide an alternative compass that guides how to interact with the self and other.

Furthermore, for public stigma, stigma-focused values exercises also highlight how individuals would choose to behave toward those in the stigmatized group. For self-stigma, a variety of exercises might help those individuals contact longer-term goals and life aspirations that relate to the areas of their life in which they experience stigma, commonly focusing on self-care, treatment engagement, and self-compassion.

Effective prosocial action versus avoidance and inflexibility. Ultimately, reductions in prejudice and stigma depend upon overt actions. As reviewed above, positive intergroup contact promotes reductions in stigma (Corrigan et al., 2001), and behavior aimed at approaching out-group members has been shown to increase self–other overlap (Phills et al., 2011), a sign of greater empathy and compassion toward self and others. Intervention protocols that focus on public stigma have typically asked participants to identify their intentions for responding to out-group members and sometimes have encouraged public statements of intentions for future action.

In terms of self-stigma, effective action may involve taking more compassionate and caring actions toward a self that is perceived as devalued or damaged. This may involve actions such as effective self-care behavior, obtaining help for problems, treatment engagement, or advocacy for other in-group members. Protocols often encourage participants to identify concrete actions that are tied to values as well as plans about how to respond to internal barriers that arise in the process of acting on these intentions.

Review of Data

To date, a psychological flexibility model has been applied to a number of types of stigma. These include weight self-stigma, self-stigma in addiction, public stigma toward mental illness, self-stigma relating to same-sex attraction, and addiction counselor stigma toward clients.

Self-Stigma

Lillis, Hayes, Bunting, and Masuda (2009) randomly assigned 84 patients who had completed a weight-loss program to receive either a one-day ACT-based workshop or a wait-list control condition. At the three-month follow-up, greater improvements in quality of life, psychological distress, weight-related stigma, and body mass were found in the ACT condition than were found in controls. Reduced self-stigma in the ACT group was mediated by improved acceptance and mindfulness. An open trial showed that an ACT intervention targeting self-stigma and shame among those struggling with substance misuse resulted in gains across a range of measures at post-treatment, including internalized shame (Luoma, Kohlenberg, Hayes, Bunting, & Rye, 2008). In a larger pilot study (Luoma et al., 2012), 133 addiction treatment patients were randomized to receive the six-hour ACT protocol developed in the open trial or to treatment as usual. The difference between conditions was small, in terms of treatment received, with the ACT intervention replacing six hours of regular programming during a 28-day residential program. The ACT condition resulted in smaller gains in shame at post-treatment but larger gains at the four-month follow-up. Those in the ACT condition also reported fewer days of substance use and more treatment attendance at follow-up. Finally, a multiple-baseline study by Yadavaia & Hayes (2012) evaluated a six to ten session intervention based on ACT for self-stigma related to same-sex attraction, showing promising findings.

Public Stigma

In a study aimed at reducing public stigma toward mental illness, Masuda et al. (2007) assigned 95 undergraduates to either a two and a half hour ACT workshop or an educational model of the same length. Both interventions were successful in reducing mental health stigma at the one-month follow-up in those who were psychologically flexible. However, the ACT group, but not the education group, was effective for those low in psychological flexibility. A second open trial (Masuda et al., 2009) of the same intervention with 22 undergraduates showed that change in psychological flexibility was correlated with change in stigmatizing attitudes at a one-month follow-up. In a third study of public stigma (Hayes et al., 2004), 90 addiction counselors were randomly assigned to attend one-day workshops based on ACT training, multicultural training, or a control lecture focused on a biological basis for methamphetamine addiction. Stigmatizing attitudes were reduced post-training in both active treatment groups, but only the ACT condition had lower scores through the three-month follow-up. The ACT intervention also decreased burnout at the three-month follow-up, suggesting that interventions targeting stigma in providers may improve their psychological well-being.

Conclusion

The burden of stigma is huge and the number of proven interventions to help those living under its weight is small. More traditional methods focusing on first-order cognitive change have generally shown limited effectiveness and have not led to robust programs of implementation in the real world. Recent developments based on acceptance and mindfulness approaches focus on second-order cognitive strategies and have the benefit of closer connections to basic research on the nature of stigma and stereotyping. While data are still preliminary, early intervention trials suggest that this approach might hold promise.

More research is needed. Of particular importance are studies that dismantle larger stigma-reduction packages and focus on theoretically defined processes of change. Longitudinal studies exploring how acceptance and mindfulness processes interact with stigma-related thinking will serve to refine intervention targets and our understanding of these processes (Livingston & Boyd, 2010). Improved measurement of stigma-related behavior is needed, rather than a sole reliance on self-report. Finally, larger trials are needed to better establish the generalizability and size of these effects.

A comprehensive approach to reducing stigma will need to cut across levels of analysis, discipline, and society. While there is an abundance of research on what stigma "is," there is limited data on how to effectively change it, and most research on stigma reduction comes from pilot studies. With time, hopefully psychological flexibility–based interventions will mature into evidence-based, organizational strategies that achieve long-lasting stigma reduction.

References

Corrigan, P. W. (2007). Changing mental illness stigma as it exists in the real world. *Australian Psychologist, 42*(2), 90–97.

Corrigan, P. W., River, L. P., Lundin, R. K., Penn, D. L., Uphoff-Wasowski, K., Campion, J., et al. (2001). Three strategies for changing attributions about severe mental illness. *Schizophrenia Bulletin, 27*(2), 187–195.

Corrigan, P. W., Rowan, D., Green, A., Lundin, R., River, P., Uphoff-Wasowski, K., et al. (2002). Challenging two mental illness stigmas: Personal responsibility and dangerousness. *Schizophrenia Bulletin, 28*(2), 293.

Dahl, J. A. C., Plumb, J. C., Stewart, I., & Lundgren, T. (2009). *The art and science of valuing in psychotherapy.* Oakland, CA: New Harbinger Publications.

Devine, P. (1989). Stereotypes and prejudice: Their automatic and controlled components. *Journal of Personality and Social Psychology, 56*(1), 5–18.

Djikic, M., Langer, E. J., & Stapleton, S. F. (2008). Reducing stereotyping through mindfulness: Effects on automatic stereotype-activated behaviors. *Journal of Adult Development, 15*(2), 106–111.

Fredrickson, B. L., Cohn, M. A., Coffey, K. A., Pek, J., & Finkel, S. M. (2008). Open hearts build lives: Positive emotions, induced through loving-kindness meditation, build consequential personal resources. *Journal of Personality and Social Psychology, 95*(5), 1045–1062.

Galinsky, A. D., Ku, G., & Wang, C. S. (2005). Perspective-taking and self-other overlap: Fostering social bonds and facilitating social coordination. *Group Processes & Intergroup Relations, 8*(2), 109–124.

Galinsky, A. D., & Moskowitz, G. B. (2000). Perspective-taking: Decreasing stereotype expression, stereotype accessibility, and in-group favoritism. *Journal of Personality and Social Psychology, 78*(4), 708–724.

Gonzalez, A., Solomon, S. E., Zvolensky, M. J., & Miller, C. T. (2009). The interaction of mindful-based attention and awareness and disengagement coping with HIV/AIDS-related stigma in regard to concurrent anxiety and depressive symptoms among adults with HIV/AIDS. *Journal of Health Psychology, 14,* 403–413.

Greenwald, A. G., & Banaji, M. R. (1995). Implicit social cognition: Attitudes, self-esteem, and stereotypes. *Psychological Review, 102*(1), 4–27.

Greenwald, A. G., Poehlman, T. A., Uhlmann, E. L., & Banaji, M. R. (2009). Understanding and using the Implicit Association Test: III. Meta-analysis of predictive validity. *Journal of Personality and Social Psychology, 97*(1), 17–41.

Hayes, S. C., Bissett, R., Roget, N., Padilla, M., Kohlenberg, B. S., Fisher, G. et al. (2004). The impact of acceptance and commitment training and multicultural training on the stigmatizing attitudes and professional burnout of substance abuse counselors. *Behavior Therapy, 35*(4), 821–835.

Hayes, S. C., Niccolls, R., Masuda, A., & Rye, A. K. (2002). Prejudice, terrorism, and behavior therapy. *Cognitive and Behavioral Practice, 9*(4), 296–301.

Hayes, S. C., Strosahl, K. D., & Wilson, K. G. (1999). *Acceptance and commitment therapy: An experiential approach to behavior change* (pp. xvi, 304). New York: Guilford Press.

Hewstone, M. (1990). The "ultimate attribution error"? A review of the literature on intergroup causal attribution. *European Journal of Social Psychology, 20*(4), 311–335.

Hilton, J. L., & von Hippel, W. (1996). Stereotypes. *Annual Reviews in Psychology, 47*(1), 237–271.

Inzlicht, M., Gutsell, J. N., & Legault, L. (2012). Mimicry reduces racial prejudice. *Journal of Experimental Social Psychology, 48*(1), 361–365.

Inzlicht, M., & Kang, S. K. (2010). Stereotype threat spillover: How coping with threats to social identity affects aggression, eating, decision making, and attention. *Journal of Personality and Social Psychology, 99*(3), 467–481.

Langer, E. J., Fiske, S., Taylor, S. E., & Chanowitz, B. (1976). Stigma, staring, and discomfort: Novel-stimulus hypothesis. *Journal of Experimental Social Psychology, 12*(5), 451–463.

Legault, L., Gutsell, J. N., & Inzlicht, M. (2011). Ironic effects of antiprejudice messages: How motivational interventions can reduce (but also increase) prejudice. *Psychological Science, 22*(12), 1472–1477.

LeJeune, J. T., Luoma, J. B., Terry, C., & Glaser, T. (2012). *ACT-based stigma reduction curriculum*. Unpublished manuscript.

Lillis, J., Hayes, S. C., Bunting, K., & Masuda, A. (2009). Teaching acceptance and mindfulness to improve the lives of the obese: A preliminary test of a theoretical model. *Annals of Behavioral Medicine, 37*(1), 58–69.

Lillis, J., Levin, M. E., & Hayes, S. C. (2011). Exploring the relationship between body mass index and health-related quality of life: A pilot study of the impact of weight self-stigma and experiential avoidance. *Journal of Health Psychology, 16*(5), 722–727.

Livingston, J. D., & Boyd, J. E. (2010). Correlates and consequences of internalized stigma for people living with mental illness: A systematic review and meta-analysis. *Social Science & Medicine, 71*(12), 2150–2161.

Luoma, J. B., & Kohlenberg, B. S. (2012). Self-stigma and shame in addictions. In Steven C. Hayes & M. E. Levin (Eds.), *Acceptance, mindfulness, values, and addictive behaviors: Counseling with contemporary cognitive behavioral therapies*. Oakland, CA: New Harbinger Publications.

Luoma, J. B., Kohlenberg, B. S., Hayes, S. C., Bunting, K., & Rye, A. K. (2008). Reducing self-stigma in substance abuse through acceptance and commitment therapy: Model, manual development, and pilot outcomes. *Addiction Research & Theory, 16*(2), 149–165.

Luoma, J. B., Kohlenberg, B. S., Hayes, S. C., & Fletcher, L. B. (2012). Slow and steady wins the race: A randomized clinical trial of acceptance and commitment therapy targeting shame in substance use disorders. *Journal of Consulting and Clinical Psychology, 80*, 43–53.

Macrae, C. N., Milne, A. B., & Bodenhausen, G. V. (1994). Stereotypes as energy-saving devices: A peek inside the cognitive toolbox. *Journal of Personality and Social Psychology, 66,* 37.

Masuda, A., Hayes, S. C., Fletcher, L. B., Seignourel, P. J., Bunting, K., Herbst, S. A., et al. (2007). Impact of acceptance and commitment therapy versus education on stigma toward people with psychological disorders. *Behaviour Research and Therapy, 45*(11), 2764–2772.

Masuda, A., Hayes, S. C., Lillis, J., Bunting, K., Herbst, S. A., & Fletcher, L. B. (2009). The relation between psychological flexibility and mental health stigma in acceptance and commitment therapy: A preliminary process investigation. *Behavior and Social Issues, 18*(1), 1–16.

Masuda, A., & Latzman, R. D. (2011). Examining associations among factor-analytically derived components of mental health stigma, distress, and psychological flexibility. *Personality and Individual Differences, 51*(4), 435–438.

McConnell, A. R., & Leibold, J. M. (2001). Relations among the Implicit Association Test: Discriminatory behavior, and explicit measures of racial attitudes. *Journal of Experimental Social Psychology, 37*(5), 435–442.

Penn, D. L., Kommana, S., Mansfield, M., & Link, B. G. (1999). Dispelling the stigma of schizophrenia: II. The impact of information on dangerousness. *Schizophrenia Bulletin, 25*(3), 437–446.

Pescosolido, B., Martin, J., Lang, A., & Olafsdottir, S. (2008). Rethinking theoretical approaches to stigma: A framework integrating normative influences on stigma (FINIS). *Social Science & Medicine, 67*(3), 431–440.

Phills, C. E., Kawakami, K., Tabi, E., Nadolny, D., & Inzlicht, M. (2011). Mind the gap: Increasing associations between the self and blacks with approach behaviors. *Journal of Personality and Social Psychology, 100*(2), 197–210.

Puhl, R. M., & Heuer, C. A. (2009). The stigma of obesity: A review and update. *Obesity, 17*(5), 941–964.

Rüsch, N., Todd, A. R., Bodenhausen, G. V., & Corrigan, P. W. (2010). Biogenetic models of psychopathology, implicit guilt, and mental illness stigma. *Psychiatry Research, 179*(3), 328–332. doi: 10.1016/j.psychres.2009.09.010.

Tajfel, H. (1982). Social psychology of intergroup relations. *Annual Reviews in Psychology, 33*(1), 1–39.

Walker, I., & Read, J. (2002). The differential effectiveness of psychosocial and biogenetic causal explanations in reducing negative attitudes toward "mental illness." *Psychiatry: Interpersonal & Biological Processes, 65*(4), 313–325.

Yadavaia, J. E., & Hayes, S. C. (2012). Acceptance and commitment therapy for self-stigma around sexual orientation: A multiple baseline evaluation. *Cognitive and Behavioral Practice, 19*(4), 545–559. doi: 10.1016/j.cbpra.2011.09.002.

CHAPTER 12

Acceptance- and Compassion-Based Approaches for Invisible Minorities: Working with Shame among Sexual Minorities

Matthew D. Skinta, Ph.D.

University of California, San Francisco

If we are holding back from any part of our experience, if our heart shuts out any part of who we are and what we feel, we are fueling the fears and feelings of separation that sustain the trance of unworthiness.

—Tara Brach, *Radical Acceptance* (2003)

For a therapist to develop cultural competency in psychotherapy, it is essential to look beyond external differences and uncover hidden diversity in assumptions, thoughts, and social expectations. Working with a client whose minority status is invisible poses additional challenges. This chapter is an exploration of culturally competent practice with invisible minorities, focusing specifically on sexual minorities (e.g., LGB persons: lesbians, gay men, and bisexual men and women). That being said, I believe that novel therapies shown to be successful with sexual minorities are also relevant to other minority communities that may not be visibly recognizable, such as persons living with diabetes, HIV, or chronic pain. Minority stress theory and recent research about shame inform the culturally competent application of acceptance- and compassion-based techniques for various invisible minorities.

Minority Stress Theory

Psychotherapists have long observed that stigma, including self-stigma (e.g., internalized homophobia), is a major negative contributor to the well-being of sexual minorities (Malyon, 1982). Mental health professionals have a checkered history of diagnostic attempts to capture this distress (e.g., ego-dystonic homosexuality; Smith, 1980). While gay affirmative therapy models that promote acceptance of one's experiences and identity as a sexual minority have been developed (Ritter & Terndrup, 2002), these protocols are general guidelines that offer atheoretical suggestions unyoked from any specific theoretically or empirically derived intervention. These models stress the internalization of widely held cultural opprobrium for same-sex attraction as the primary source of this distress. Fortunately, recent research informs the recommendation of more specific approaches functionally specific to the needs of sexual minorities.

Currently, the dominant theoretical lens used to observe the impact of stigma is Meyer's minority stress theory (1995), which emphasizes the wide array of mechanisms by which societal views can be conveyed and might impact the individual. Minority stress theory describes how long-term stress caused by social difficulties results in chronic health problems among minority members. The theory posits that one can only measure—and presumably mitigate—the impact of societal stigma when the full range of proximal to distal effects is assessed. This list is generally composed of internalized homophobia, the expectation of stigma, outness/concealment, and discrimination (e.g., overt acts of discrimination or violence); more recent, the case has also been made to include community connection within the LGB community (Frost & Meyer, 2012).

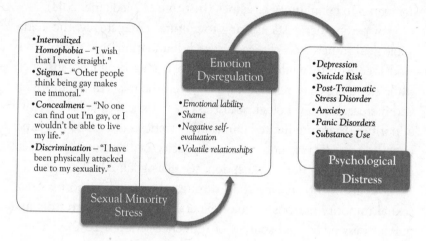

Figure 1. The link between sexual minority stress and psychological distress.

As shown in Figure 1, emotion dysregulation has been identified as the most likely link between minority stress and psychological distress, which creates an important avenue for clinical intervention (Hatzenbuehler, 2009; Hatzenbuehler, McLaughlin, & Nolen-Hoeksema, 2008). Emotion dysregulation refers to the difficulty individuals experience in controlling or coping with strong emotions, and high levels of emotion dysregulation are associated with a broad array of psychopathological outcomes (Aldao, Nolen-Hoeksema, & Schweizer, 2010). A number of variables associated with emotion dysregulation, such as rumination and emotional lability, are present among psychologically distressed sexual minorities. Recent prospective studies of sexual minority adolescents reflect a linear sequence in which stigmatizing events led to emotion dysregulation, which in turn led to psychopathological symptoms (Hatzenbuehler, 2009; McLaughlin, Hatzenbuehler, 2009). Increased dysregulation was observed in the days immediately following stigmatizing experiences (Olatunji, Mimiaga, O'Cleirigh, & Safren, 2006). These findings help to explain the consistent report that minority stress is related to marked elevations in psychological distress among sexual minorities compared to community baselines (Institute of Medicine, 2011).

For psychotherapists aspiring to cultural competency, the epidemiological rather than clinical research foundation of minority stress models constitutes a major shortcoming of this approach. For instance, while there are clear relationships between the expectation of stigma and increases in psychological distress in statistical samples of sexual minorities, there are limited clinical descriptions of individuals experiencing this distress and an equal paucity of literature on clinical conceptualization (for an exception, see Glassgold, 2009).

It is also worth noting that, through the lens of minority stress, sexual minority persons of color experience additional stressors and may possess additional sources of resilience (Meyer, 2010). There is also evidence that the importance of each aspect of minority stress may differ between White and community of color sexual minorities (Moradi et al., 2010), and unique histories of systematic distress impact the risk of HIV seroconversion among sexual minorities of color (Hoyt et al., 2012). In both popular rhetoric and the cultural competency literature, the presence of sexual minorities within communities of color is neglected, heightening the invisibility of persons of color even within the LGB community. Cultural differences among ethnic groups may contribute to recent findings that differences exist between the experiences and impact of minority stress among LGB African American, Latina/o, and Asian and Pacific Islander groups (Balsam, Molina, Beadnell, Simoni, & Walters, 2011; Nabors et al., 2001; Szymanski & Gupta, 2009; Szymanski & Sung, 2010; P. A. Wilson &

Yoshikawa, 2007), such as an increase in behavioral avoidance among African-American gay men experiencing minority stress (Tucker-Seely, Blow, Matsuo, & Taylor-Moore, 2010). In exploring the applicability of mindfulness- and acceptance-based interventions for various forms of minority stress, recent research has extended the use of these interventions into communities of color (Fuchs, Lee, Roemer, & Orsillo, 2013).

The Role of Shame

Shame is an important aspect of the sexual minority experience that merits clinical consideration, yet it is not well described in minority stress approaches (Downs, 2012). Shame, while not a clinical diagnosis, has been linked to a number of different problems and psychopathologies, including depression (Orth, Berking, & Burkhardt, 2006; Thompson & Berenbaum, 2006), PTSD (Lee, Scragg, & Turner, 2001; Leskela, Dieperink, & Thuras, 2002; J. P. Wilson, Drozdek, & Turkovic, 2006; Wong & Cook, 1992), substance abuse (Dearing, Stuewig, & Tangney, 2005), and suicide (Hastings, Northman, & Tangney, 2000; Lester, 1998). While the minority stress concept of self-stigma focuses on the content of particular self-referential thoughts, shame is both an affective consequence of those thoughts and a stimulus for self-critical mental content (e.g., "I am damaged").

In the therapeutic interaction, treatment of shame requires both therapist and client to pay careful attention to attempts to hide "shameful" content in verbal interactions, and to directly address avoided content in the absence of the approbation that reinforces hiding. Past attempts to treat shame have focused on the principle of reciprocal inhibition: practicing an alternate and mutually exclusive behavior in response to a stimulus weakens the strength of a conditioned response. One promising pilot incorporated sustained eye contact and an assertive posture in the presence of personally relevant shaming cues (Rizvi & Linehan, 2005). Another example of this would be Gilbert and Procter's (2006) Compassionate Mind Training and its application to shame. Training for compassion toward others, which weakens a conditioned response of attributing undesired outcomes to flawed selves and instead attributes these outcomes to undesirable contexts or behaviors, also creates opportunities to be compassionate toward one's self.

Acceptance and Commitment Therapy for Stigma

There are few interventions for the experience of stigma, and even fewer that have been empirically based and assessed. Third-wave behavioral therapies, such as functional analytic psychotherapy (FAP; Kohlenberg & Tsai, 1991), dialectic behavioral therapy (DBT; Linehan, 1993), acceptance and commitment therapy (ACT; Hayes, Strosahl, & Wilson, 1999), mindfulness-based cognitive therapy (MBCT; Segal, Williams, & Teasdale, 2001), and compassion-focused therapy (CFT; Gilbert, 2010), have yielded the greatest promise. Theoretically and staunchly within the behavioral tradition, these therapies are unique in their focus on the function of private events (thoughts, feelings, etc.) in the present moment; acceptance of adverse internal states; and a perspective that thoughts about the content of the self are subject to learning histories, rehearsal, and the internal reinforcement that consistency yields. These approaches contrast with more traditional cognitive and behavioral methods that seek instead to alter the form or frequency of private events (e.g., automatic thoughts).

Among these behavioral interventions, ACT has been most examined for the treatment of self-stigma and shame. ACT for stigma focuses on the fears, shame, and identification with a stigmatized group that poses a barrier to living a life consistent with one's values (Luoma Kohlenberg, Hayes, Bunting, & Rye, 2008). ACT has been demonstrated to reduce shame and self-stigma with substance users (Luoma et al., 2008) and overweight individuals (Lillis, Hayes,

Bunting, & Masuda, 2009). It has also been used with the general public and service providers to reduce stigma associated with mental illness (Masuda et al., 2007), substance use (Hayes, Follette, & Linehan, 2004), and racial minorities (Lillis & Hayes, 2007). ACT focuses on the verbal processes that underlie experiential avoidance and fusion. "Experiential avoidance" refers to avoidant behaviors that occur in response to internal stimuli and "fusion" is one's attachment to these stimuli. For example, a man with HIV might have a frequent thought, such as "I will be rejected if people know of my HIV status." This thought can occur in the absence of experience with such an event and might lead him to avoid disclosure to his parents, reducing his ability to utilize them as valued caretakers. He might also choose not to disclose to sexual partners or suggest the use of condoms in response to this private event, putting others at risk of contracting HIV and himself at risk of contracting additional sexually transmitted infections. ACT has demonstrated effects on emotion regulation (Forman et al., 2012; Goldapple et al., 2004), which may make it particularly effective for sexual minorities, given the connection between minority stress and emotion regulation.

Most recent, a single case pilot of a group therapy format found ACT to successfully reduce self-stigma and depression and increase quality of life and social support among a small sample of gay men and lesbians experiencing conflict about their sexual orientation (Yadavaia & Hayes, 2012). As noted in Table 1, the primary ACT strategies of the hexaflex correspond in meaningful ways with the effects of minority stress.

Table 1

Component of Minority Stress	Behavioral Expression	Corresponding ACT Principles
Self-Stigma/ Internalized Homophobia	Self-as-Content, fusion with anti-gay stereotypes	Defusion, Self-as-Context
Expectation of Stigma	Rumination, fusion with negative beliefs about others	Acceptance
Concealment	Restricted behaviors, avoidance of attention	Values, Committed Action
Discrimination	Reliving traumatic events, fear of unanticipated danger	Contact with the Present Moment

ACT interventions for stigma may also benefit by incorporating strategies and techniques from compassion-focused therapy (CFT; Gilbert, 2010). The basic science of shame indicates that shame is fundamentally the result of an overfocus on one's internal agency in negative events; one feels shame because one is to blame (Tangney & Dearing, 2002). This would imply some benefit to skills training toward noticing causal relationships between external or contextual factors and a given outcome. Functionally, compassion might be thought of as exactly this: an orientation toward the role of contextual factors that is incompatible with the self-focused blame that is the hallmark of shame (Tangney & Dearing, 2002). As described by Gilbert (2010), CFT is a set of techniques that may be incorporated into a variety of compatible therapeutic techniques.

Acceptance- and Compassion-Based Group Therapy for HIV Stigma

To illustrate these principles, a protocol is described below that the author utilized in a community-based mental health clinic. This intervention was developed based upon existing ACT protocols (e.g., Eifert & Forsyth, 2005; Hayes et al., 1999; Luoma et al., 2008) and buttressed with compassion-focused exercises (see Tables 2 and 3 for examples) for use with gay men living with HIV who self-referred for HIV-related shame. Five men participated in eight 90-minute weekly groups, and three men participated in interviews eight weeks after group completion. These participants' impressions are described below.

Session 1. The first session focused on introducing and attuning the client to core ACT perspectives. Specifically, this began with a discussion of the problem (e.g., HIV stigma), what purposes it might serve (e.g., protecting a participant in a situation in which it is unsafe to disclose, etc.), and how it has become a problem in the participant's life through attempts to avoid contact with feelings of stigma or shame. Following this there was a discussion of the treatment focus on *valued action* and finding ways to experience greater quality of life, which may include continuing to experience thoughts about HIV stigma and the fears that it elicits. This session ended with a brief *grounding* exercise (Najavits, 2002, p. 133) allowing clients the first chance to mindfully observe their thoughts about the group and sharing their experiences with HIV without being overwhelmed by them.

Session 2. This session covered the costs and unworkability of responding to HIV stigma. Specifically, this relates to the ACT concept of *experiential avoidance* and how attempts to control or avoid aversive responses to one's HIV status have impacted participants. Participants were encouraged to reflect on the costs of efforts to avoid HIV stigma, ways HIV stigma may have reduced the quality of other areas of life, and the need for more workable solutions (*creative hopelessness*). This session ended with a five-minute *mindfulness* exercise, in which the participant observes rising thoughts and feelings associated with HIV stigma.

Table 2
Loving-Kindness Meditation Script

Sit in a comfortable position and, when you're ready, close your eyes.

Focus gently on the breath for one to two minutes.

Gently bring to mind the image of someone you love or like very much. It could be a lover, a parent, or a dear friend. See if you can bring that sense of presence into the room and picture that person here with you. Imagine yourself saying to this person...

(Repeat exercise for each category below.)

Someone you like/love

May you be happy and peaceful.

May you be free from fear or pain.

May you be free of harsh treatment.

May you live comfortably and with love and compassion in your life.

Someone you have positive-neutral feelings toward

May you be happy and peaceful.

May you be free from fear or pain.

May you be free of harsh treatment.

May you live comfortably and with love and compassion in your life.

The self

> May I be happy and peaceful.
>
> May I be free from fear or pain.
>
> May I be free of harsh treatment.
>
> May I live comfortably and with love and compassion in my life.

Session 3. This session began with a ten-minute *mindfulness* exercise observing thoughts and emotions about HIV. ACT utilizes a variety of metaphors, such as that of the Chinese finger trap (Hayes et al., 1999, p. 105) discussed in this session, to illustrate the role of control in maintaining *experiential avoidance* and explore the possibility of reducing those attempts at control. Following this was a discussion on identifying *values-driven behaviors* (e.g., Dahl, Plumb, Stewart, & Lundgren, 2009, p. 63; Eifert & Forsyth, 2005, p. 47) to replace control efforts, as well as a discussion of which valued behaviors participants may have given up in an attempt to control information about their HIV status or minimize the possibility of others finding out their status.

Session 4. This session continued with a discussion of *acceptance* and *mindfulness*, and how to apply these to concerns regarding HIV. This includes disclosing that *acceptance* is not a "clever fix" for worries related to HIV but rather a skill intended to choose valued life directions despite feelings and thoughts associated with HIV. The rest of the session was devoted to the exploration of values and defining values in contrast to goals.

Session 5. This session introduced the underlying principle of *self-as-context* vs. *self-as-content* (Eifert & Forsyth, 2005, p. 180). This is a reflection of ACT's core focus on reducing cognitive fusion that occurs when a person's self-identity becomes conflated with thoughts related to, in the case of HIV, being a diseased, shameful, or toxic being. This will lead back to an exploration of what valued behaviors participants have been practicing, how acceptance and mindfulness have worked for each client in the past week, and any barriers that arose.

Session 6. This session explored the importance of *willingness*—that is, a return to valued behavior in one's life and the importance of being willing to engage in behaviors that elicit fears of stigma and thoughts of HIV, without attempting to control or stop those thoughts. This session included some psychoeducation on how traditional exposure works and how this might work when one is experiencing/exposed to aversive, internal experiences.

Session 7 and Session 8. The final sessions introduced the role of self-compassion, particularly as it relates to the experience of living with HIV. This included a loving-kindness meditation in place of the mindfulness practice (see Table 2), writing a compassionate letter to one's self, and guided visualization with the hand-on-heart meditation (see Table 3). Participants were asked to provide progress reports on attempts to increase *valued behaviors* and explorations of obstacles to valued behaviors.

·Table 3
Hand-on-Heart Visualization Script

1. Assume a comfortable seated position, close your eyes, and begin to gently rub the palms of your hands together.

2. When your palms become warm, place your dominant hand flat over your chest, above your heart. Gently bring your awareness to the physical sensation of warmth in your heart.

3. Bring to mind a particularly loving interaction, preferably recent, that you can imagine vividly in your mind. Imagine the feeling of closeness you had in this moment—it is often helpful to focus on your memory of this loved one's face, looking into

her or his eyes, while maintaining an awareness of the warmth in your heart (cue client to the feeling of warmth and the mental image, particularly the person's eyes, during the next three to five minutes).

4. Now, imagine if you can what it might be like to look at yourself through this loved one's eyes—to see yourself as precious, deserving of receiving love, and worthy of time and affection. See if you can deeply connect with how she or he saw you in that moment.

Note: This variation from Neff's (2011, p. 203) loving-kindness exercise has been further modified to incorporate the core ACT process of perspective taking and increase attention to the accompanying physical experience of affects.

Participant Responses

Most participants reported experiential avoidance of HIV-related content and distress related to self-disclosure that impacted discussions with treatment providers, friends, and romantic partners. As the group progressed, the relationship between disclosure and the reduction of shame was noted by most participants. In describing the shift in his hopes and expectations about status disclosure, one participant noted:

I'm gonna tell you I'm positive, and you're gonna have a good reaction, and then I'm gonna get to feel better about myself—when step one is really me disclosing to myself and me dealing with it with myself, and that doing that work changes how I disclose to somebody else and what I expect their response to be, or what I need their response to be.

This participant realized that the suffering in disclosure—in being labeled as a member of a stigmatized group—derived largely from the expectations, hopes, and fears of how that information would be handled. Specifically, he noted that the responses he feared, such as rejection or negativity, were a reflection of his own feelings about his HIV status and what he "needed" as a response. Through working to be more accepting of his status, and to invite in the experience of this present moment, he was able to reduce his concern that he would be defined by a negative reaction from someone else when he disclosed. He continued:

> The other thing I've gotten from this group and from the thoughts and feelings thing is that everything passes and don't put so much weight on every little moment, every little feeling, and every little reaction. I mean, I can't tell you how grateful I am about this group.

The experience of suffering from stigma appears related to fusing with the content of one's story of stigma. As in the chessboard metaphor (Hayes et al., 1999, pp. 190–192), in which a client is oriented toward the experience of self-as-context and not defined by thoughts or emotions, this participant was able to gain freedom from "every little feeling, and every little reaction" that had previously encouraged him to withdraw, hide his HIV status, or become overwhelmed with emotion when the topic arose. Another quote further describes this process:

> If you do get kind of what the goals are first, it doesn't take into consideration that once you learn meditation, and once you learn acceptance of thoughts and feelings, and once you pry off all the stigma, you're going to go through a period, or at least this is what's happening with me, and I'm like, "Man, I'm not who I thought I was…" It's like the revolution of the self. At least that's how I'm experiencing it.

Concluding Remarks

In this chapter, we have explored the integration of minority stress theory and the application of acceptance- and compassion-based approaches to culturally competent care for invisible minorities. The specific changes in emotion regulation give acceptance-based approaches an edge over earlier therapeutic approaches in treating the underlying difficulties associated with shame and stigma experienced by sexual minorities. Men living with HIV who have participated in a treatment based upon this model stress the relationship between disclosure, self-acceptance, and a changed relationship with the self. Compassion-based approaches may enhance the effects of mindfulness, perspective taking, and acceptance present in ACT.

References

Aldao, A., Nolen-Hoeksema, S., & Schweizer, S. (2010). Emotion-regulation strategies across psychopathology: A meta-analytic review. *Clinical Psychology Review, 30*(2), 217–237.

Balsam, K. F., Molina, Y., Beadnell, B., Simoni, J., & Walters, K. (2011). Measuring multiple minority stress: The LGBT People of Color Microaggressions Scale. *Cultural Diversity and Ethnic Minority Psychology, 17*(2), 163-174.

Brach, T. (2003). *Radical acceptance: Embracing your life with the heart of a Buddha.* New York: Bantam.

Dahl, J. C., Plumb, J. C., Stewart, I., & Lundgren, T. (2009). *The art and science of valuing in psychotherapy: Helping clients discover, explore, and commit to valued action using acceptance and commitment therapy.* Oakland, CA: New Harbinger Publications.

Dearing, R. L., Stuewig, J., & Tangney, J. P. (2005). On the importance of distinguishing shame from guilt: Relations to problematic alcohol and drug use. *Addictive Behaviors, 30*(7), 1392–1404.

Downs, A. (2012). *The velvet rage: Overcoming the pain of growing up gay in a straight man's world* (2nd ed.). New York: Da Capo Press.

Eifert, G. H., & Forsyth, J. P. (2005). *Acceptance and commitment therapy for anxiety disorders: A practitioner's treatment guide to using mindfulness, acceptance, and values-based behavior change strategies.* Oakland, CA: New Harbinger Publications.

Forman, E. M., Shaw, J. A., Goetter, E. M., Herbert, J. D., Park, J. A., & Yuen, E. K. (2012). Long-term follow-up of a randomized controlled trial comparing acceptance and commitment therapy and standard cognitive behavior therapy for anxiety and depression. *Behavior Therapy, 43*(4), 801–811.

Frost, D. M., & Meyer, I. H. (2012). Measuring community connectedness among diverse sexual minority populations. *Journal of Sex Research, 49*(1), 36–49.

Fuchs, C., Lee, J. K., Roemer, L., & Orsillo, S. M. (2013). Using mindfulness- and acceptance-based treatments with clients from nondominant cultural and/or marginalized backgrounds: Clinical consideration, meta-analysis findings, and introduction to the special series. *Cognitive and Behavioral Practice, 20*(1), 1–12.

Gilbert, P. (2010). *Compassion focused therapy: Distinctive features.* New York: Routledge/Taylor & Francis Group.

Gilbert, P., & Procter, S. (2006). Compassionate mind training for people with high shame and self-criticism: Overview and pilot study of a group therapy approach. *Clinical Psychology & Psychotherapy, 13*(6), 353–379.

Glassgold, J. M. (2009). The case of Felix: An example of gay-affirmative, cognitive behavioral therapy. *Pragmatic Case Studies in Psychotherapy, 5*(4), 1–21.

Goldapple, K., Segal, Z., Garson, C., Lau, M., Bieling, P., Kennedy, S. et al. (2004). Modulation of cortical-limbic pathways in major depression: Treatment-specific effects of cognitive behavior therapy. *Archives of General Psychiatry, 61*(1), 34.

Hastings, M. E., Northman, L. M., & Tangney, J. P. (2000). Shame, guilt, and suicide. *Suicide science: Expanding the boundaries,* 67–79.

Hatzenbuehler, M. L. (2009). How does sexual minority stigma "get under the skin"? A psychological mediation framework. *Psychological Bulletin, 135*(5), 707.

Hatzenbuehler, M. L., McLaughlin, K. A., & Nolen-Hoeksema, S. (2008). Emotion regulation and internalizing symptoms in a longitudinal study of sexual minority and heterosexual adolescents. *Journal of Child Psychology and Psychiatry, 49*(12), 1270–1278.

Hayes, S. C., Follette, V. M., & Linehan, M. M. (2004). *Mindfulness and acceptance: Expanding the cognitive-behavioral tradition.* New York: Guilford Press.

Hayes, S. C., Strosahl, K. D., & Wilson, K. G. (1999). *Acceptance and commitment therapy: An experiential approach to behavior change.* New York: Guilford Press.

Hoyt, M. A., Rubin, L. R., Nemeroff, C. J., Lee, J., Huebner, D. M., & Proeschold-Bell, R. J. (2012). HIV/AIDS-related institutional mistrust among multiethnic men who have sex with men: Effects on HIV testing and risk behaviors. *Health Psychology, 31*(3), 269.

Institute of Medicine & Committee on Lesbian, Gay, Bisexual, Transgender Health Issues, Research Gaps, Opportunities, Board on the Health of Select Populations. (2011). *The health of lesbian, gay, bisexual, and transgender people: Building a foundation for better understanding.* Washington, DC: National Academies Press.

Kohlenberg, R. J., & Tsai, M. (1991). *Functional analytic psychotherapy: Creating intense and curative therapeutic relationships.* New York: Plenum Press.

Lee, D. A., Scragg, P., & Turner, S. (2001). The role of shame and guilt in traumatic events: A clinical model of shame-based and guilt-based PTSD. *British Journal of Medical Psychology, 74*(4), 451–466.

Leskela, J., Dieperink, M., & Thuras, P. (2002). Shame and posttraumatic stress disorder. *Journal of Traumatic Stress, 15*(3), 223–226.

Lester, D. (1998). The association of shame and guilt with suicidality. *Journal of Social Psychology, 138*(4), 535–536.

Lillis, J., & Hayes, S. C. (2007). Applying acceptance, mindfulness, and values to the reduction of prejudice: A pilot study. *Behavior Modification, 31,* 389–411.

Lillis, J., Hayes, S. C., Bunting, K., & Masuda, A. (2009). Teaching acceptance and mindfulness to improve the lives of the obese: A preliminary test of a theoretical model. *Annals of Behavioral Medicine, 37*(1), 58–69.

Linehan, M. M. (1993). *Cognitive-behavioral treatment of borderline personality disorder.* New York: Guilford Press.

Luoma, J. B., Kohlenberg, B. S., Hayes, S. C., Bunting, K., & Rye, A. K. (2008). Reducing self-stigma in substance abuse through acceptance and commitment therapy: Model, manual development, and pilot outcomes. *Addiction Research and Theory, 16,* 149–165.

Malyon, A. K. (1982). Psychotherapeutic implications of internalized homophobia in gay men. *Journal of Homosexuality, 7*(2–3), 59–69.

Masuda, A., Hayes, S. C., Fletcher, L. B., Seignourel, P. J., Bunting, K., Herbst, S. A. et al. (2007). Impact of acceptance and commitment therapy versus education on stigma toward people with psychological disorders. *Behaviour Research and Therapy, 45,* 2764–2772.

McLaughlin, K. A., & Hatzenbuehler, M. L. (2009). Mechanisms linking stressful life events and mental health problems in a prospective, community-based sample of adolescents. *Journal of Adolescent Health, 44*(2), 153–160.

Meyer, I. H. (1995). Minority stress and mental health in gay men. *Journal of Health and Social Behavior, 36*(1), 38–56.

Meyer, I. H. (2010). Identity, stress, and resilience in lesbians, gay men, and bisexuals of color. *The Counseling Psychologist, 38*(3), 442–454.

Moradi, B., Wiseman, M. C., DeBlaere, C., Goodman, M. B., Sarkees, A., Brewster, M. E. et al. (2010). LGB of color and White individuals' perceptions of heterosexist stigma, internalized homophobia, and outness: Comparisons of levels and links. *The Counseling Psychologist, 38*(3), 397–424.

Nabors, N. A., Hall, R. L., Miville, M. L., Nettles, R., Pauling, M. L., & Ragsdale, B. L. (2001). Multiple minority group oppression: Divided we stand? *Journal of the Gay and Lesbian Medical Association, 5*(3), 101–105.

Najavits, L.M. (2002). *Seeking safety: A treatment manual for PTSD and substance abuse.* New York: Guilford Press.

Neff, K. (2011). *Self-compassion: Stop beating yourself up and leave insecurity behind.* New York: William Morrow.

Olatunji, B. O., Mimiaga, M. J., O'Cleirigh, C., & Safren, S. A. (2006). A review of treatment studies of depression in HIV. *Topics in HIV Medicine, 14*(3), 112–124.

Orth, U., Berking, M., & Burkhardt, S. (2006). Self-conscious emotions and depression: Rumination explains why shame but not guilt is maladaptive. *Personality and Social Psychology Bulletin, 32*(12), 1608–1619.

Ritter, K. Y., & Terndrup, A. I. (2002). *Handbook of affirmative psychotherapy with lesbians and gay men.* New York: Guilford Press.

Rizvi, S. L., & Linehan, M. M. (2005). The treatment of maladaptive shame in borderline personality disorder: A pilot study of "opposite action." *Cognitive and Behavioral Practice, 12*(4), 437–447.

Segal, Z. V., Williams, J. M. G., & Teasdale, J. D. (2001). *Mindfulness-based cognitive therapy for depression: A new approach to preventing relapse.* New York: Guilford Press.

Smith, J. (1980). Ego-dystonic homosexuality. *Comprehensive Psychiatry, 21*(2), 119–127.

Szymanski, D. M., & Gupta, A. (2009). Examining the relationship between multiple internalized oppressions and African American lesbian, gay, bisexual, and questioning persons' self-esteem and psychological distress. *Journal of Counseling Psychology, 56*(1), 110–118.

Szymanski, D. M., & Sung, M. R. (2010). Minority stress and psychological distress among asian american sexual minority persons 1ψ7. *The Counseling Psychologist, 38*(6), 848–872.

Tangney, J. P., & Dearing, R. L. (2002). Our "intrapersonal" relationship: The self in shame and guilt. *Shame and Guilt,* 52–77.

Thompson, R. J., & Berenbaum, H. (2006). Shame reactions to everyday dilemmas are associated with depressive disorder. *Cognitive Therapy and Research, 30*(4), 415–425.

Tucker-Seeley, R. D., Blow, A. J., Matsuo, H., & Taylor-Moore, R. (2010). Behavioral escape avoidance coping in African-American men who have sex with men. *Journal of Gay & Lesbian Social Services, 22*(3), 250–268.

Wilson, J. P., Drozdek, B., & Turkovic, S. (2006). Posttraumatic shame and guilt. *Trauma, Violence, & Abuse, 7*(2), 122–144.

Wilson, P. A., & Yoshikawa, H. (2007). Improving access to health care among African-American, Asian and Pacific Islander, and Latino lesbian, gay, and bisexual populations. In I. H. Meyer & M. E. Northridge (Eds.), *The health of sexual minorities.* New York: Springer.

Wong, M. R., & Cook, D. (1992). Shame and its contribution to PTSD. *Journal of Traumatic Stress, 5*(4), 557–562.

Yadavaia, J. E., & Hayes, S. C. (2012). Acceptance and commitment therapy for self-stigma around sexual orientation: A multiple baseline evaluation. *Cognitive and Behavioral Practice, 19*(4), 545–559. doi: 10.1016/j.cbpra.2011.09.002.

Editor **Akihiko Masuda, PhD,** is associate professor of psychology at Georgia State University. He was born and raised in Nagano, Japan, and moved to the United States for his psychology career. His primary areas of interest include acceptance- and mindfulness-based behavioral therapies, diversity psychology, and Zen Buddhism. He is the author of over seventy peer-reviewed papers and book chapters.

Index

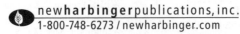